D0214943

Jean-Baptiste Say

This volume is the first full-length biography of Jean-Baptiste Say (1767–1832), the most famous French classical economist. During his lifetime Say actively took part in three revolutions: the French Revolution, the Industrial Revolution and the establishment of economics as an academic discipline. He struggled with Bonaparte, was the owner of a cotton spinning mill and published his famous *Treatise of Political Economy* and many other economic writings.

Say was a child of the Enlightenment. At first trained for a commercial career, after 1789 he became the managing editor of the literary and political journal *La Décade*. Briefly close to Bonaparte, he was forbidden by him to publish a second edition of his *Treatise* (first edition 1803) as it heckled government intervention. As a cotton mill owner Say prospered until Napoleonic trade policies created a slump. The *Restauration* government commissioned him to report on the industrialisation of Britain. On his trip he met Bentham, Ricardo and James Mill. As a republican and a liberal, he had a hard time in post-Napoleonic France while his international reputation grew. In 1819 he was appointed to the first professorship of economics at the Conservatoire des Arts et Métiers. After the July Revolution of 1830, he became the first professor of economics at the Collège de France.

This biography is the first balanced account of Say as a historical figure and as an economist. After his literary editorship, he came relatively late to economics. A new perspective is presented on the relationship between his entrepreneurship and his theory of the entrepreneur. He is described in the context of liberal circles, of a Protestant Huguenot network and of his 'overseas membership' of the British milieu of Philosophical Radicals. Many quotations from letters sent and received give a lively impression of his tempestuous lifetime.

Evert Schoorl (1940) was director of graduate studies in the economics department at the University of Groningen, the Netherlands.

Routledge studies in the history of economics

Jean-Baptiste Say

Revolutionary, entrepreneur, economist

Evert Schoorl

Routledge
Taylor & Francis Group

LONDON AND NEW YORK

First published 2013
by Routledge
2 Park Square, Milton Park, Abingdon, Oxon OX14 4RN

Simultaneously published in the USA and Canada
by Routledge
711 Third Avenue, New York, NY 10017

Routledge is an imprint of the Taylor & Francis Group, an informa business

© 2013 Evert Schoorl

The right of Evert Schoorl to be identified as author of this work has been
asserted by him in accordance with the Copyright, Designs and Patents
Act 1988.

All rights reserved. No part of this book may be reprinted or reproduced or
utilised in any form or by any electronic, mechanical, or other means, now
known or hereafter invented, including photocopying and recording, or in
any information storage or retrieval system, without permission in writing
from the publishers.

Trademark notice: Product or corporate names may be trademarks or
registered trademarks, and are used only for identification and explanation
without intent to infringe.

British Library Cataloguing in Publication Data
A catalogue record for this book is available from the British Library

Library of Congress Cataloging in Publication Data
Schoorl, Evert.
Jean-Baptiste Say : revolutionary, entrepreneur, economist / Evert Schoorl.
    p. cm.
    1. Say, Jean Baptiste, 1767–1832. 2. Economists–France–Biography.
    3. Economics–France–History. I. Title.
    HB105.S25S36 2012
    330.15'3092–dc23
    [B]

ISBN: 978-0-415-66517-9 (hbk)
ISBN: 978-0-203-07356-8 (ebk)

Typeset in Times New Roman
by Wearset Ltd, Boldon, Tyne and Wear

Printed and bound in the United States of America by Publishers Graphics,
LLC on sustainably sourced paper.

To my granddaughters
Anne-Martje and Renée Schoorl

If our goal is modern relevance, we ought to focus on the ideas alone. If, by contrast, we are intrigued by how it is that ideas are created and how they change over time in response to multiple influences, then we have to undertake the far more difficult task of actually to reconstruct those forces acting on a particular person at a particular time.

Evelyn Forget (1999), *The Social Economics of Jean-Baptiste Say*

Contents

Introduction

When I defended my dissertation on Jean-Baptiste Say's life and economics in 1980, scientific interest in the French classical economist was at a low ebb. The definitive statements on Say's Law had been, or at least seemed to have been written by Thomas Sowell (1972) and William Baumol (1977). Otherwise he was duly credited with some original thoughts on entrepreneurship. On the other side of the globe, Hitoshi Hashimoto published another dissertation on Say, and several translations of his work. However, to most historians of economics, the objectivist paradigm of economics, or the Ricardo–Marx–Sraffa heritage, seemed to be the mainstream rather than Say's subjectivism.

But what happened? The owners of the Say papers, the Raoul-Duval family, generously took my advice and donated the papers to the Bibliothèque Nationale. At the Institut Walras in Say's native city Lyon, Pierre Dockès and André Tiran set up the project of the Oeuvres Complètes de Jean-Baptiste Say. And between the bicentenary of the French Revolution in 1989, and the one of Say's *Traité d'Economie Politique* in 2003, numerous conferences, books and articles gave testimony of renewed interest in Say's work. André Tiran and Philippe Steiner – to name just two Frenchmen – and Evelyn Forget, Richard Whatmore and Sam Hollander – to name just three others – have drawn different pictures of their J.-B. Say as economist, political thinker and historical figure. Even the great historian of the French Revolution period, Robert Palmer, has produced a book on Say as 'an economist in troubled times'. Steven Kates has shown up as a diehard believer in the validity of Say's Law in modern economics. Among these, my favourites are Evelyn and Philippe. I am also indebted to Hitoshi Hashimoto who has brought together, from all over the world, many copies of letters written by and addressed to Say.

This book aims at bringing together a picture of Say's life as revolutionary, entrepreneur and political economist, as these different dimensions have until recently been in the separate domains of history and economics, and to some extent in that of political science. In this book, the accent is upon his life; regarding Say's economics, his treatment of value, of entrepreneurship and of Say's Law have been singled out as the most important topics, and as (at least in part) fit for a relativist approach in the sense of Evelyn Forget's quote above. There is a close link between Say's entrepreneurship and his theory of the entrepreneur.

His lifelong struggle with Ricardo centred around problems of value and price. His discussions with Malthus, Sismondi and Everett concerned the true meaning and validity of 'Say's Law'. Finally I briefly compare the recent evaluations of his intellectual achievement.

The hospitality of Professor André Tiran, of the 'Institut Triangle' at the Université Lyon 2 *Lumière*, and the assistance of the administrative staff of this institute, are gratefully acknowledged. Parts of the manuscript were read by Lex Lammen, Ben Gales and Hiske Schoorl. I thank them for their comments; all errors and false choices in style and composition remain the author's responsibility.

1   Youthful revolutionary

Early youth

Jean-Baptiste Say was born in Lyon on 5 January 1767, the oldest child of a Huguenot family. This Protestant lineage was one of the formative elements of his life. In his early career as well as in later life he was often in the company of other Huguenots and Calvinists. After the revocation of the Nantes Edict in 1685, his great-grandfather Louis Say had found refuge in Amsterdam where he took the oath as a citizen. He was a member of the Église Wallonne and had a very modest account at the Amsterdam bank of exchange. His Amsterdam merchant's passport is still in the possession of his descendants. Jean-Baptiste's son Horace Say, in his introduction of 1834 to his father's *Oeuvres Diverses*, still wrote about the basket kept by the family in which Louis Say had carried his belongings to Holland, but it has not survived since.

By 1694 Louis had already moved to Geneva, where his son Jean became a registered citizen. This gave his descendants the right to call themselves *citoyen de Genève*, which continued after Jean's son Jean-Estienne Say, the father of Jean-Baptiste, moved to Lyon. Louis and Jean Say were merchants of woollen and serge cloth, Jean-Estienne primarily traded in silk. For some time the latter kept a little diary in which he noted the registration of his children as Genevan citizens. He did not explicitly mention this with regard to his oldest, but Larousse's *Grand Dictionnaire Universel du XIXe Siècle* even (wrongly) classifies J.-B. Say with Rousseau, Necker and Sismondi as *born* in Geneva. Still one century later Sismondi and Say could address each other as 'Cher concitoyen' in their correspondence. There were regular childhood family visits to Geneva which as late as 1814, when he walked on British cobblestones, revived Say's boyhood memories of the Protestant capital's pavement.[1]

Genevan family relationships were to remain an important factor in Say's life and career. His mother was Françoise Castanet, whose parents were Honoré Castanet and Elisabeth Rath. Say's younger brother Honoré, called Horace, was named after his grandfather; he married his full cousin Alphonsine Delaroche, the daughter of Daniel Delaroche and his mother's sister Marie Castanet. Doctor Daniel Delaroche (1743–1812), a remarkable medic and botanist, was born in Geneva, studied abroad and finally settled in Paris.

Members of the Castanet, Rath and Delaroche families were lifelong close relations, correspondents and sometimes business contacts of Jean-Baptiste. Other Genevan families figuring prominently in his life were the Duvoisins and Dumérils; after the death in action during Napoleon's Egyptian campaign of Horace Say, his widow Alphonsine Delaroche married Constant Duméril. Jean-Baptiste's aunt Duvoisin, née Say (his father's sister), was to be a financier for his cotton mill which he started in 1804. She clearly cared about her nephews, as she wrote to the Genevan physicist Georges-Louis le Sage (who gave private lessons of mathematics) in 1786 about the education of her little nephew Horace.[2]

In his diary, Say's father Jean-Estienne wrote very frankly about his family planning. This is worth noting by itself, and even more so because of his son's future Malthusian notions. Among demographers Geneva is known as a clear example of eighteenth century birth control practice. The French historian Flandrin writes about the introduction of 'coïtus interruptus', specifying that

> demographers see proof of the diffusion of this practice among the elites in the fact that as from the beginning of the eighteenth century the legitimate birthrate of the French nobility and of the citizens of Geneva has very notably lowered.

He even calls this the beginning of the Malthusian revolution.[3]

Jean-Estienne and his wife had planned to have two children. But after Jean-Baptiste and Denis (1768) an unplanned third one announced itself in 1770. Jean-Estienne wrote that he could live with the idea of having a daughter, but another son was born: Jean-Honoré, called Horace. Three days later, Denis died. Another son, Louis Auguste, was born in 1774. Because of his mother's complicated pregnancies Jean-Baptiste – or simply Say, as his father called him in his diary – was sent to Genevan relatives for almost that entire year. On 30 June his father wrote: 'Say has started his writing lessons with Mr. Borde.' In the only completed chapter of his autobiography, Say mentions receiving lessons in physics at an early age – possibly from le Sage.

New Enlightenment insights on education and teaching did not go by unnoticed to the Say family. Say's mother was the author of a manuscript called 'Projet d'Education Nationale', and Horace wrote another, called 'De l'Education'. He also published a pamphlet under the title 'Plan d'Education dans les principes de J.J. Rousseau', in which he writes that he was brought up according to those principles. And he unfolds a plan for a boys' boarding school to be situated near Paris, led by himself. It is unknown whether it received any acclaim, but it is not unlikely that this was the same project which Jean-Baptiste and his wife Julie considered establishing, after their marriage in May 1793 (see Figure 1.1). Horace's choice for a military career might have been an obstacle to its execution, although both Jean-Baptiste and Horace would publish on the subject of education in *La Décade*. Teaching and education remained lifelong interests to Jean-Baptiste.

Figure 1.1 Jacques-Augustin-Catherine Pajou (1766–1828) served with the 'sous-lieutenant' Say in the Parisian 'Arts Company' in the campaign of 1792, under captain (and sculptor) Lemercier. He painted Say's pair of marriage portraits in 1793. From the collection of Dominique Raoul-Duval (all rights reserved).

At the age of nine, he was sent to a boarding school run by a French priest and an Italian layman. Although precisely at that time the archbishop of Lyon strengthened his grip on the schools in the region, for fear of the 'esprit philosophique' of the century, Say's overall recollections of the teaching and atmosphere were positive, with an exception for the endless hours of prayer on his knees. By contrast to the 'fable convenue' of the contemporary schoolbooks, he wrote that 'grammar and the Italian language were taught quite well, and Latin pretty badly. Like Jean Jacques Rousseau I could say that I was destined to learn Latin all my life, and to never really master it.'[4]

Say's father exported silk to European countries, and even to Turkey. When business was slack at the end of the 1770s, 'his debtors were dispersed all over Europe, and his creditors at his front door', as his son noted.[5] He went bankrupt and the family moved to Paris in 1780, where Jean-Estienne managed to re-establish his credit as a currency broker. His son Jean-Baptiste became a bank clerk at the age of fifteen with the firm of Laval and Wilfelsheim, and later with Louis Julien.[6] Eighteen years old, at the end of 1785, he was sent to England, together with his dear brother Horace, aged fourteen.

During this stay in London he resided in Croydon, where he worked for the trading company of James Bayle & Co., doing business with the Antilles, and later for Samuel & William Hilbert, trading with India.[7] He became well versed in English and caught his first glimpses of the Industrial Revolution. Both assets would later be extremely valuable to his career. His first theoretical economic notions were traced back by him to observations made in Croydon. There they were lodged in a fairly new house where one day a mason came in to fill up an entire window with bricks, as a new law levied a tax on the number of windows. So the owner suffered 'one enjoyment less' while the treasury gained nothing. At the end of his life, Say was to write an entire chapter in the *Cours Complet* about taxes that do not produce any fiscal revenues, without however mentioning the Croydon case again.[8] In the archives of the Borough of Croydon, the oldest map of the village kept there was drawn by J.-B. Say (see Figure 1.2).

Youthful revolutionary

At his return to Paris in 1787, Say became secretary to Clavière, like himself a man of Genevan Protestant stock. Etienne Clavière (1735–1793) was one generation older than Say, and the first of many Genevan Protestants who would play a role in Say's career. He was a clever financier and speculator, but also bridged the gap with literature and politics. With Mirabeau, Lafayette and others he founded the Society of Friends of the Blacks in 1788.[9] In that year he also became the director of a life insurance company. After the revolution he was one of the founders of the assignats system – where he was in the company of Say's father Jean-Estienne – and was also suspected of forging false assignats. Twice a finance minister, he was arrested with other Girondins in 1793 and found guilty of channelling funds away from the insurance company as well as from the treasury to emigrants abroad, who had fled from France since the Revolution.

Next to his directorship of the insurance company, Clavière was at least as active as a pamphleteer and pre-revolutionary activist. He went further than Turgot and Necker in proposing radical reforms for France: politically by advocating the general male franchise; economically by pleading against the prominent role of the nobility, which he believed stood in the way of a commercial society, and in favour of simple tastes and of public credit. So he took up clear positions on topics that were hotly debated at the time and would continue to be so during the first ten years of the Revolution period. Say's economic rejection of luxury and his plea for simplicity can to some extent be traced back to his first boss. These themes would recur in his *Décade* articles, in *Olbie* (1800) and in his later writings.

Whatmore writes about the evolution of the ideas of Clavière and his companion Brissot, from justifying popular sovereignty in small states to pleading a republican constitution for France. This was a truly revolutionary idea, as for most political and economic reformers the concept of France as a kingdom had been unassailable. Rousseau's ideas on the importance of virtuous popular manners for the development of a flourishing state were a guideline to them: 'From 1785, Clavière, Brissot and other members of their circle made Rousseau's idea of manners the linchpin of proposals to transform France into a different kind of republic: one whose merits Say would quickly be persuaded to support.'[10] Egalitarianism, meaning the abolishment of the aristocracy in the first

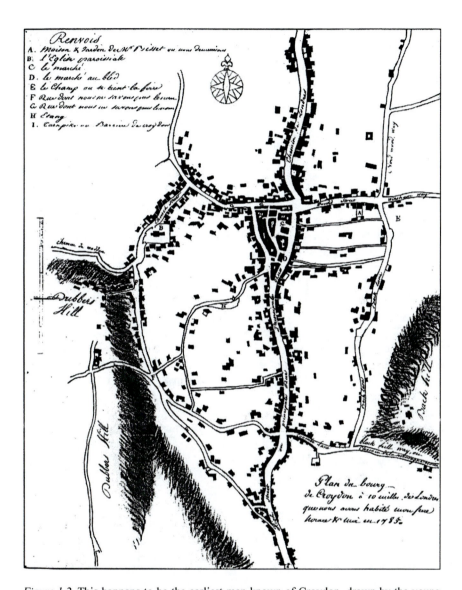

Figure 1.2 This happens to be the earliest map known of Croydon, drawn by the young J.-B. Say: 'Plan of the Borough of Croydon where we have lived, my brother Horace and me, in 1785'. The brothers stayed with Mr Alexander Bisset on Pound Street. Courtesy of the Borough of Croydon (all rights reserved).

place, was another essential idea. Aristocracy and luxurious consumption belonged to the past, the future was to commercial activity and simple manners.

Clavière may have strengthened Say's early republican beliefs. He has certainly influenced, or at least awakened, Say's turning to economics by lending him his copy of the *Wealth of Nations*. Say immediately felt so inspired that he rapidly ordered his own copy of its fifth edition (1789). This three-volume edition has survived, with Say's annotations on practically every page – summaries on top of the page, critical notes in the margin. It was donated by his grandson Léon Say to the Bibliothèque de l'Institut in Paris in 1888. We shall come back later to the content of the notes.

However, more grandiose events took place in 1789 than the printing of Smith's fifth edition. The Estates-General were called to meet, and the young Say contributed to the stream of publications overflowing all of France on this occasion. At the age of twenty-two he wrote a pamphlet on the freedom of the press. In rhetorical language he proposed the institution of a tribunal that would represent *La République des Lettres*, and would perform as an 'ideal nation', to be a tribunal in case of abuse of this freedom: 'There I will denounce the brutal libel, and will proudly ask for an explanation of what it contains against me, my family, my king and my country.'[11] In his own copy he afterwards crossed out *mon roi* in heavy black ink. Also in this annotated copy he describes this early work as 'quite mediocre', seeking an excuse in his age and in the atmosphere of the epoch. And precisely as a reflection of the age it is an interesting first product of the young Say, not yet an economist, and already more than an economist as well. There is also some irony in the fact that in the three first decades of the next century he would himself encounter serious problems of censorship: as the author of the *Traité d'Economie Politique*, a second edition of which was prohibited by Bonaparte; as a contributor to the occasionally censored *Censeur Européen*; and as a Conservatoire professor under surveillance by the French secret police.

When we turn to the events of 1789, we do not find Say's name among those of the 'vainqueurs de la Bastille'. But he must have been on the spot pretty rapidly, at least soon enough to collect a souvenir: a leaf of a seventeenth century prisoner's interrogation, marked in his son Horace's handwriting as 'a piece found by my father at the taking of the Bastille'.[12] His employer Clavière joined the Legislative Assembly, and through him Say obtained a job with the younger Mirabeau's *Courrier de Provence*.

Honoré Gabriel Riqueti, Count Mirabeau (1749–1791) was a colourful nobleman who had been elected to the Legislative Assembly as a representative of the Third Estate. According to the *Biographie Universelle*, in 1789 he was in the company of Clavière and other citizens banned from Geneva, all of them 'experienced publicists'. It can be imagined that Say's pamphlet on the freedom of the press was something of a recommendation as Mirabeau also wrote one on the same subject. The latter had wished to 'take this freedom stormingly' by the printing of more than ten thousand copies of his *Journal des États-Généraux* which aroused the anger of Louis XVI's minister Necker, and led to its confiscation within a week after its first printing in May 1789.[13] In spite of an edict forbidding reports of the Assembly, Mirabeau continued to publish under a different label, and again as the *Courrier de Provence* from July 1789 till his death in April 1791. His journal continued for another six months, until the end of September. Writing to Etienne Dumont in 1829, Say recalled that while the Genevan reverend was advising Mirabeau, all he did was to administer subscriptions. Whatmore thinks that this administrative experience, together with his writing talent demonstrated in his pamphlet on the liberty of the press, made him the qualified managing editor of the *Décade* in 1794.[14]

Clavière and Mirabeau belonged to the group of moderate bourgeois revolutionaries known as Girondins, and both spoke in the Assembly on the proposals of monetary reform. Clavière is considered by Tiran as the Girondins' foremost monetary theorist, and critic of the monetary practices of the *Ancien Régime*.[15] He and Mirabeau advocated a silver standard and an identical nominal and real value of coins, so as to avoid the earlier debasement of currency by the king. Regarding Clavière's ideas on the real economy, Tiran quotes from one of his pamphlets of 1790: 'Now less demand brings about less industry, less industry employs less individuals; less individuals being occupied, less will be produced, which means less population, less public force.'[16] It is tempting to read this sentence as an elementary summary of themes that would be recurrent in Say's economic thought, in particular Say's Law and his linking of economic and population growth.

Say's work on the *Courrier* was followed by his participation in the campaign of 1792, the first military trial of revolutionary France. He volunteered for recruitment into a Compagnie des Arts, about which he later wrote:

> However security and even joy reigned in the tents of the French almost within cannonballs reach. In the one where the author of this article found himself, the volunteers coolly discussed questions of agriculture, of political economy and even of literature.[17]

The same questions of political economy, in particular those of monetary matters and of the viability of the assignats system, were hotly debated in Paris. They determined the ill fate of Clavière, who as a minister of finance had been unable to restore the republic's finances. In June 1793, one month after Say's demobilisation and marriage (and three months before the beginning of the reign of the Terror) he was arrested with other Girondin ministers, on charges of being an English agent and forging assignats. He killed himself in prison in December.

Say's recent military action saved him from the possibility of becoming suspect as a result of his close alliance with Clavière. In the theatre of shifting dominances and alliances during the first decade of the French Revolution, he was still on the right side of events, and on the way of coming even closer to the centre of it.

The first portrait known of the young Say dates from this period. It is a drawing by (or at least attributed to) Isabey. The only known persons among his fellow volunteers are the poet Andrieux, his later associate of *La Décade*, and the painter Pajou, who painted the pair of wedding pictures of Say and his wife Julie Gourdel de Loche whom he married on 25 May 1793. She came from a Roman Catholic family in the Calvados, but a church wedding never took place and their children received a Protestant education.

In a later reconstruction of important events in his life during the years 1793–1807, the beginning certainly reflects the 'troubled times' he lived in, as the first three notes reveal:

- *My marriage*
- *Beginning of the Terror*
- *The Girondins executed and outlawed*[18]

The sources of Say's income during the first year of his marriage, when the couple lived on the Rue Montmartre, are unclear. The *Courrier de Provence* had ceased to exist in 1791. There was the unfulfilled plan of a boarding school. Say did not come from a wealthy family; his wife Julie's father, a lawyer, might have supplied some means. He might have sold a few articles. And he was working on translations of works by Helen Maria Williams and by Benjamin Franklin. In any case he made it clear at the founding of *La Décade* in 1794, that material considerations were an important factor in his personal decision to join the founders of this journal. At least he proudly reported about his situation in a letter to his aunt Delaroche in Geneva, who was staying there with his aunt Duvoisin,[19] just after the first issues of the *Décade* had been printed:

> As to my position, in spite of twenty sorts of worries through which I have passed and of which I am not yet entirely relieved – but I will spare you the details – I am quite satisfied with my present position. I find myself the director of a printing house with a salary of one thousand écus, plus one tenth of the interest [profit] promised.[20] It has always been my ambition to be at the head of a manufactory and nothing is more agreeable than a print-ing house. I do not dissimulate however the risks of such an enterprise; but what would one do at all if one only looked at the risks? Our printing firm, primarily dedicated to Literature, arts and sciences is perhaps in a more favourable position than others. I live in a small apartment on the third floor in the same building, with an excellent wife and a wonderfully pros-pering child, one must be as happy as it is possible to be here.[21]

La Décade

The first issue of *La Décade philosophique, littéraire et politique, par une Société de Républicains*, appeared on the tenth floréal of the Republican year II (29 April 1794). Its title reflected the revolutionary calendar, dividing each month in three ten-day 'weeks'. There were seven members in the journal's society, six of whom were also editors. The seventh, Charles Arnault Aumont, was only a financier taking part in the venture with six thousand livres. At twenty-seven, Jean-Baptiste Say was the youngest and probably the least known of them all. Yet he was the *Rédacteur Général* (managing editor) of the journal during its first six years.

Of the others, Pierre Louis Ginguené (1748–1816) and François-Guillaume-Jean-Stanislas Andrieux (1759–1833) had already established their literary reputations. The latter had served with Say in the 'Compagnie des Arts'. Amaury Pineux Duval (1760–1838) had been a brilliant young lawyer, and had served as embassy secretary under Talleyrand in Naples. His brother had been another companion of Say in the arts company. The former monk Joachim le Breton (1760–1818) had in 1792 been one of the authors drafting the defence of the *Constitution Civile du Clergé*, to be sent to the Pope. One year later, he was one of the official reporters to the Minister of the Interior about the economic state of the French *départements*. Finally the naturalist Georges Toscan (1756–1826), the librarian of the Musée d'Histoire Naturelle, was not a very conspicuous member.[22]

Say continued to be the managing editor till 1800, when his membership of the Tribunat commenced to ask too much of his time. Soon after the foundation of the journal he had made it clear that he not only expected it to spread the republican message – so clear from its title – but to make some money for its owners as well. To Duval, then residing in Rennes, he wrote in the autumn of 1794 that he estimated the interest in the whole of France to be large enough so as to 'make an annual income for each of us of at least 25,000 livres' – more than four times the sum he had proudly reported to his aunt Duvoisin. This remark was intended as an incentive for recruiting new subscribers. In an earlier letter he had asked Duval for the addresses of the most important cafés in Rennes, Nantes, Brest and Rouen, in order to send around presentation copies 'as our fate depends upon it'.[23]

For an era of many short-lived periodicals the continuity of *La Décade* was remarkable, so it cannot have been a commercial failure. But it is difficult to tell whether the commercial success did entirely live up to Say's optimistic expectations. The society of the owners possessed its own printing house, where books such as the works of Chamfort were published, along with Say's French edition of Benjamin Franklin's *Poor Richard Saunders*.[24] There are no figures available regarding the society's profits, but the author's fee for each article was twenty-four francs.[25] Say himself kept an account of his personal finances in the former livres as well as in francs till late in 1810, but only started doing this after his *Décade* editorship. The Duval papers show him to have received fees of F464 over six months in 1801 when, as a Tribun, he contributed much less than during his editorship. Soon after the fall of Robespierre in 1794, he asked his younger brother Louis to come over from Lausanne to work at the *Décade* office. This could only mean that business was running satisfactorily.

According to Kitchin, the reputation of the editors was such that they could have sold their articles for more than the *Décade* was willing to pay. It can be questioned whether this was also true for the young Say, certainly in the early phase of the journal. Within a year of its founding, the periodical's existence was threatened by the provisioning problems of Paris at the end of 1794, when inflation and food scarcity had risen enormously after the end of the Terror. Say sent money to Duval in Rennes in order to try to purchase sugar, butter, meat, coffee and candles. These were only available in Paris at extravagant prices. Especially the candles were of the greatest importance, as the printers had threatened to leave *La Décade* if they could not attain their usual production level (the measure by which they were paid). Say wrote ironically to Duval: 'Look, my dear friend, how much closer to nature this revolution has brought us.'[26]

As to the editorial programme, the flyer introducing the journal mentioned politics, science, literature and art. Economics was explicitly named as being an element of philosophy, and defined as follows: 'Political Economy, or the social art [i.e. science] with all its subdivisions among which Public Instruction will certainly occupy an important position.' In the Republic, new forms of literature and criticism were expected to flourish. Kitchin classifies the *Décade* editors as belonging to an elite of moderate republicans, who after Thermidor made their career, albeit not without compromising, in the Institut and in politics. The 'Institut National des Sciences et des Arts' was set up by the Convention in 1795. It was intended to replace the Academies which had been suppressed in 1793. Its aim, Whatmore writes, 'was to unite the best minds in a variety of disciplines for the furtherance of truth and the support of the French republic'.[27]

The Institut was divided into three 'Classes' for the arts and the sciences. Between the first for 'Physical and Mathematical Sciences' and the third for 'Literature and the Fine Arts, the *Seconde Classe* was devoted to the *Sciences Morales et Politiques*. The latter had sections for political economy, history, geography and statistics, as well as morals, social science and legislation, and the Condorcetian subject of 'analysis of feelings and ideas'. With this subdivision it was 'unlike any other educational establishment in Europe'.[28]

But already in 1803, the Institut was reorganised by Bonaparte into four Classes, roughly corresponding to the earlier seventeenth and eighteenth century Academies.[29] The class of 'moral and political' sciences was suppressed altogether, only to reappear in October 1832 as Académie des Sciences Morales et Politiques – ironically one month before Say's death. Its reinstitution by Louis Philippe had been prepared by Guizot and Roederer. Of course this long gap tells as much about Napoleon's dislike of the social sciences as it does about the reactionary climate of the *Restauration*. We shall return to this matter, when discussing Say's efforts in trying to become an *Académicien*.

From the start of the Institut National in 1795, an interest was shown by the *Décade* in the reports of all classes, which leads Kitchin to the conclusion that the journal supposed its readers to be participating in a unity of culture and in a continued cosmopolitanism. For in spite of the war with England and Germany, the *Décade* also had a clear orientation towards foreign publications and scientific work in other countries.[30] Say's own background, with his formative period in London, accounts for the large attention given to British publications. At his boarding school he had already received Italian lessons, which is reflected in his

Décade articles. Also, events in Germany and the US were commented upon at length.

A glimpse of the details of business is provided by a letter Say wrote to the bookseller and publisher Paschoud in Geneva in 1797. He began by pronouncing his hope that 'the times of peace will be favourable to the book trade, which is quite weak at present'.[31] Say further informed him about the success in Paris of Edward Gibbon's *Memoirs* (which had been published in 1796), and announced the mailing of twenty-four copies of its French translation, produced by the printing house of the *Décade*.[32] He also proposed to him to have printed, at the expense of the *Décade*, a hundred posters for the journal of which he included the text with his letter. This had worked quite well in French cities; Paschoud was to administer the subscriptions, and would receive four sous for every registration. As Say had noted that the high cost of international postage was a barrier for potential Swiss subscribers, he proposed to him to have the journals delivered to Paschoud; he could then further distribute these by the Swiss mail. Say concluded by writing that his journal was 'the highest estimated literary journal' in France, and he offered Paschoud publicity for his books in it, as well as a free copy for his reading room if he succeeded in acquiring subscriptions.

The organ of the *Idéologie*

It is impossible to improve upon the introductory statement of Lécuyer and Oberschall in their encyclopedia article on the so-called *Idéologues*: 'Social science began after the fall of Robespierre.'[33] The foundation of the Institut gave a powerful incentive to the movement of the *Idéologie*, a label coined in 1796 by Destutt de Tracy. With this name he intended to make a clear distinction between 'metaphysics' in the meaning of Condorcet's analysis of the senses and of ideas, and the 'old metaphysics' (*ancienne métaphysique*). Originally it was Destutt's idea to call the new social scientists 'Idéologistes', but the nickname of 'Idéologues', invented by their opponents, became the household name. Lécuyer and Oberschall even call the Idéologie, laid down by Destutt de Tracy and Cabanis, the official doctrine of the Second Class: 'This doctrine, with its stress on the analysis of language and of signs and its notion of a perceptible relationship between the moral and the physical influenced empirical social research in ethnography and hygiene and also affected government administration.'[34]

F. Picavet distinguishes between two groups of Idéologues. The first group contained a number of people already – or about to become – famous in 1789 such as Condorcet, Sieyès, Roederer and Laplace:

> Under the Directoire, the second group realises at the Institut (the living Encyclopédie) the intimate alliance of the arts ['lettres'], the sciences and philosophy. Cabanis and Destutt de Tracy are working at the progress of the physiologic and rational idéologie, theoretical and applied; they are assisted or followed upon by Daunou, M.J. Chénier, Andrieux, Benjamin Constant and J.B. Say; ... by Saint-Simon and Aug. Comte.[35]

It was the intention of the two branches, the 'rationnels' or social scientists and the 'physiologues' or physical and medical scientists, to integrate their findings into one Science of Man, with the ultimate objective 'to change the face of the world'. 'Progress à la Condorcet' was written on their banner. In Kitchin's opinion the doctrine of the *Décade* coincided to a large extent with the programme of the Idéologie, as was shown by the journal's agnostic zeal and its republican conviction.[36] The editors' belief in progress was evident from the large attention given to the ideas of Helvétius, Rousseau and Diderot. The two 'classics' of the idea of progress, Condorcet's *Esquisse* (1795) and Mme de Staël's *De la Littérature* (1800), were immediately reviewed at length. When a second edition of the latter work came out only a few months after the first, it was again reviewed by Say.

As a youngster he could not yet aspire to the Institut, but he met many members of its Second Class in the salons of Madame Helvétius and others, and one of them, Ginguené, was his colleague at the *Décade*. The latter was in the section 'Analysis of Sensations' with Cabanis and Volney; Sieyès, Roederer and Dupont de Nemours were members of 'Political Economy'. Say must enthusiastically have absorbed their ideas, in particular the necessity of separating religious beliefs and virtuous civil practices. In the *Décade*, launched at the height of the Terror, a central topic was the question: how to make the Revolution work by solidly founding republican manners in France. In his first book, *Olbie* (1800), Say was to deal with this question. But in his *Décade* years, he was a very generalist commentator and reviewer.

His contributions were sometimes signed JBS; his pseudonyms were 'Boniface Véridick' and 'Atticus'. Judging by the number of recognisable contributions from his pen, his interests in this period were not so much economic as literary and philosophical. In the papers he left behind, a sizable amount of literary manuscripts can be found. Tiran has noted that he was the author of a number of plays, only one of which was actually performed.

For one year, Say's brother Horace was responsible for the section on national politics. He also contributed reviews of books on mathematics, physics and astronomy. According to Tiran, the two brothers put their mark on the *Décade* in the period of the Directoire (1795–1799).[37] Forget quotes Staum on three criteria for being a true representative of the Idéologie movement: (a) visiting certain salons; (b) publishing in the *Décade*; (c) being a moderate republican, and critical of Bonaparte. Jean-Baptiste Say answers to all three.[38]

Regaldo has identified a total of about 300 authors who wrote for the journal, 40 of whom were regular contributors. Over the years, no less than 60 members of the Institut published in the journal. The number of subscriptions to the *Décade* ranged between 350 and 900.

2 At the crossroads of literature, politics and economics

A promising young man of letters

In the second half of the 1790s, the young father Say was moving upward on a career path of literature and politics.[1] Economics still seemed just a secondary field of interest.

His detailed commitment with purely literary contributions in the *Décade* is evident from his correspondence with François Vernes, another writer originating from and living in Geneva.[2] Say wrote to him as Citizen Vernes, Man of Letters, or alternatively, *Administrateur*. In 1797 he told him that a lot of poetry was submitted for publication, and he advised Vernes to be more critical of his own work: 'There is a lot of esprit in the ideas and turns of several couplets, but there are many passages lacking poetry and others wanting harmony.'

In August 1799 he reported on literature and politics. He started with apologising for his delay in replying on Vernes' last letter, because of the multitude of events happening in Paris:

> *I am overwhelmed by them and still I have to behave decently and keep up the appearance of freedom of spirit, like those sluts who are starving from hunger and who lively pretend to give the impression of love ...*
>
> *In the next issue of la Décade philosophique I will put the Verses to Molé which you sent me.[3] They have been very well made, but truly you are giving too much credit to this comedian. Be more careful with your talent. If these people receive love-letters from distinguished authors, they will end up by believing they are great men ...*
>
> *I have no literary news to report apart from what you can read in my journal; regarding political news, this is less sinister than a few decades* [of the republican calendar] *ago. Siey[è]s seems to take the upper hand in the directoire, and the friends of peace and of a moderate system are drawing favourable predictions from this. We ordinary Frenchmen are only doing well on certain moments, when we urgently feel the need to do so; but then we are doing great, and when the kings do not grab the opportunity to conclude peace, they will be badly off. If unfortunately the campaign will be reopened next year, you will see the denial of my prediction.*

The first and last of these paragraphs are illustrative of the confusing political climate of the period, in which Say sometimes felt like a prostitute of the pen, and was inclined to optimistically bet on the wrong horse – not for the last time in his life. The second echoes his interest in literature and the theatre. A number of mostly undated small letters about theatre tickets demonstrate that Say and his wife liked to see stage plays. The addressee of these notes was Charles Mahérault, professor of literature at the Ecole Centrale du Panthéon, as well as government commissioner of the Theatre of the Republic, close to the Palais-Royal. Say corresponded with him in both capacities. He asked him to 'keep pushing the sale of my *Olbie*' and promised him an announcement of his literary work in the *Décade*. Also, on several occasions he asked for theatre tickets for his wife so that she could accompany him, or be seated next to her husband.[4] In *Olbie* he wrote that 'Theatre gives us a more intense abiltity to sympathise with others.' Therefore he recommended for the Olbians a theatre such as the French possessed already, where 'models of humanity and greatness of soul were constantly offered'.[5] In the introduction to his *Traité d'Economie Politique* (1803) he would even draw a parallel between the fully developed theatrical models, understandable to all layers of society, and the reasonings of political economy, still to be discovered and taught. In the former, Racine's masterpieces as well as simple farces reflected the nature of man. But in the latter discipline, the most elementary truths were yet to be explained to administrators and simple citizens alike.

Many years later, in 1819, when Say had just been appointed to the chair of Economie Industrielle at the Conservatoire, the same author Vernes was the bearer of a letter to Say's old friend and colleage Andrieux. The latter wrote back that (the playwright) Picard had given theatre tickets to Vernes; and that he had also told the theatre director about Say's 'good intentions'. Whatever these may have been, the theatre clearly remained a focus of Say's interest.

Revolution and progress

When a right-wing, confessional movement started to question the revolutionary results after 1795, by suggesting a relation between a naïve belief in progress and the excesses of the reign of the Terror, the *Décade* editors came to the defence of the eighteenth century's achievements. Towards the end of his editorship, Say reacted to one of Duval's contributions in an almost emotional letter:

> *What is this outrage breaking loose against the eighteenth century? …*
> *Because a horrible revolution has characterised its last ten years, has it*
> *therefore soiled the entire century?*

He attributed the outrage to 'a few despicable pamphleteers' and denied the second accusation:

> *[by agreeing] you would admit that this [revolution] has soiled the last ten*
> *years; and those are, taken altogether, the most beautiful years of the*

century, and equally the years that will have the longest and the greatest consequences.[6]

Not only did the *Décade* editors wish to defend the revolutionary heritage against reactionary movements, but also against people who might wish to go further. They had come to belong to that part of the bourgeoisie which had something to lose after the Terror. This became evident from their support for the not so democratic census constitution of the year III, and from their opposition to revolutionary-egalitarian plans like Babeuf's. Say's opposition was also manifested in practice. His own provisioning problems for the *Décade* at the end of 1794 have been mentioned above. In his reconstructed diary of life events he noted for May 1795: 'The faubourg St. Antoine wants to reestablish the Terror; with my battalion I march against the faubourg.'[7] And the subsequent note made abundantly clear on which side he stood: 'The sections of Paris conquered by Bonaparte. The constitution of year 3 established. The victory.'

The fear of a revolution of the fourth estate made him and his colleagues blind to the needs of the proletariat. Not for a second did they regret the decision to take the franchise away from them. Horace Say wrote with praise about the Directoire's decision to stop food aid to Paris in the winter of 1795–1796. He also put the blame for the workman's poverty on himself, because of his careless spending and alcoholism. Even ten years after the appearance on stage of Gracchus Babeuf and his 'niveleurs', their actions were still an alarming memory to the *Décade*.[8]

With regard to the discussion on the constitution of 1795, Tiran – following Regaldo – notes that the editors started taking a more partisan position than they had done before as just commentators. Say found it unnecessary to have the constitution preceded by a declaration of human rights. For him the following preamble would suffice:

> The French people, willing to assure to all its constituent individuals their tranquility, their personal security and their right of property, and the freedom compatible with a great association, has agreed to organise its government as follows.[9]

Even if the revolutionary bourgeois of the *Décade* had become a little more conservative, they still had an eye for social injustice. Say in 1796 published an allegory, *Les Enrichis*, on the practices of swindling food dealers. And Andrieux in 1800 warned the bourgeoisie against an attitude of complacency that might go hand in hand with taking over the position of the old aristocracy. Horace Say wrote in favour of a progressive tax on estates and of equal inheritance rights, in order to attain a more even distribution of income and wealth. But the journal did not suggest a coherent economic programme. Laissez-faire was the only recurrent recipe. On monetary reform, Horace was a more outspoken writer than his brother. The revolutionary 'assignats', paper money, had suffered an enormous depreciation. Incidentally Jean-Estienne Say, the father, had been one of the founders of this system, the demise of which would make him bankrupt for the second time (after his first bankruptcy had driven him from Lyon to Paris). Horace's plan was to peg the value of the new currency by indexation to the monthly average of the corn price. When a plan for a national circulation bank was proposed, the *Décade* suggested a kind of free banking plan: the safety of such a bank would be beyond doubt if it were seen as a private bank of very secure credit.[10]

Say's younger brother Honoré, called Horace (1771–1799), probably was better known than Jean-Baptiste when he died in Napoleon's Egyptian campaign. In 1794, the founding year of the *Décade*, he had gone into the army as a cavalry captain and afterwards joined the School of Engineers. He had not only been in charge of the *Décade* section of national politics, but he had taught the art of fortification at the Ecole Polytechnique, and was a member of the Institut d'Egypte. As a true polymath in the spirit of the Idéologie, he had published on physics, literature, language and Egyptology. He died after getting wounded in Napoleon's siege of Acre. In a letter, Bonaparte paid a tribute to three of his generals, and wrote: 'the engineers battalion commander Say and the company commander Croizier, my aide-de-camp, fallen in Syria, were officers of the greatest merit'. Jean-Baptiste Say wrote his brother's obituary in the *Décade*.[11]

Say's eldest Horace Emile, born in 1794, was named after his uncle. Adrienne – later also known as Andrienne – was born in 1796. After the birth of Hippolyte in 1799 the family moved to the Rue de Tournon, which reflected not only Say's growing family but also his rising social status.

Regarding his achievements as an Idéologue, Jean-Baptiste Say is classified by Kitchin in the same category of people as Sieyès and Chénier. They had no great merits in its theoretical deepening or refinement, but as authors and politicians they spread the message of the Idéologie. The close scientific and political relationships, often tied in with friendship, between many Idéologues are reminiscent of those between the Physiocrats. Their meeting point was the 'salon' of Helvetius' widow in Auteuil,[12] and later the one of Madame Lebreton. Say also visited the salon of the English poet Helen Maria Williams, who had come to Paris after the Revolution and whose work he translated. Finally the salon of Madame de Salm attracted the company of Say, and of many other authors, scientists, artists and composers.[13] An engraving of the visitors to the salon of Princess Constance de Salm shows the young Say, pictured as quite bald-headed, in the company of his fellow editors Andrieux, Ginguené and Amaury Duval, the painter Pajou, the German discoverer von Humboldt and some thirty others, depicted with their heads above the clouds.[14]

The salons were informal gatherings. In these circles, a special purpose could occasion the founding of a formal society, like the Société des Amis des Noirs of which Say became a member.

La Société des Amis des Noirs

The second Society of the Friends of the Blacks 'and of the colonies' was first and foremost a political society. But its foreign and female members, like the prominent Swedish abolitionist Wadström and the English poet Helen Maria Williams, also made it look like something of a salon.[15] The first society by this name was founded by Brissot and Clavière in 1788, and actively campaigned for the abolition of slavery till 1793. In 1798 and 1799, Say and his wife were active members of the second, which also counted a number of former slaves among its members. In the words of Gainot, 'The discrete but real presence of Cabanis, the brother-in-law of Condorcet, testifies the essential involvement of the future Idéologues in the second Society of the Friends of the Blacks.'[16]

Its revival had very practical reasons. In 1794 the first French Republic had abolished slavery in principle, but its effective ending in the West Indian colonies was a complicated story. In 1791 the black commander and later general Toussaint Louverture had started a successful rebellion in the French part of Santo Domingo (Haiti), and in 1793 he proclaimed the abolition of slavery there.

After the French official abolition he switched alliances from the Spanish on the other half of the island – the present Dominican Republic – to the French. But between him and the former French governor Sonthonax, an ardent revolutionary and opponent of the aristocratic white plantation owners, tensions mounted and in 1797 the latter was expulsed from the island. At the same time it became clear that the French Directoire government was considerably less revolutionary than pretended, and suspicions began to brew that it might reconsider the abolition of slavery. So the second Society of Friends of the Blacks 'and of the colonies' had a clear cause to defend. Although its members might in principle be opponents of colonialism altogether – like the later J.-B. Say would testify – for the time being they wished to defend the status quo of colonies with free labour. The expulsed governor Sonthonax was a very active member. Say's involvement started in 1798 with the publication in the *Décade* of a report on the production costs of cane sugar in the Dutch East Indies. In that system with free labour, costs were lower than those under slavery in the French West Indies. Wadström ordered no less than 2000 copies of this *Décade* issue, to be distributed among members of the legislative assembly and to be sent to the colonies. At the next session in May 1798, Say was present for the first time. Occasionally he served as the secretary of the meetings. Mrs Say joined in 1799, after Mrs Wadström and Miss Williams. Cabanis was registered on the membership list as 'representative of the people'.

After a number of meetings held in private houses, the Society came together in the Ministry of the Navy and the Colonies. In 1799 minister Bruix of this department wrote to the Directoire, in order to exonerate himself from any complicity in the true character and objectives of the society. It had been reported to the Directoire that a Society under the name of Friends of the Blacks, chaired by the notorious Sonthonax, held its meetings in a room of his ministry. His predecessor, Bruix wrote to his defence, had granted the use of a room for meetings of a number of citizens wishing to improve colonial agriculture. When citizen Grégoire – the famous anti-slavery abbé – had asked him the favour to continue this practice, he had wished to

> assure myself of its true objective; whether these citizens did not intend to form a political society, with a president and secretaries; and I remained convinced by their confirmations that here was no question of such a thing, but only of the meeting of several citizens solely occupied with the improvement of colonial culture, of the elevation of animals, of the progress of plantations, of cultivating the soil, and altogether this meeting was only presented to me as the model of a true colonial institute.[17]

He concluded his letter as follows:

> If in good faith, and willing to do good, I have committed a fault, so punish me, but render me justice in believing that I have been more afflicted than you might be displeased. So many traps have been set for me since I have entered the ministry that it is not surprising I have fallen into this one.[18]

His letter demonstrates that the formal organisation of a society as either a series of informal meetings like a 'salon', or a full-fledged 'society' having its meeting place at a ministry, could carry a heavy political load for the acting Directoire government. This was neither the first nor the last occasion on which Say himself, or an organisation or periodical in which he was involved, would meet with political suspicion or obstruction.

The sequel of events with regard to French colonial slavery is well known. Napoleon's general Leclerc invaded Haiti and made Louverture a prisoner; he died in France in 1803. Slavery was continued in the French colonies of Martinique and Guadeloupe. Say would again discuss the economics of slavery in his *Traité* and his *Cours Complet*. In 1814 he sent a copy of the second edition of his treatise to the Haitian president Boyer, and in the 1820s he was involved in a debate with the British abolitionist Adam Hodgson on the profitability of the slavery system.

Enlightenment and economics

At the age of thirty, Jean-Baptiste Say already had a background in commerce, literature and journalism, but his future in economics was not yet clearly visible. About France's economic potential, in the perspective of an industrial revolution, he wrote the following recommendation in 1796:

> I wish that its agriculture and all branches of industry will be in a state of most brilliant activity; that its seaports full of ships, its canals and rivers

covered with boats, its markets clean and well provisioned, will show a picture of abundance. I wish that every field worker in the country, every city craftsman will have perhaps not an independent property, but at least the perspective of acquiring one in old age, even if it be only a small life annuity. I wish that in every household there be convenient and well maintained utensils, dresses of good tissues, and white linen, giving everywhere the impression not of opulence but of ease; that every person will be able to read, and will have in his chest at least a few books to instruct himself about manufacturing processes, and a few journals too so as not to be a stranger to the interest of his country ... I wish that in this great republic there will not be ... one miserable person who might complain being unable to earn, by work and good behaviour, a decent living, and lead a life which the English would call 'comfortable'.[19]

In a footnote Say even suggested the introduction of this word in the French language: 'After a long day's effort when we feel the need of restoring our strength, a solid dinner and a glass of good wine are comfortable.' And he recommended the inclusion of this notion in the French dictionary.

Among all his literary and political contributions in the *Décade*, Say's perspective for France gives a first glimpse of the economist who wished to convey the message of the Encyclopedists to a wider audience, and would continue to do so with a political programme in his *Olbie* (1800), and an economic one in his *Traité d'Economie Politique* (1803). Commentating on his youthful pamphlet on the freedom of the press, he wrote that he had wished 'to open all influence to Enlightenment ideas'.[20] So he may rightfully be labelled a worthy Enlightenment character as well as an Idéologie figure.

It is remarkable that Jonathan Israel in *Democratic Enlightenment* (2011), the last of his three books on 'Radical Enlightenment', fails to mention the *Décade* as an enlightenment organ, and only once in passing writes about Cabanis. It may be true that he cares more about ideas than about institutions – for example in belittling the influence of Mme Helvétius' salon – but the Condorcetian, value-free approach to social science and the role of Say who had started his publishing career with a pamphlet on the freedom of the press and continued with Olbie, deserve more than a footnote in an Israel-like approach of Enlightenment writings.[21] Freedom, universalism and progress, three of Israel's essential elements in his definition of Enlightenment, would continue to be central themes in Say's economics. Two others, agnosticism and republicanism, were already mentioned above as recurrent subjects in the *Décade*. Perhaps the explanation of Georges Gusdorf, given in 1975, may account for Israel's neglect and perhaps a more general disinterest in the achievements of the Idéologues:

the thought of the idéologues has been lost in the sands of an ungrateful memory ... every man whose active life is situated between the fateful dates of 1789 and 1815, or more largely between the disappearance of the last philosophes and the ascent of Romanticism, inevitably seems a dwarf.[22]

For a balanced judgment, it seems necessary to distinguish between ideas, characters and events. We may no longer agree to the first of Say's two statements quoted above on the last decade of the eighteenth century as 'the most beautiful years of the century', but we can hardly disagree on the second as 'the years that will have the longest and the greatest consequences'.

3   A dissident under the Consulate

Political theory and practice

In the years of Say's editorship, the political influence of the *Décade* grew slowly but steadily. In its editorial policy after the Terror, the centre of gravity was moved from foreign to national affairs. It remained a convinced advocate of laissez-faire, while disapproving of the frivolousness of the nouveaux riches. After the coup of 1797 the linkages between the editors and the executive power became visible. Ginguené was appointed as ambassador to Turin, after an unsuccessful attempt to succeed Carnot as a member of the Directoire. Andrieux became a member of the Council of Five Hundred. But as the *Décade*'s political editor he continued to criticise the Directoire sharply for its corruption and its waste of public means. When war broke out again in 1799, the journal exercised a violent criticism of the Directoire policy, and in this way helped to pave the way for Brumaire. (In the letter to Vernes from August of that year, quoted above, Say had ranked himself among the 'friends of peace'.) Kitchin does not exclude the possibility of a certain participation of the editors in Bonaparte's coup, in view of Cabanis' active role. The future First Consul had even taken the trouble to pay a visit to the salon of Madame Helvétius, posing as a philosopher-statesman. If, two centuries before him, King Henry IV might have said 'Paris is well worth a mass', Napoleon may have thought 'Paris is well worth some philosophy and anticlericalism'. At any rate, Andrieux as well as Duval and Say did write in positive terms about the coup and the new constitution.

Four of the editors were appointed as members of the Tribunat: Andrieux, Ginguené, Le Breton and Say. For the latter this meant that he had to give up the managing editorship of the journal, but all four continued to contribute to it.[1] There was certainly an overlap of the subject matter of their legislative duties and their editorial work. As Tribuns they had to discuss – and no more than discuss – the draft bills coming from the Conseil d'État. Subsequently the Legislative Body had to vote – and no more than vote – on the proposed laws. 'Legislative eunuchs' is the judgement of the Dutch historian Jacques Presser with respect to the actors in this show.[2] Nevertheless the Tribuns received an annual salary of 15,000 francs.

Still the *Décade* editors did not refrain from criticism with their pen, in spite of the bridles that were soon proclaimed for the press. Already in 1800 Ginguené became a suspect of the secret police as a possible conspirator against the First Consul. When this became known in 1801, the *Décade* censored itself for one month by dropping the section on French domestic politics. Inside the Tribunat quite rapidly a kernel of a liberal opposition became noticeable, centred around Benjamin Constant. By this development the influence of the *Décade* and its circle waned, almost immediately after it had reached prominence in the political developments and in the careers of its editors.

For the time being however, Say could sit quietly behind his desk and write. At the end of 1799 he wrote in his reconstructed journal: 'I publish my Olbie', and subsequently for 1800: 'Nothing remarkable [*sic*]. I start writing my Treatise of Political Economy.'[3]

So *Olbie* was still the fruit of his *Décade* period. In 1797 the Institut had organised an essay contest on the subject: 'What are the most appropriate means to establish the morals of a people?' On behalf of the Morals section of the *Seconde Classe*, it was soon announced by Roederer that this should be read as 'What are the most appropriate *institutions*' to this purpose.

None of the contenders was judged worthy of the prize, but Say's submission was praised as the second among three works of commendation. In the *Décade* it was reviewed favourably by Théremin, and critically by Ginguené who could not discover 'a system and a theory' in it.[4] For Say this was enough encouragement to rewrite and publish his long essay himself.

In the first part of his book on Say's 'republicanism', Richard Whatmore has given an admirable survey of the evolution of the discussion on manners and morals in the first ten years of the Revolution.[5] Abolishing the Old Order had been a lot easier than establishing a new one. Proclaiming a republic and a commercial society did not automatically bring about economic growth, and trust in orderly public finance. An education in republican manners, supported by new institutions, was necessary to establish the confidence and structure which would make the republic work. Whatmore describes the increasing radicalisation of the solutions proposed by Clavière and Saint-Just, and the return to more realistic plans for republican education of Condorcet, of Sieyès and finally Roederer – if we do not give too much weight to the calendar of national fêtes for every possible local crop or for 'visible nature' proclaimed by Sieyès, and to the salutary effects of 'republican music' praised by Roederer.[6]

Olbie

Say's *Olbie* was a worthy successor to these plans. In the *Décade* milieu, two kinds of approaches to the problem of moral elevation were proposed. Some Idéologues, like Ginguené, Andrieux and Duval, had a firm belief in the value of education and in the positive influence of good examples in art, literature and the theatre. Republican fêtes could work in support of such a programme. Others like Cabanis and Destutt de Tracy expected more from a programme of economic reform measures, aimed at providing space for personal development of the individual. Specific measures proposed by the latter were aimed at restoring order in public finance, establishing economic freedom and equality before the law, an equal distribution of heritage portions, the possibility of divorce and the exclusion of the religious orders from public office.

In Say's book elements of both approaches can be found. In his imaginary 'blessed state' *Olbie* (from the Greek adjective *olbios*), France could easily be recognised. After the overthrow of an absolute monarchy, good laws had not been enough to fulfil the promise of a just and incorrupt republic. Therefore a programme of legislation leading to virtuous manners would be necessary, but for the Olbians their first and foremost necessity was to possess a good textbook of economics:

> Sufficient wellbeing for the indigent can only result from a wise sharing of general wealth which, itself, can only be the fruit of a good system of political economy. This science is important, the most important of all, if morality and the happiness of human beings deserve to be regarded as the most worthy object of research.

> [To which he added the footnote:]
> Whoever writes an elementary treatise on political economy, capable of being taught in public schools and understood by all public bureaucrats even of the lowest level, by countrymen and by artisans, would be the saviour of the country.[7]

In Olbian society there would be no luxury or conspicuous consumption. And in principle all trades were equal, while idle incomes were condemned. For the organisation of retirement funds a system of savings banks was institutionalised. As 'great wealth is devastating for good morals', the acts and fortunes of all citizens would be made public information. This would help in making non-financial considerations an incentive for work as well.

Exclusively commercial societies, like Carthage and Venice in the past, had encouraged luxury and idleness. By contrast, 'the Olbians knew the love of gain to be a sin almost as dangerous as idleness'. Really 'industrious' societies would be fairly egalitarian. For Say and many of his contemporaries the United States of America, as a successful large republic, was an inspiring example. Yet he warned the Americans against the 'general tendency of the minds in your beautiful republic': their virtuousness might be corrupted by an increasing wealth.

To Olbian women, those professions which 'make the heart rude and the character mordant' were forbidden. But as the household and caretaking jobs were reserved for them, the government also made them responsible for the national well-being.

This echoes Cabanis' conception of the role of women, published in 1798 in his *Rapports du physique et de moral de l'homme*: they should be mothers and caretakers rather than politicians or heads of households.

Moral elevation was expected by Say to result from 'useful recreation', which however should not be too tiring! The theatre and national fêtes were considered most appropriate to that purpose. At the fêtes a tribunal of *Gardiens des Moeurs* – Say's second tribunal, after the one proposed for the Liberty of the press ten years before – would distribute distinctions and rewards. In a *Panthéon* the statues of Orestes, Pylades, Henry (the fourth?), Sully, Montaigne and Laboétie were to be erected as an example to the citizens.[8] Once they had entered it through the gate, under the inscription 'To Friendship', they would be able to read wise statements on friendship, zeal and thrift.

None of these recommendations, with the possible exception of the one about economics education, was very new in 1800. The Olbian economy is reminiscent of what he had written in the *Décade* in 1796 about the desirable future of the French economy. So it is not surprising that Say's essay was not prize-winning. Two centuries later, the modern reader will recognise many elements proposed earlier by other Idéologues and their forerunners; he may also feel some aversion to the amount of social control proposed for this rather dull and honest society.

Olbian economics

Say starts his pamphlet by defining 'Morale' as the science of social conduct, and 'Moralité' as the exclusively human faculty of considering the rules of social science in one's behaviour: 'The goal of all rules of morality is to gain for human beings all the happiness compatible with their nature.' (This is where eighteenth century Idéologie and modern economics of happiness meet.) Say continues by distinguishing two motivating forces of human conduct, either the promotion of one's own safety and welfare, or the well-being of others. In the intriguing first two notes at the end of the book, he establishes a link between virtue and utility:

Note A
I cannot imagine that there can be duties perfectly useless for other creatures or for ourselves. All virtue which does not have utility as its immediate object appears to me futile, ridiculous, similar to that accomplishment of Talapoin [a Buddhist monk], which consists of standing on one foot for years on end, or to some other humiliation harmful to ourselves, useless to others and which even God must regard with pity.

Note B
It may be believed that it is superfluous to search for ways to make man faithful to those responsibilities which have for goal his own wellbeing, since self-interest must naturally lead him to fulfil them. That would be true if man always knew his true interest; but he often sacrifices them, either to passions, to false and even ridiculous opinions.[9]

Let us try to rephrase this in modern vocabulary, as it is essential for understanding Say's later notion of utility as a central concept in his theory of value. To begin with, all human action must have a purpose for the actor or for another person. Some actions may have been labelled 'virtuous' in the past (or even today, in some religions) but this does not make sense if they do not produce 'utility'. However, man can be confused about his true interest, and can (mistakenly) follow passions or fashions in a way that will not produce true utility.

Later, in his economic textbooks, Say would stress the individual appreciation of usefulness of goods and actions. But in Olbie, a work suggesting recipes for social cohesion, he still pretended to be able to distinguish between truly virtuous and useful behaviour, and other acts resulting from passions and false opinions.

The older Say had become a modern political economist, for whom utility instead of virtue was the economic agent's driving force, without however denying the importance of institutions and civilisation. Unfortunately he did not come around to completing his treatise of politics, in which he might have explained the relationship between private and public utility. But in later editions of the *Traité*, and in the *Cours Complet*, the sovereign consumer is entitled to his own values and utilities:

> Sometimes, vanity is for man an equally imperative need as hunger. He alone judges the importance which goods have for him, and the need he feels for them. The utility of things, conceived like this, is the first foundation of their value; but the consequence is not that their value is as high as their utility: it is not higher than the level of utility which is attributed by man. The surplus of utility belongs to natural riches, which remains unpaid.[10]

A persistent theme running through Say's political thought, and his economics, is that of a moderate egalitarianism. The 'contemptuous wealthy' are inclined to exhibit 'obscene' economic behaviour. In a footnote in *Olbie*, he used the metaphor of prostituting one's talent which he also used in a letter to the *Décade* author Vernes:

> We must ensure that one is not forced to prostitute one's talents any more than one's person in order to live. If it is distressing to see courtesans selling, at the first opportunity, those favours which ought to be exchanged with the most tender sentiments, it is not less distressing to see the man of letters selling his approval to powerful and corrupt persons in power, and the artist lending the magic of his colours to the obscene commissions of the contemptuous wealthy.[11]

Say had of course absorbed the eighteenth century debate on luxury and taken the position, which would remain unchanged through his entire life, that luxury must be denounced as socially disruptive. Luxury production would cause necessary goods to be underproduced, and thus be the cause of poverty:

> All countries, by their agriculture and their commerce, create some or many products, but these are never without limits; one cannot consume in a

country more than is consistent with its soil and its industry; if one finds persons there who consume an abundance of the products of the soil and industry, there must also be others who endure proportional deprivation. This is the reason that luxury and poverty always go together.[12]

When people choose 'useful professions' and produce 'useful things', every person may be fed and clad decently. But when the 'fashion of ornamenting clothing with braid spreads among the richest inhabitants', a misallocation results which engenders poverty. Say would always remain an Idéologue for whom the ideal society would be characterised by a large 'classe mitoyenne'. In rejecting luxury he was in the good company of Bérenger and Sieyès, who both published pamphlets against the nobility.[13] According to the former (1789), luxury was the critical failing of the nobility. And the latter (1788) suggested that because of their luxury, nobles were more interested in money than others.[14]

The young Say, who was to praise the efficiency of the market in his *Traité* and *Cours Complet*, warned that the love of work must not only be stimulated by the desire for gain:

> ... the happiness and even survival of society demands that a certain number of people in each nation pursue the sciences, the fine arts and letters; noble wisdom that engenders elevated sentiments combined with useful talents. Some writer, in his modest office, works more effectively at establishing the glory, power and happiness of his country, than the general who wins the battle.[15]

Olbian legislation 'gradually eliminated all that was contrary to political economy'. This included abolishing lotteries and gambling houses, and forbidding the 'publication of books of magic'. Following Beccaria, Say recommended the institution of prizes for virtuous actions as an alternative incentive.[16] In this way, the Olbians were taught to value merit above gold. As a consequence, luxury and conspicuous consumption were condemned, and investment encouraged. This would even result in public works – canals, roads and harbours – being undertaken by private persons: 'finally, they pursued the glory of being called the benefactors of the country, and their wealth was pardoned'.[17] He may have borrowed this idea from Roederer, who suggested in 1793 that 'honors' might be an inducement for the rich to put their money into public projects.[18]

Working class people were to put aside their savings by depositing them in mutual aid societies, and in this way build up their old age pensions. Say also favours progressive taxation as a means of encouraging moderate wealth. In a lengthy paragraph on the subject, he suggests 'a geometric progression in the tax tables rather than an artithmetic progression'. He refutes the objection that putting a heavier burden on the wealthy would discourage industry:

> For example, for each increase in revenue, the share of the state may only take one tenth of the increase above the last contribution; industry would

not be discouraged because the industrious individual would always profit from nine tenths of the increase produced by his industry. Once this distinction is made, this seems to be the only equitable approach; because the needs of man do not increase in proportion to his wealth, the surplus increases progressively as wealth grows. And the tax must be in proportion to the surplus only; the necessary income, that is that portion without which one cannot live, must never be taxed.[19]

Adam Smith is quoted twice, and approvingly. First, on his anti-mercantilistic position. In Say's wording: 'if a nation is entirely composed of shopkeepers, how will they raise themselves to those liberal ideas which, alone, can ameliorate human faults?' And second on not trusting the morality of humans too much: few people will, by conviction, care to avoid purchasing smuggled goods. Therefore morality in legislation is necessary, as well as in administration.

It is one of Kitchin's comments that Say's rejection of large fortunes, which is equally pronounced in the *Décade* and in *Olbie*, is remarkable because of his reputation as one of the prophets of nineteenth century capitalism, with its enormous inequalities in the distribution of wealth. But we have seen that in the circles of the Idéologues and other revolutionaries, the ideal of moderate egalitarianism was shared by a majority. And in his later economic writings Say continued to expect that the functioning of the market would skim monopolistic profits quite rapidly. So there is no real contradiction here.

In the longest of the notes at the end of *Olbie*, the agnostic Say dwelled equally upon the morally corruptive effect of religion, and upon its economically counterproductive result. On the one hand, 'religions do not eliminate those vices and crimes to which they are most opposed'. On the other, 'religious practices absorb time and talents that could be employed productively'.[20] He seems to have been unaware that the same could be said of the labour of his proposed 'moral guardians'.

Say's comments on his own book, written many years later, are revealing about the development of his economic and political ideas:

> *If I were to rewrite my Olbie, I would base it on an entirely different foundation. I would demonstrate that the morality of nations depends on the degree of their instruction ... I would show that eras one could call enlightened were exceedingly few ... I will not give men the honour of believing that they will ever see a time when there will not be tyrants among them; but I see that their work becomes more difficult in proportion as nations become more enlightened; and note that it is not necessary for a nation to be composed of scholars to be what I call enlightened.*[21]

It is clear that the older Say was a lot more sceptical than the youthful man of letters. The *Cours Complet* (1828–1829) is much less optimistic about the perfectibility of the individual and of the institutions of society. The author of *Olbie* still expressed many ideas of the eighteenth century political economist for whom politics and economics had a large overlap, and in whose vocabulary virtue was still a central concept. This leads Whatmore to the provocative conclusion that *Olbie* really was a treatise of political economy, and the *Traité* a republican political tract.[22] He defends this statement very elegantly, but Say's remarks on the importance of education and enlightenment seem to effectively falsify it with regard to *Olbie*.

From manners to markets – the *Traité* of 1803

According to Philippe Steiner, Say may have seemed 'poorly qualified' for the job of writing his treatise in the years 1800–1803.[23] Whatmore thinks that Say's handwritten annotations in the margins of his copy of the *Wealth of Nations* were the result of his rereading Smith in the years 1799–1801.[24] The Swiss botanist, Augustin Pyramus de Candolle (another Genevan Protestant living in Paris), wrote in his memoirs that he had seen the *Traité* 'so to speak, expanding in his [Say's] head'.[25] It has been pointed out above that in the first thirty-three years of his life, Say had shown an equal interest in literature, politics and economics. Whatever may have been the precise path leading to his becoming an economist, his first professional training in commerce, followed by his moving around in Parisian salons and Idéologie circles, and his editorship of the *Décade*, were not the least appropriate qualifications for writing an economics textbook.

The first edition of the *Traité d'Economie Politique* by 'Jean-Batiste [*sic*] Say, Membre du Tribunat' was published in two volumes in 1803. 'You will see that I have followed Smith on all principal points', he wrote to Sismondi in the letter accompanying his complimentary copy. This is certainly true with respect to his treatment of value and price. His comment on Smith's labour theory of value, *I believe this is an error*, written on the first page of his own copy of *The Wealth of Nations*, is nowhere to be found. It only appears in the second edition of 1814. In the first, the treatment of value is not his starting point as it would be in later editions. The subject is discussed in book 3, after 1. Production, and 2. Money, and followed by 4. Revenues, and 5. Consumption.

The treatise starts with a historical and methodological introduction. First, the domain of economics is defined, and Adam Smith is praised for separating economics from politics:

> Until Smith's work, Politics, which ought to be understood as the science of government, was confused with Political Economy, which shows how wealth is created, distributed, and consumed. This confusion was perhaps uniquely caused by the name that has inappropriately been given to research of this kind. Since the word *economy* signifies the laws which regulate the household or home affairs, and the word *politics* appears to apply this idea to the political family or city, some have desired that political economy takes care of all the laws which regulate the affairs of the political family. It was therefore not necessary to involve research into the creation of wealth.[26]

Surprisingly, the republican autor of *Olbie* continues by stating that 'wealth is independent of the nature of government'. Under any system, a well-administered state may prosper. Sometimes a democratic government has turned out ruinous, and some absolute monarchs have enriched their nations. This is because individual people are responsible for the largest part of wealth creation, and the system of government only has an indirect influence.

Say's approach is that of the positivist Idéologue. A science must be based upon facts. Now there are *general* or *constant* facts, and *particular* or *variable* facts. An example of the former is the law of gravity, which may seem to be disturbed when we observe the particular fact of a feather floating in the air. This inductive methodology must be practised in every science. Say warns against deductive system building, from which not even Smith is exempt:

> In Political Economy, as in physics, and indeed in everything else, thinkers have constructed systems before establishing truths, for a system is more easily built than a truth is discovered. But our science has benefited from the excellent methods that have brought progress in the other sciences. It now admits only the rigourous consequences of facts carefully observed, and rejects the prejudices and authorities which, in science as in moral philosophy, formerly interposed between the observer and the truth.[27]

Economics should not only be distinguished from politics, but from statistics as well. This discipline

> demonstrates the state of production and consumption of one or more nations in a certain period or in several successive periods, as well as the state of its population, of its forces, of ordinary facts, which are susceptible to arithmetical observation.

But without an insight in the causalities linking them, these are nothing but the knowledge of a lower clerk.

Say's introduction draws a parallel between the progress of economics and the recent progress of the sciences, physics in particular. Then he discusses the theories of doctor Quesnay and his followers, the 'sect' of the Economistes or Physiocrats. According to Say, they were guilty of system building by 'posing abstract generalities', instead of carefully observing facts and deriving general truths from them. They have been rightfully criticised by Voltaire, who knew to find the ridiculous everywhere around him; but while he could demonstrate the impertinence of the boring nonsense of Mercier de la Rivière and of *l'Ami des hommes* of Mirabeau (the elder), he could not explain why they were wrong.

However, the Economistes deserve praise, 'as their writings have all been favourable for the strictest rules of morality, and for the liberty which people must have for their persons and their possessions, a liberty without which social happiness and private property are idle words'.[28]

Turgot is praised highly for not having fallen into the physiocratic trap: although he appreciated the Economistes, he did not judge by their code, but by the facts. It is sad that his political career was frustrated because the king did not fully support him. But when one reads Adam Smith, it becomes apparent that before him there was no true political economy. Yet 'he is lacking clarity in certain places, and lacking method almost everywhere'. Say is ambiguous about his master. He praises Smith's treatment of taxes and of money: 'Where my steps are supported by Smith, my work is perhaps not useless.' But his 'long digressions' do not belong in a work designed to explain general principles.

Regarding economic education, Say recognises the importance of 'enlightened' administrators. But even more important is the enlightenment of the middle class:

> In the 'classe mitoyenne', far from the worries and the pleasures of greatness, far from the fears of misery; it is in this class where honest fortunes meet with leisure, joined with the habit of work, and with the free communication of friendship, the taste of reading and of travelling; in this class, I say, enlightenment is born; from here it expands to the upper classes and to the people: for the upper classe and the ordinary people do not have time for reflection; they only adopt the truth when it comes to them in the form of axioms of which they do not need proof.[29]

This paragraph remained unchanged from the first to the sixth edition of the *Traité*. Here we recognise the author of *Olbie*, who wishes to picture his ideal society on the basis of general economic principles. He concludes by comparing again the progress of science and the diffusion of true economic knowledge: 'We are at the beginning of a century destined to harvest a glory which will be above any other.' Say would never lose his Condorcetian-ideological belief in progress. It was voiced again on many occasions, and finally even in the concluding sentence of vol. 6 of his *Cours Complet*, published three years before his death in 1829.

Say's entrepreneur in 1803

Say's treatment of value in 1803 is still fairly Smithian. Say's Law is already there, but in a very elementary and largely microeconomic representation. The true and original Say is essentially present in the treatment of the entrepreneur.

Schumpeter (1954) is ranking Say in the French tradition of Cantillon and Turgot. It is remarkable that while Say praises the latter, he nowhere mentions Cantillon in his published works (nor can any reference to him be found in his papers). One can hardly believe that he was not familiar with Cantillon's work, so this is an enigmatic gap in his own references.

Regarding the possible connection between Say's own experience as an entrepreneur and his ideas of the *Traité*, Forget notes 'that the entrepreneur was fully present in 1803, so Say's knowledge, if derived inductively, had to have come from more general sources'.[30] She suggests the influence of Cantillon. However, in my opinion, Say's entrepreneurial and managerial problems as managing editor of the *Décade*, especially in its turbulent founding period with riots and shortages of all kinds, can explain the fact that already in 1803 his theory of the entrepreneur was at least partly based upon his own experiences.

Say himself employs a somewhat old-fashioned vocabulary. So he uses the word *profit* for the income of the worker ('profits de l'ouvrier'), as well as for the entrepreneur's reward ('profits de l'entrepreneur').

Palmer (1997) gives due credit to Say's reputation as a thinker on the subject. Also he has done an excellent job by making available in English a number of hitherto untranslated texts of Say.[31] Among these are large parts of the 1803 chapter on the *Profits of the entrepreneur*.

This is placed in book 4 – on income distribution – of the second volume. Say starts by distinguishing between the income of the entrepreneur and that of the capitalist: even if the entrepreneur is the owner of all or part of the capital employed in his firm, the profits of stock must be distinguished from the entrepreneur's income proper. Sometimes even all the capital has been borrowed by him; the difficulty of *finding the funds* is one of the two 'principal causes' which, according to Say, do limit the supply of entrepreneurs. The other one is the required *judgment and knowledge*. And he continues:

Those who, by presumption, undertake this kind of work without sufficient ability make products whose value does not pay for the costs of production, and so does not pay enough for their own labour and the interest on their funds. Sometimes, indeed, far from being able to remunerate their own efforts from the value of the product, they are obliged to provide the wages of their workers and the interest of capital from their own pockets. Matters cannot long continue in this way, and their own labour will soon go out of circulation. Those left will be the ones who can continue with success, that is, with the needed ability. In this way the requirement of ability restricts the number who can provide the work of the entrepreneur.

Not all kinds of industry require in those who undertake them the same amount of ability and knowledge. A farmer who is an agricultural entrepreneur need not know as many things as a merchant dealing with distant places. As long as the farmer is familiar with the routine methods involving two or three crops, from which he derives his income, he can come off successfully. The kinds of knowledge needed for carrying on a long-continuing trade are of a higher order. It is necessary not only to know the nature and qualities of the goods on which one is speculating, but also to form an idea of the needs and markets in places where one expects to sell them. Hence the entrepreneur must keep constantly informed of the price of each of these goods in different parts of the world. To judge these prices accurately he must have knowledge of various currencies and of their relative values, or what is called foreign exchange. He must know something about means of transportation and must measure the risks and the costs that they impose;

the laws and usages of peoples with whom he is dealing; and enough knowledge of man not to be deceived in the confidence he puts in them, the missions he charges them with, and any other relationships that may arise. If the knowledge that makes a good farmer is more common than the knowledge that makes a good merchant, it is not surprising that the labours of the former are less well rewarded than those of the latter.

This is a fairly detailed summing-up of the qualities required for being a successful entrepreneur, even including a capacity for doing business cross-culturally. So already before he had the experience of being an industrial entrepreneur, Say knew that:

[The head of an enterprise] is the intermediary between the capitalist and the landowner, between the man of science and the worker, between all classes of producers and between them and the consumers. He manages the work of production, is at the center of several interrelationships, and profits from what the others know or what they do not know and from unforeseen developments in the course of production. So it is in this class of producers, when events are favorable and reinforce their abilities, that almost all the largest fortunes are made.[32]

Not only is Say's entrepreneur already clearly present in 1803, but also his definition of a product as 'something that must at least be worth its production cost in the market' is there. In his second edition of 1814, he would be even more specific about the entrepreneurial capacities, as we shall see below.

Bonaparte

Not Sieyès and the 'friends of peace', as Say had optimistically expected in 1799, had taken the upper hand in the Triumvirate, but the First Consul Napoleon. At first this development seemed to favour the Idéologues and *Décade* editors, who were nominated to higher offices like the membership of the Tribunat for Say. Before he grabbed power, Bonaparte had courted them in the literary salons. But true liberals and republicans soon discovered that he would not tolerate any criticism, and very rapidly he changed his position from 'Idéophile' to 'Idéophobe':

Metaphysicians are my *bêtes noires*. I have classed all that crowd under the denomination of *idéologues* ... The word has caught on, I believe, because it was my own ... Yes, they are obsessed with meddling in my government, those windbags! My aversion for this race of *ideologues* amounts to disgust.[33]

In the summer of 1802, Say took some time off for a holiday 'to Geneva and the glaciers'. On that occasion he was invited to Coppet by Necker.[34] His daughter

Mme de Staël and her partner Benjamin Constant were also present. The latter had been eliminated from the Tribunat in January by Bonaparte for speaking up against 'the régime of servitude and silence'. Say made an autobiographical note of the visit:

> *Finding myself in Geneva in 1802, I was invited to monsieur Necker at Cop[p]et. Mad. De Staël was charming like she always was in company. The reverence she bore to her father, laid in his presence a certain transparent veil on her sharp wit which – without altogether masking it – softened its most brutal traits and gave them a new attractiveness. As usual, Benjamin Constant was there, and his biting spirit shared in the same mood. The conversation discussed the over-crowdedness of the streets in Paris, and the little space left to pedestrians. It was remarked that the choice was between being crushed and crushing the others. 'If I must choose,' remarked Benjamin Constant, suppressing a smile … and halted there, undoubtedly for fear of offending the virtue of the master of the house. One of the others spoke and added: 'From your philanthropic look, it is easy to see what choice you will make.'*
>
> *I had the pleasure of making monsieur Necker laugh and that made me feel very happy after all the misfortunes which his political miscalculations had heaped upon such an excellent man. We spoke of monsieur de Calonne. 'According to Mr. De Calonne', I added, 'there are two kinds of economy: that of Mr. Necker, which means saving, and his own, which means throwing money out of the windows.'*
>
> *If these are not the precise words of this honest man in his reply to the work of monsieur Necker, it is certainly their exact meaning.*[35]

In such company of course Say rapidly drifted away from Bonaparte, even if he had voiced a suggestion of Milan Decree-like measures one year earlier in *La Décade*:

> If sugar and cotton were to be delivered to Europe (as they might be) by way of Sicily and Egypt, if tea were to be brought through Russia, and if the inhabitants of the Continent, closing their harbours to England, would dress in cloth of their own industry, we cannot see what means would remain to Great Britain to sustain its considerable benefits in order to pay interest for its enormous debt, and to feed a population which has already, by its profits and commercial needs, been extended far beyond the capacity of its territory.[36]

In view of his later occupation as owner of a cotton mill, and of his continuing concern about the sustainability of British public finance, these are remarkable words. But first back to Bonaparte. Not only had Say's brother Horace taken an active part in the Egyptian campaign, Jean-Baptiste himself had been asked to compose Napoleon's travel library for this expedition. And even in 1803 the

First Consul, the Idéophobe who had come to label all his opponents in the Tribunat as Idéologues, thought that he could call upon Say as a house intellectual in spite of his deteriorated relationship with practically all republican and liberal politicians.

In the Tribunat, Say was a member of the finance committee. In this capacity he was asked, in April 1802, to prepare a report on the spending of 300 million francs, in anticipation of its collection in the following tax year, and for unspecified purposes. Say looked back upon the pattern of French public finance in the eighteenth century, and argued for stricter budget controls. The committee exercised self-censorship on this draft, rightly judged to displease Napoleon, and decided to ask the Legislative Body to act. The First Consul duly received his 300 million. On his copy of the draft report, Say noted that it had been replaced by 'a few words for the gallery'. It was published posthumously by Charles Comte and Horace Say in the *Oeuvres Diverses*.

When the *Traité* had been published in 1803, Bonaparte invited its author to his domicile at Mailmaison in September and asked him to rewrite certain free-market parts in a more interventionist vein.[37] He must certainly have disliked the sentences in the introduction about the fundamental principles of economics, which are not the work of man but derive from 'the nature of things', and are above lawmakers and princes 'who never violate them with impunity'. Upon his refusal to comply, Say lost his membership of the Tribunat. Nevertheless he was offered a tax collectorship as director of the *Droits Réunis* in the Allier department, far away from Paris. Towards the end of his life, in the *Cours Complet*, he would remark that these indirect taxes were originally kept by Bonaparte at a low rate: 'It is a maxim in public finance that in order to extract a lot of money from the people, you must start by asking them little.'

It is a matter of speculation whether Bonaparte wished to see Say far away from Paris, or whether he contemplated using him again in the future. But Say equally refused the tax directorship. Ten years later, when finally he was about to deliver his second edition to the printers, he recalled Bonaparte's offer in a letter to Dupont de Nemours. In April 1814, a few days after the allied forces entered Paris, he wrote:

> *During my period as Tribun, not wanting to deliver orations in favour of the usurper, and not having the permission to speak against him, I drafted and published my Traité d'Economie Politique. Bonaparte commanded me to attend him and offered me 40 thousand francs a year to write in favour of his opinion; I refused, and was caught up in the purge of 1804.*[38]

He also refused the tax collectorship, at a salary of 30,000 francs. Considering both the political situation and his private circumstances, these decisions required a strong backbone. The proposed bribery sum was enormous, and even the tax collector's salary was twice the amount of a Tribun's remuneration. In the letter to Dupont, his argument was that 'the principles of the government became every day more hostile to the citizens'.

But already before the summer of 1803 he had been considering other activities, as he paid a visit to Sedan, considering to invest in a factory there. In February 1804 he wrote in his diary: *I go to the Conservatoire in order to learn spinning.*

With the exception of a brief membership of the Conseil général de la Seine in 1830, from which he resigned after his nomination to the chair of political economy at the Collège de France, he would never hold a political office again.

4   Reluctant entrepreneur

Auchy

For a thirty-seven-year-old father of four, with a fifth under way, it is no small step to go back to school and learn a new trade. Yet this is what Say did in 1804. He went to the Conservatoire des Arts et Métiers, unaware that he would return there fifteen years later as its first professor of economics. His oldest son Horace, aged ten, joined him as his little assistant holding the spools.

Already in the first edition of the *Traité*, Say had cleverly discussed entrepreneurship. In later editions he would add elements based upon his own experience in Auchy. His first practical lessons as an entrepreneur had been his experiences as managing editor of the *Décade*, in the post-revolutionary period of unrest and sudden scarcity of elementary products, for example the lack of candles for the printing department. He was well aware that improvising and coordinating capacities were essential to being an entrepreneur. And he certainly would be put to the test with respect to these qualities.

Unfortunately we know little about the years 1804–1807, when finally the Auchy factory started to make a profit. From September 1806 Say kept a very summary diary, *Acta*, and from May 1810 until May 1831 he administered his finances in a *Journal des affaires personnelles*. Already in July 1804, he started a cotton spinning mill in Maubuisson, in the Oise department, about which little is known. A few months later, in October, together with a partner named Isaac Louis Grivel, he set up another one in Auchy, in the Pas-de Calais department. There the old Benedictine abbey had been acquired from the nationalised church properties by the Protestant 'venture capitalists' Grivel and Delessert. It is highly probable that the banker Delessert, who had sold out to Grivel, would have established the contact between his partner and Say. Delessert's daughter was married to Michel Delaroche, whose sister was the widow of Say's brother Honoré ('Horace'). The Delaroche family was also of Genevan Protestant stock. The successful businessman Michel was about the same age as Jean-Baptiste, and regularly advised him in business and in investments and speculative transactions.

Preparations in Auchy seem to have been more thorough than in Maubuisson. After almost one year, in September 1805, the Say family moved there. During the first year and a half, spinning in Auchy went by hand. Simultaneously the factory, powered by a watermill, was constructed. In August 1806, Say described it in a letter to Duval:

> *I am still in the infancy of our great mechanism. It is still unfinished without this being anybody's fault, but because it is a very considerable and very peculiar work, which will honour the engineer who has made the plan and who is at present with us to supervise its execution.*[1]

The engineer, Mr Delcassan, had already accompanied Say and Grivel to Auchy in December 1804. His visits – but not his precise doings – are mentioned in Say's *Acta*.

Mechanical spinning was still the exception in Revolutionary France. The unreliable statistics counted between three quarter and one million spindles in 1812. A significant jump in output, from two to four and a half million kilos of yarn, was made between 1806 and 1808. The completion of Say's 'moteur hydraulique' on 26 February 1807, happened in the middle of this period. This important event was of course recorded in the *Acta*, as well as its reporting to his brother Louis Say and to the shareholders aunt Duvoisin in Geneva, and Louis Grivel. Delcassan was rewarded with a share in the factory. Five months later, in July, Say recorded the working of a 'Mule-jenny'.

Not just the spinning, but also the carding of the raw cotton was done mechanically. In March 1807, his seems to have been the first smoothly running process in the factory. A man by the Scottish sounding name of MacLaod (a misspelling of McLeod?) was mentioned a few times as chief carder, Sometimes a whole family was hired like the Le Blancs from Savoy, in July 1807. Father and daughter were admitted to the factory, the mother worked at home. The fragmented information about the production process is much less than that on the construction activities. In the letter quoted above to Duval Say described his household as a 'little world':

> *All professions are executed. We are masons, blacksmiths, carpenters, philosophers and a little bit writers.*

Yet his letters to Duval convey an impression of intellectual isolation. Writing from Maubuisson he still seemed to be happy with his new environment:

> *Every morning, from five o'clock, I am busy putting together machinery and training workmen, and I am so happy to know nothing about events happening elsewhere.*

But from Auchy he commented bitterly upon the Voltairian world of 'tigers and monkeys' which he witnessed. In October 1806 he cynically wrote about Bonaparte and his own practical problems with payments through bills of exchange:

In Auchy we live with our head in a bag; we see nothing, we know nothing. We only read in a second rate journal that our imperial sovereign has departed to Mainz; which makes us predict the most glorious events for the reign of this worthy prince. Is there in Paris an enthusiasm, proportional to the grandeur of this illustrious chief, and do people have all the confidence in the events which he was designed to inspire? That we do not know. All I know is that while we trade here with bills of exchange, we are required to specify them as payable in specie. Which seems to prove that the provinces do not have all the confidence they ought to have, and that they fear that banknotes will, sooner or later, be transformed by the authorities into forced paper money, a chimerical fear under a government which has proved that it is the slave of its promises.

Technical and commercial problems

In the construction of the watermill, one technical problem was mentioned repeatedly in Say's diary. This concerned a part of the fly-wheel to which the connecting rods with the machine were attached. It often broke down, and in May 1807 caused a stand-still of half a month. Shorter breaks occurred in September and December 1807, February 1808 and April 1809. In this last month, Say completed the canalisation of the little river upward from the village. Finally he decided to replace the wooden construction by one of wrought iron. But after one year this showed signs of tear and wear, and broke repeatedly between May and September 1810. Say then decided to replace the wrought iron parts by cast iron, and travelled to Mons to order these. But in February 1811 he suddenly mentioned in his diary that a new wooden wheel had replaced the wrought iron one. These problems demonstrate that technical progress was no straight road, and also illustrate the words of David Landes that 'the first decades of industrialization were a ceaseless war against breakdowns'.[2]

There is a parallel between Say's experiences in the cotton industry and the mechanisation of the French wool industry in the same period. Many former convents were used, many English experts recruited. But the machinery for the wool factories benefitted from active government support, both financially and by protection of designs.[3] In Auchy the construction of machinery seems to have been done on the spot, as Say's diary mostly mentions the purchase of machine parts. However, in October 1807 someone was sent to Paris 'in order to find machinery'.

By analogy to what is known about other factories, Teilhac supposes that a vertical axis from the watermill propelled the spinning machines on the first floor.[4] On the upper floor the yarn was rolled on spools, and these were stored in the attic. When the machines were out of order, spinning went by hand. Initially the higher costs this caused were no great problem. But as more and more parts of the factory functioned on water power and the entire French cotton industry was mechanised, while the French economy and the cotton industry declined, breakdowns caused a real problem. In September 1810 Say recorded an extension of the spinning by the water-powered machine, but just before and after this event the fly-wheel broke down repeatedly. And one year later he wrote to his partner Grivel about the business figures for 1811 that these were unfavourable, but that the extra costs incurred by spinning by hand during the replacement of the fly-wheel were an important cause.[5]

The first year showing business profits was 1807. All shareholders received a 6 per cent dividend. Besides Say and Grivel this certainly was Say's aunt Duvoisin from Geneva. According to Say's financial *Journal*, she had furnished 7200 francs, and when the company was dissolved in 1812 she received a lifelong rent.

The *Journal* (or what is left of it) starts in 1810, and it is impossible to reconstruct the early financial history of J.-B. Say & Cie. Schmidt (1911) and Teilhac (1927) report that in the peak year 1810 between 300 and 400 people worked in the factory, spinning between 100 and 125 kilogrammes of yarn every day. They record a gross profit of 300,000 francs, a third of which was spent on machinery maintenance.

Say's own figures of September 1810 seem a little more modest, as he recorded in his *Journal* a sum of 8600 francs as 'my disposable part' of the profits, and an equal sum as 'non-disposable'.

Apart from their interest in the spinning factory, Say and Grivel participated in the cotton weaving mill in nearby Abbeville, owned by Say's brother Louis. Stockings were the product mentioned explicitly in a number of Say's letters. Louis was a customer of part of the produce from Auchy. An interesting technological experiment took place at Louis' mill in 1808, when J.-B. Say wanted to try out the quality of a chain thread spun from a combination of Pernambuco and Georgia cottons. This experiment must have decided which of the two could be resold as raw cotton, because Say and Grivel privately traded in cotton as well. As some of Say's copied letters show, he sometimes had to remind his partner about an equal distribution of their profits.

Grivel was the travelling salesman, based in Paris, and Say the managing partner in Auchy. When in 1810 the departmental Prefects were questioned by the Minister of the Interior about possible members for a Council of Factories and Manufactures, the one of Pas-de-Calais described Say as 'very active and very hard-working, the soul of the company'.[6] The Prefect also predicted that the firm, which had employed 80 in 1807, would expand to double its size of 1810, of more than 300 workers. But the economic climate, with imperial trade policy as its most important factor, determined otherwise.

Decline

The effects of Napoleon's *Blocus Continental*, or Milan Decree (1808), are reflected in the raw cotton purchases of Say and Grivel. In 1807 they still primarily bought South American cotton, and in second place bales from Georgia. In January 1808, 50 bales of Georgia were bought (at 3 livres 8 sous the most expensive ones) beside 14 'Kirgaga du Levant' and 10 'Surate' (from India, the cheapest at 52 sous).[7] In January 1808, Grivel purchased large quantities from the Levant. Remarkably, from November 1810 bales of 'Louisianne' are reappearing beside those from Macedoine. But at that time Bonaparte had started to become 'his own smuggler' by admitting colonial produce at high import tariffs.[8]

Regarding exports of cotton yarn, its prohibition in 1808 had caused a crisis in the recently mechanised sector. In 1809, exports were liberated again, and a survey was conducted among cotton manufacturers about the desirability of prohibiting all yarn imports. Already in 1806, import duties had made the import of cotton cloth practically impossible. The outcome of the survey was that only the weavers in Tarare, who were dependent on importing very fine-spun yarns, and Jean-Baptiste Say protested.

According to Teilhac, 'Say was able to sacrifice his own advantage to the general interest.' One might add that since his suggestion of 1802 in the *Décade* he had slightly changed his mind about protection. He proposed raising import duties on cotton yarn, while completely liberating import of raw cotton. Of course this implicit plea against the Milan Decree, and against the profitable duties on cotton bales, was neglected and all imports of yarn were prohibited. After 1810 the supply of raw cotton became a real problem. Napoleon himself, who had originally encouraged the cotton industry, now became disgusted with it and in 1811 even banned all cotton textiles from his palaces.

By the greater availability of letters and business figures, a much clearer picture of the decline of J.-B. Say & Cie can be drawn than of its rise. A parallel with the rise and decline of the entire industry in France was sketched above. Therefore Say's earlier biographers, like his son-in-law Charles Comte (1834) and Ernest Teilhac (1927), have praised Say for his achievements without blaming him for the failure of the company.

In 1810 the weaving mill had still shown a profit, paying Say an interest twice (310 and 266 francs respectively) and a profit share of 5064 F. But in 1811 the interest received of 971 francs was outweighed by far through the loss of 8397 F reported in the books.

As from February 1811, Say started making copies of his letters. These offer an insight in the dealings of spinning and weaving in Auchy and Abbeville, as well as glimpses of the general economic decline. In February he wrote to Grivel, who was in Rome – travelling in Italy for reasons of health – about the continuing state of commercial crisis, and the bankruptcy of a customer which cost the firm 11,000 F. Apparently Grivel did some business as well, as Say wrote at the end of February:

> *I am angry that you have bought Napoli [cotton] which will cost us 6 Frs 5 cts. We could at present have Louisiana, which has always produced better results, at 5 Frs 10 cts …*
>
> *I have cut down the production of warp-thread number 30 to 10 [pounds per day?]. When we would only earn our fixed costs, we must produce because otherwise we would lose these altogether.*

Discouragement increases and increases. The majority of spinning factories in Rouen have closed down. But that does not discourage me.

Our engine has never been running better. We take advantage of this by making the planned improvements.[9]

He still had time to read, as he ordered books by Castellan and Chateaubriand from the Parisian publisher and bookseller Deterville, together with a copy of Destutt de Tracy's *Idéologie*. A few months later he asked him for the two most recent volumes of Turgot's *Works*, the *Mémoires de Mme Roland*, the (French) *Cotton Producers Guide* and Chaptal's *Applied Chemistry*.

In April he wrote to Grivel urging him to buy only the best quality of cotton, and only upon explicit orders from Auchy. The same letter reported lower wages being paid. In the same month he advised standard loss-minimising behaviour to his brother Louis: 'It is better to compensate only one third or fourth of our fixed costs, than to lose all of it by doing nothing.' In May he reported to Grivel, then in Milan, that Louis had written to him that all his sales in Paris resulted in losses; he told him about sending all personnel on leave for three days. In the same month he had come to the conclusion that if he could not even earn back his fixed costs, he must send no more yarn to the weaving mill. To Grivel he wrote that their customers were getting more and more difficult about prices and qualities, but occasionally he managed to conclude new deals: 'I will not let myself be discouraged.' However, business continued to slow down, and in October 1811 he proposed to his brother to liquidate the Abbeville factory. When its sale to the firm of Grivel and Say had been concluded in November, he wrote to Louis about Grivel's 'violence' in the negotiations:

Also, as I think that you must not be treated by your brother as rigorously as by a greedy stranger, I permit myself to beg you to accept annually that I will keep for you an interest in the Abbeville weaving mill of one tenth of my net revenue in this business.

In December he further showed his concern for his brother by promising him a 6 per cent loan of 8500 F – in addition to Louis' own capital of 26,000 F – to set him up as a partner in 'a good house': *upon the condition that I will have a signed bond of the house you will join, and only if it has a good credit and a good reputation.*

A very detailed calculation of cost price was recorded in a letter to Grivel of that same month. The new ownership relation between Auchy and Abbeville necessitated this restatement, as well as the difficult times for spinning and weaving mills alike. The calculating unit of production was the French pound. According to Say, in the 13 preceding months a quantity of 65,000 pounds of spun cotton had been produced – 5000 per month.

On the raw material, he counted 2 per cent of 'false costs' for brokerage, transport and damage. The waste in production had so far been calculated at 18 per cent, but 25 per cent seemed more realistic. Labour costs were 90 centimes per pound, but Say's expectations were still optimistic. Less spinning by hand, and a better utilisation of the engine-driven spindles, would reduce this amount. 'General costs' were computed at 1.25 F per pound.

Interest paid was 74,000 F, and interest received 8000. On top of these net 66,000 F came the 'commercial costs' of 59,000 F.[10] The resulting cost price was just over 1.80 F per pound of cotton spun. It was Say's conclusion that the reduction of costs already realised, plus a further one together with a growth in output, would produce more satisfactory results:

> *We already work till nine in the evening. As to interest paid, we must seek to reduce this by putting out less work. We will have to buy bales of cotton in very small quantities, and only upon formal requests that we will address to you. In Auchy we will seek to evaluate those parties which are on our arms since a long time.*

These concluding remarks seem to go against his pretended optimism. They might as well be read as: we are obliged to stock no more raw material than absolutely necessary.

Also in December 1811, in a long and very personal letter to his cousin Michel Delaroche, he showed much less optimism in explaining the structural and accidental causes of the recent developments:

> *... you are one of the very small number of people who understand me. For quite a long while I have accepted being blamed by those who do not understand me, but I must say that I would feel quite unhappy being blamed by the few who do ...*
>
> *My brother has wished to pull out of the weaving mill at Abbeville, shocked by the loss this mill has suffered last year, a loss which should not have surprised him as it was occasioned by extraordinary causes, the likes of which had not occurred in human memory, to wit the crisis which has paralysed all branches of industry. This crisis has been accompanied by some particular circumstances like the journey of Mr Grivel necessitated by the state of his health, precisely at the time when it could harm us most, when we had pushed up our output, and had a considerable stock of merchandise to be sold, left to the care of young people with very little experience, too light, too busy with other things than governing sales, precisely at a time when all the ability of a man well versed in affairs was necessary to dispose of it in an acceptable manner.*

He described the details of the sale of the Abbeville mill to Grivel and 'the house of Auchy' (the spinning factory). As Say owned half of Auchy, he became one-quarter participant in Abbeville. Louis purchased a small spinning mill of 1220 spindles on the northern outskirts of Paris, and expected to sell his output to the Abbeville factory. His brother continued the letter to Delaroche with a little lecture on entrepreneurship:

For a long time he [Louis] *has had the idea in his head that the big profits were made in spinning, and that he would work wonders at the head of a spinning mill. And undoubtedly with a lot of effort, activity and the knowledge he already partly possesses, he can hope for some success, but he will also encounter many difficulties which one does not see from a distance, and will not find the results as brilliant as he expects. On top of this he has the advantage of not having invested much in this spinning mill, and will always be able to get a decent return from the larger part of this small capital if he wishes.*

He continued by describing his own strategy for Auchy, of producing no more yarn than those quantities that had already been ordered, or were to be sold very probably. And he complained about the subversive behaviour of two of his production chefs he could hardly command himself, and against whom Grivel was powerless. The letter was concluded by thanking Delaroche for taking on as his young assistant Horace Say, who was employed as a trainee in his trading company in Nantes. For his lodging, Say paid 100 F a month. And as a father he promised to pay for his music lessons.

Reorientation

Late in 1811 or early in 1812 Say must have started to consider his total withdrawal from Auchy. At first the responsibility he felt for his family stood in the way of this decision, as he wrote to Michel Delaroche in February 1812. But in the same month he arranged to have a pied-à-terre in Paris, in the same house where Madame Ginguené lived, on the Rue du Cherche Midi. In April and May he sometimes wrote a weekly letter to his friend and relative. This correspondence is not only revealing about his business dealings, but also about his preparations of a second edition of the *Traité*, and about the reorientation of his brother Louis towards a sugar refinery. And the letters include a report of Say's efforts in Paris, on behalf of Delaroche, to obtain export permits which is revealing about the beginning of the end of the Napoleonic reign.

In February 1812 he approvingly commented on Delaroche's plans for an early retirement from business, at an age where he could still enjoy the pleasures of life. He wished he could do the same, as his wife noticed that his spirits went lower and lower. If it were not for the 'dead years for business' he would already have split up with his partner Grivel by 'pulling out my needle from the game', and would continue by 'living quietly'. Now he expected he would have to go on for a few more years 'as long as destiny does not work to our advantage'. Grivel, he wrote, was even less capable than Say himself to handle their chief engineer, who cheated them by employing part of their staff and using part of their iron, wood and other materials to his own advantage in his private mills. He apologised to his friend for elaborating so much on private matters, and begged him for confidentiality. Then he continued on:

> *... another thorn hurting me badly, this poor Louis, who when not yet a spinner believed that a spinning mill was a goldmine, that all the profits were for us and that he was the victim, and now believes exactly the opposite. He shares his worries with me with a weakness that hurts me, and demonstrates to me that he does not have a character strong enough to direct a business without being pushed aside. You told me that you were going to close down a factory: I believe a sugar refinery. I am sure you would receive a lot of gratitude from Louis by employing him in some way in this business. He is altogether discouraged, and would do much better when he felt some support. He is perfectly honest; I can tell after a seven years association; he has an insight and a talent in a lot of trades. I submit this idea to you and I think you might suggest any proposition that would fit your plans.*

In April, after congratulating Delaroche with the birth of his son, he mentioned for the first time his work on a second edition of the *Traité*:

> *I devote all my leisure time to the second edition of a work which has long been sold out, and which one cannot obtain either for gold or for silver. This second edition will be better beyond comparison than the first, as I have for ten years profited from my own experience and from that of others. My work advances rapidly, and to have this judged by you I would, when I find a means of sending it to you, let you have a copy of a chapter containing very fundamental matters, which one would fail to find in Smith and other authors before me, and which I have too imperfectly discussed in my first edition. When might all this be printed? God knows, but he does not seem to care much.*

Say himself cared a lot, as he wrote again on the subject in May, joining the relevant chapter to the letter:

> *You will give me your counsel the first time you will write to me. The subject, which was only indicated in my first edition, is still quite novel. I believe it has not only been totally ignored by the governments – who ignore quite a number of other things – but also by the people who run the various industries, in agriculture, in manufacturing and in trade for whom it is nevertheless of high interest.[11] One would search for it in vain in Smith and people are commencing to note that even in my first edition there is a whole lot of things and even important principles that are absolutely new. This testimony has been given to me by various people of merit in Paris, and by Jefferson who has told so to Mr. Warden in America. It is a sweet satisfaction to see a glimpse of the dawn of justice under the eye of injustice. I am working at this second edition with the same ardour as when I would have the possibility to have it printed. Maybe the moment will come. So when you would be so benevolent as to send me a criticism of the chapter on which I*

consult you, I would still have the time to take advantage of it. If such a chapter would be generally recognised, people would know the origin of one of the causes of the present lack of sales, and of the one threatening us. There are still other causes, but therefore one would have to see the entire work. What an indignation people would feel if they knew the entire present misfortune.

The chapter, of course, is the expanded text in the second edition on Say's Law.

The gloomy economic situation in France is reflected in a letter written in April 1812 to Grivel about the possible provision of 'soupe économique' to their workers.[12] Say had received an official instruction to that purpose, but he was sceptical about it:

In our position, I believe that it would bring us extra costs and little advantage. The workers would not care! Nothing would get them away from their slices of bread; the more uncivilised people are, the more obstinate they are too. If hunger would force the poorest to have recourse to it, they would not give us any money, we would have to deduct it and we experience the near-impossibility to do so. We would end up by paying the soup as well as the cost of the firm.

One week later he wrote again to his partner, who apparently had laid down two business proposals, one on how to continue together, and another on how to split up:

Whatever may be, I am maturely considering your two propositions, but you will not judge me badly in not precipitating anything. I have a fairly large family, and needs and relationships dat do not allow me to live on too little; and I am too old to start again in founding a new business.

He dwelled upon the depressed economy:

I hardly dare to propose to anyone with a large fortune to engage it in commerce in an era where commerce has been erased, misery is profound, consumption reduced to half in goods of first necessity, to one quarter in goods of second necessity, and to one tenth in many others ...

I continue seeking to make economies, but these are becoming very difficult as they have to be taken on the most essential maintenance.

In April he also discussed the subject of payments by bills of exchange. (Already in 1806 he had complained to Duval about this long-winded monetary system.) Delaroche had warned him against the risks of transferring these bills to others than the originally favoured payee. 'I never take reimbursements on an acceptor', he wrote back. And he continued by commenting on the work of his son Horace and his brother Louis in the new beetroot sugar factory:

...which makes me think of poor Louis; I say poor in all respects, as he is quite pitiable to find himself in a position from which your friendship is trying to pull him out, and even more pitiable in not knowing to accept his fate or to change it, his letters demonstrate a dejection which hurts badly. I do believe that he will appreciate your good will and the necessity to take good advantage of the business you trust him with, and where I believe that the weaknesses he may have will not lead to evil consequences, at least not so close under your eyes.

Louis had told him in a letter that the sale of the spinning mill to Grivel had resulted in a modest loss of 8000 F, and Jean-Baptiste considered this a fair price to be paid for such a lesson:

What remains for him is to pull himself together for managing your beet-roots. I am quite happy that he is unburdened from his other affairs which absorb[ed] the small amount of courage he has.

The sequel to the sugar story is well known. From manager of the refinery, Louis became an associate of Delaroche, and then the owner of a beetroot and cane sugar refining empire lasting for more than a century and a half. He cleverly switched from beet to cane sugar after the fall of Bonaparte, and profited enormously from his location in the port of Nantes where the cane arrived from the Antilles. The firm merged into Beghin-Say in the 1970s. The name of Say was dropped in another, more recent merger. Louis also was an economist in his own right. He would criticise his brother's opinions in a number of publications.

Imperial bureaucracy

In two letters written to Delaroche from Paris in May 1812, Say reported on his efforts on behalf of Delaroche to obtain imperial export permits for him. His verbatim reproduction of his dealings with the responsible civil servant amounts to a hilarious sketch for two. It also illustrates the fact that, if the Napoleonic empire had not gone down in Russia and at Waterloo, it would soon have succumbed to bureaucratic implosion. In the first letter he described the administrative process cumulating in Bonaparte's own signature, who only signed the 'Permits and Licenses' on certain days, 'but when he does not fix such a day, people hardly dare to address him on the subject'. Say was to see Monsieur Le Moyne, the 'chef de division' preparing the permits at the Ministry of Commerce, and he would stress the importance of Delaroche's firm as 'a house equally recommendable by the extent of its customers as by the large sum of its capital and its commercial skills, and how unpolitical it would be to put limits upon its activities, so favourable to the general interest and particularly to the treasury'. But another contact, a Monsieur Benjamin, might be in a better position to promote Delaroche's interest, first because Say's name was 'so directly contrary to the ideas of the Master', and second because Benjamin's titles, decorations and functions gave him direct access to high officials.

Nevertheless, Say went to see Le Moyne who told him that the single permit which Delaroche had received was just 'a bone to chew on'. Say then asked for the six that Delaroche had already applied for. That was far too much. Say politely asked how many would be feasible:

- *It is difficult to allow more than one or two.*
- *Monsieur, it seems to me that it would be in the interest of the country at large, in the interest of the treasury, and consequently in that of the government to oblige a house so respectable, with affairs so solid, by asking twelve instead of six; please note that here is the only way still open to international trade, that all other trades suffer at this very moment, and that the whole of France is deploring a stagnation of its industry [economic activity] of which there is no comparable example till the present day, that its factories suffer equally, that the loudest complaints are voiced everywhere, that hindering the efforts of industry in one part means paralysing them in ten others. I cannot believe that it is the government's intention to destroy the source of its power and its revenue.*
- *You are preaching to someone already converted, but the government does not want to multiply its favours too much.*
- *Why is it a favour to allow activities that are evidently useful?*
- *That is true, but the Emperor does not want to multiply his signatures infinitely.*
- *The Emperor, I have observed, has departed for the Russian frontiers, and I suppose that he has authorised the Minister to sign permits in his absence.*
- *Not at all.*
- *So one must send permits to be signed in Warsaw, for exports from Nantes or Bordeaux?*
- *Absolutely.*
- *You are too well versed in commercial matters to ignore that the success of commercial operations almost always depends upon the capacity of the entrepreneur to grab the favourable moment. Also, the right season for sailing is determined by nature. In most cases, causing a delay in a certain operation amounts to prohibiting it altogether.*
- *I know all that ... but ... he wants it that way.*
- *In that case I beg you to promptly send the permits that have been requested and to engage the Minister in sending them as soon as possible to receive the Emperor's signature.*
- *The Minister only dares to send them when he is asked to do so.*
- *What! In order to perform a commercial operation, it is necessary that the Emperor dreams of permitting it without having been asked for it?*
- *(Nodding of the head meaning* Just like that.*)*
- *But – I dared to ask – these gentlemen are doing the same amount of business as all the other traders of Nantes together. If you will allow only two permits, how can they at the same time take their freights on board in six cities of the United States?*

- *(That seemed to make some impression with him.) Upon your recommendation I will do everything possible with a certain probability of success.*
- *And when do you expect to send these pieces to be signed?*
- *When he will ask for it.*
- *Could you send them directly to me in order to let the arrive more rapidly than by way of the administration?*
- *It is necessary that it will pass through the Departmental administration. But the house will be informed directly after.*

Say still managed to put some optimism into his concluding remarks, but he also reproduced the scepticism of public opinion about the emperor's last big project:

> *I presume that the number of permits will be bigger than when we had said nothing; it remains to know whether the other Olibrius [cruel bluffer] will wish to sign. I have always found it necessary to inform you of the bureaucratic atmosphere to guide your steps. H.M. has departed last Saturday. The preparations have been immense. But everybody is shrugging his shoulders. And quite openly so.*

The 'shoulder-shrugging' suggests that in practice many people just did as they pleased, and that perhaps Delaroche did not care too much about his official permits. For one month later, Say wrote again on the subject:

> *I have not received from you any new instructions regarding the permits you requested; which makes me think that either you know how useless this is, or that you have given them up altogether, as I don't think you have already obtained them. Anyway, I would like to learn what has come of it.*

Leaving Auchy

It is clear that by May 1812, Say had already spiritually left Auchy. In April he had asked for some time to consider Grivel's two proposals. He also wrote that one of the leading employees had for years been counteracting him. Very probably this was Delcassan the engineer, about whom he wrote to Delaroche in August:

> *A last incident, which looked like an attack on our cashier, has finally disgusted me. It happened under the eyes of my wife and my daughter. Such a state of things could not suit an honest, quiet and well educated family like ours.*

But he also resented the behaviour of Grivel and a nephew of his who was employed by the company. In August he wrote to the notary or financial advisor, who was to draft the final settlement with Grivel, that he hoped everything would have been arranged when he would move out of Auchy, the place 'so disagreeable to my family'. Then he would no longer have to sit at the table with others 'with knives drawn'.

The confidential letter to Delaroche mentioned the essence of the settlement. The firm was to be continued by Grivel, who split up with his partner on the basis of the figures of the most recent balance sheet. Half of the weaving mill was owned by the spinning factory, so one-quarter of it belonged to Say. Altogether fixed assets were valued at 410,000 F, which meant a depreciation of only 12,000 F from their cost price. A stock of 'inferior calico's, which are difficult to sell at any price, and the interest on which was eating us out', was valued at 200,000 F. Even the unspecified sum of the bankrupt debtors on the balance sheet was shared. Say's figures do not allow precise conclusions about the final outcome of his spinning venture, as he did not distinguish between the value of the spinning and the weaving mill, and their stocks. The precise proportions between his own original investment and those of others cannot be reconstructed. It was arranged with Grivel that Say would immediately receive a sum of 100,000 F. For Say this way of accounting meant that on paper – and by his own calculation – he lost 56,600 F.[13]

> *To conclude* [he wrote] *after a few more years of a costly exploitation because of interest payments, and also quite hazardous because of the nature of the engine, new investments and rigorous revaluations would have been necessary which might have left me with nothing.*
> ...
> *I will be occupied in transporting my family, and those belongings which I will keep, to the Paris region. We will live there with more thrift, until we decide on something else. If you have any good idea about the employment of my capital, I beg you, dear friend, to let me participate in the expectation that it will bring me 6% a year, with the possibility of reimbursement at two months notice.*

In the confidential letter to Delaroche he still believed that his capital of 100,000 F was 'clear, net, disposable, free from any obligation or any consequence of affairs'. He felt free to employ his capital in a less engaged way in any business he might like, or even 'wrap it in a package' and walk off to 'breathe a lighter air, more favourable to my health'.

In September he wrote a detailed letter to his aunt Duvoisin about her investments, and how he proposed to pay the interest on her capital. He started by thanking her for reducing this to 5 per cent. When business was booming, he had doubled her lifelong rent of 250 F on 'an old loan in assignats, the value of which has vanished from my hands and the principal sum of which you have transferred to me'. Now he wished to reduce it again from 500 to 250 F. Together with 5 per cent interest on two other loans totalling 7200 F, he was to pay her 610 F annually. Grivel was to pay her back a sum of 6960 F which was 'in depot' with him. Other correspondence makes it seem probable that Say's other aunt Castanet (his grandmother's sister) and perhaps also his mother-in-law were among the investors in the Auchy mill.

It is not easy to confirm these sums from Say's correspondence by comparing them with those in his *Journal*. One of the reasons is that he only consolidated his private figures again in August 1813. But as early as September 1812 he had already booked the loss of 56,600 F on his share in the factory, the same amount as already recorded in his letter of May to Delaroche. Grivel's entire debt to him was valued at 90,679 F. Three months later, in December 1812, it stood at 84,940 F. So the contractual 100,000 F did not flow as agreed.

After leaving Auchy, he also tried to liquidate what was left of the real estate inheritance of his wife in the Calvados department. A local relative by the name of Serant had taken care of the rents, and had been the cashier for sums of money due to Say's mother-in-law, madame Deloche.[14] On his behalf, Say bought a bale of cotton in January 1813 at a price of 708.30 F. He advised Serant to resell it as soon as possible, as cotton was going down. In the same letter he thanked him for poultry he had sent.

In the consolidated figures of August 1813, Grivel stood as a debtor of 61,342 F. This sum accounted for almost two-thirds of Say's private capital of 95,492 F, while he had written off a total of 65,455 F over the past year and a half.

What do these figures mean by comparison to Say's current spending at the time? In the years 1811 and 1812, his monthly expenditures were between 500 and 1000 F. The furniture he sold in Auchy was worth 2500 F.

After his splitting-up with Grivel, he still felt the necessity to explain to Delaroche his moving away from Auchy. In a letter of September 1812, he complained again about the characters of his partner and the nephew who assisted him, as well as about the general economic climate. In Say's absence, the Grivels were sloppy managers:

What happened? Nothing was ever really fixed in our mechanical operations; and in the productive ones, a cotton was produced which did not sell at all and which depreciated in a staggering manner; such a small quantity was produced that the fixed costs were spread over 5 thousand [pounds] instead of 8 or 9 thousand. There I could no longer get any sleep. Within two years I would have seen disappear everything I had gained. – On top of this I have a very low opinion of the influence of the general affairs upon trade. You tell me that foodstuffs are wearing out, which is true;

but alas! the depopulation and the growing misery of the surviving part of the population prevent their restocking. In all our provinces in this part of the country, three quarters of the population no longer have a shirt, nor stockings, nor shoes. Two years ago they still had them. Surely there still remains a certain level of consumption, but it is getting lower and lower, and accordingly the production and the commerce providing for this consumption are going down as well. Now the first result of this development is that prices are going down, as the demand for almost all goods which are not purely alimentary, always stays a little behind the supply from industry of these goods.

In the first part of this quotation, Say the entrepreneur is speaking (who would be more specific about the entrepreneur's role in the second edition of the *Traité*); in the second, the economic observer is looking at the relationship between supply and demand he elaborated in Say's Law.

In the last paragraphs of the letter he looked forward, and again asked Delaroche's advice about how and where to move and to invest his capital:

> *I am fully aware that my fortune is not big enough to renounce all profitable work; but I am very hesitant to start a new factory although I have an experience in that direction, very favourable for success; but I am afraid to engage my funds up to the point where they might fail to bear fruit, and keep my feet on the ground; I derive some happiness from being able to transform them into merchandise and to move with them to a hemisphere where prosperity is growing, which must more or less be favourable to everybody and to all employments. Help me, my dear friend, to determine my ideas on all that. My heart and my mind are open to all trades that might favour my fortune and my family.*

This is the first reference to a possible moving away from France and emigrating to the US. Three months later, in December 1812, he still started another letter to Delaroche with a few remarks about the two villains in Auchy who were now pestering Grivel. Say himself regretted being out of business, but was glad to have left the cotton trade. Current prices did not allow the smallest margin above the cost of production. He had been informed that the value of stocks left unsold in Auchy amounted to 300,000 F. As to his own finances, he asked Delaroche for help. With only Bordeaux and Nantes left as ports of international trade, the latter's company was thriving:

> *As I have been reduced to live on my small capital, I would like to be admitted in participating in one of the profitable deals which your happy situation and your excellent judgement allow you to perform. ... You understand that I am not well enough informed about your affairs to say anything more specific; but full of unlimited confidence in your insight, I say: here is 40 or 50 thousand fr. which I beg you to join with one of those [affairs] belonging to you without asking you for other accounts than those you are executing for your personal advantage.*

He told Delaroche that he could keep this account entirely out of his books or letters, and could simply inform him about it by reporting to his son Horace. The latter had also received a small sum for speculating on behalf of his father, just to improve his experience in commerce. And he continued by recommending to Delaroche a Mr Perturon, his former cashier and bookkeeper from Auchy. This demonstrates his employer's concern with former loyal staff:

> *He is an excellent person whom I would like to see well employed; if you could take him as a clerk, or have him taken by another company from*

Nantes or Bordeaux, you and the others would be entirely satisfied. It is im-possible to put more intelligence and zeal than he has shown into the man-agement of the interests we left behind in Artois.

It is clear that the problems between Grivel and some of the factory managers on one side and Say on the other, were the paramount reason to leave Auchy. The ailing state of the entire French economy and cotton industry had aggravated the situation, and determined the moment to sell his part of the firm to his partner. In other correspondence he also referred to the intellectual isolation he experienced. Already at the end of 1808 he had written to Duval:

I live in an awful isolation from all my former friends ... I earn some money but what is the purpose of that if it does not procure Living according to one's tastes.[15]

5   A rentier in a depressed economy

Family man

From Say's correspondence, a picture emerges of a warm father and family man, who enjoyed the company of friends and relatives and took the trouble to write to them regularly. There was always the Geneva connection: the Duvoisin, Castanet, Delessert, Rath and Delaroche families. With some of these, family ties and financial ones were intertwined: aunt Duvoisin was one of the financiers for the Auchy project, and Michel Delaroche was a sounding board and financial advisor. Of his *Décade* associates, Amaury Duval remained a regular and trusted correspondent.

In Auchy his daughter Octavie was born (1804), his son Hippolyte died (1805) and his youngest Alfred arrived (1807). Births and deaths, and health problems in general, were an important subject in his letters. In 1807 he wrote to his uncle, the physician Delaroche in Paris, about the success of the treatment with leeches which he had recommended for the twelve-year-old Adrienne, and which was to be supplemented by mercury chloride, or ultimately vesicatory medicine. In 1810 he wrote to the doctor's younger son François, Michel's brother, about an aching inflammation in his wife's ear. The main content of this letter was a message about his daughters Amanda and Adrienne, who were staying in a boarding school in Paris, run by two ladies. It was 'necessary for their character to pull them out of Auchy'. When living with her parents, Adrienne 'did not even know English', and now she could read it.

In February 1812 he wrote to Michel Delaroche in Nantes about the latter's wife's pregnancy, possibly of a 'crown prince', although he did not wish him a kingdom, 'neither for his happiness nor for ours'. In April he could congratulate him on a safe delivery, and again in May when apparently the baby had recovered from a grave illness. But in June he had to write him a letter of condolence at the loss of his son: 'You have all the courage and the force of reason necessary to carry it well, and what I would have to say would probably add little to what your firm and enlightened reasoning is suggesting.'

In December he wrote a long letter about the death and funeral of the old doctor Daniel Delaroche. Apparently his son Michel had been unable to attend the ceremony in Paris. It had been carried out 'in the most recent manner' and

Reverend Monnot had spoken for more than fifteen minutes. The burial took place at the Père Lachaise cemetery, the preferred place for Protestants (where Say himself was to be buried twenty years later).

Regarding more mundane matters, in 1811 he asked the older Delessert, the Paris banker and father-in-law of Michel Delaroche, to buy a horse for him. With the saddle and harness, this cost him 386 F. Other daily affairs asking his attention were the purchases of wine and provisions. In October 1811 he ordered a 'feuillette' (half a hogshead) of Tonnerre 1811 wine, 'second quality' for 92 F from a merchant in Abbeville. In the same month he was settling his account with a grocer in Paris of 545 F while ordering at the same time two bushels of beans, two of lentils and one of 'hard peas', plus one cask of anchovy.

One year later, liquidating his cellar in Auchy, he offered 250 bottles of Pouilly white wine to a Mr de Gouy in the nearby village of Wavin for 260 F, together with thirteen bottles of Hermitage rouge and fourteen Hermitage white at 3.50 a bottle, ten Côte Rôtie at 3, nine St Péray white at 2 and ten Château Grillet at 2. He also offered him bell-glasses and flower pots. So he managed in detail his moving from Auchy to Paris. The correspondence with a wine merchant from Mâcon, about the resale of an unconsumed cask of white Pouilly, was prolonged from September 1812 till March 1813 and ended with its purchase by Grivel.

In April 1812 his daughter Adrienne, aged seventeen, had been sent to live with her aunt Duvoisin in Geneva for her education. She carried in cash the interest of 520 F, due to her aunt as a former investor in Auchy. Say was to pay 40 F a month for her household charges. In an accompanying letter he asked his aunt to specify a certain loss she had suffered in cashing a bill on Paris, for which he would compensate her. Adrienne was also carrying a portrait of her mother, painted by Say's niece Miss Rath, which must be paid for by Mrs Duvoisin. And finally, Adrienne was to receive a religious instruction, following 'the established cult'. Of course in Geneva this could only mean Protestantism, but aunt Duvoisin was of a different conviction.

As an agnostic, Say was not in favour of a religious upbringing, and even less so when it would be a Roman Catholic one. But as a loyal nephew, he did not wish to confront his aunt too much. In May, he wrote her a very long letter on this delicate subject:

> *I see that you wish Adrienne to follow a course in religion and take her first communion, and you are giving me excellent reasons for this interference. The main thing for me would be to please you and to exclude any grief regarding this subject; also I will start by telling you that I will conform, and that Adrienne will conform for the same reason; but on the other hand you cannot expect that a man of 44 years, who is not accustomed to judge matters lightly, and whose opinion has been formed by instruction, by long meditations and by love of the good, does not have motives of his own and must organise his conduct and that of his children after the opinion of other people rather than his own. I will gladly explain to you these motives which*

would rather be the subject for a book than for a letter, but I will just react to those which you believe will make me decide, primarily that I do not deprive my children at all from the consolations which people derive from resignation and confidence in the divine justice and goodness, for this confidence is quite independent of any cult whatsoever. I do believe that it must be seated on even better foundations than those found in a course of religion, where many documents which I believe to be false are harmful to truths I consider constant, and identical for our ancestors who did not yet know Christianism, and for us who know it, and for three quarters of the world population who will never know it.

You are attributing the qualities I might have to my own Christian instruction, and I can assure you that I feel that I am worth more and am happier because specific and much more profound studies have let me put things in their proper place, and let me judge everything with my own assessment. And otherwise my experience has proved that in all beliefs and human opinion, there are vices and virtues, and the virtues are much less due to speculative opinions than to habits and a solid appreciation of the advantages and inconveniences of good and bad conduct; and upon this solid appreciation I am founding the good conduct of my children, as I have experienced this myself in a more certain manner.

Then he became more specific about his daughter's character, and possible ways to improve this. In his opinion she was a bit superficial and pleasure-oriented, and too much occupied with her jewellery. But in time she would become aware that modesty and gracious behaviour would be worth more. A girl with 'simple taste, love of order, and devotion to her duties' would always be able to get 'the attention of an honest man'. He was right in cherishing these expectations, as Adrienne was to marry Charles Comte, lawyer, journalist and editor-to-be of the posthumous *Oeuvres Diverses* of his father-in-law.

He fully realised that his aunt believed the Christian religion to be an essential condition for eternal salvation. And he wrote down two alternative concluding sentences:

(1) *My only motive, I repeat, which can make me change my mind, is the grief I would have in hurting you, and this reason will let me advise Adrienne to submit herself to whatever you believe you must ask from her.*

(2) *But once more I will make it my duty to subordinate my opinion to yours and I wish only that if you are determined to have Adrienne taught a course of religion, that she fully agrees herself and that Mr. Dicor will instruct her.*

These long quotations illustrate in the first place how much Say was occupied with the impact of religion and of institutions in society at large, and in economic life. He speaks about virtue and good behaviour, which in his opinion should be more or less the same in Christian and non-Christian societies alike. But his remark about 'the advantages of good behaviour' has a decidedly utilitarian flavour of reasoning.

Second, his remarks about girls of simple taste and devotion to their duties who will always find a husband, are revealing about his opinions on the place of women in society. Apparently these had not changed in the eleven years elapsed since he published his *Olbie* in 1801.

In November 1813 he replied to Michel Delaroche, who had written him three letters in the preceding week. (In October the battle of Leipzig had been Napoleon's decisive defeat.) The occasion was Horace's planned departure for the United States, which gave some grief to his mother. But Say expected to see his son back safely, or perhaps to join him in the United States, for at the time he was 'not living, but choking'. Of course he was hinting at the end of Bonaparte's reign, but he still only dared to write about the mood of the Parisians in metaphorical terms:

> *Regarding the news you say the Parisians are flattering themselves with, I will tell you nothing, but I will recall a scene from the classic Italian theatre. Arlequin has been thrown out by his mistress Colombine, and meets Scapino in the street, who asks him about his marriage plans with Colombine: It's halfway accomplished. – What do you mean halfway? – Well, don't we need my consent and Colombine's? – Yes. – All right, I've given mine; you see that it's halfway done.*

Managing a rentier's fortune

After leaving Auchy, Say would have to wait two more years before he could publish his second edition. As the rooms he had rented in Paris could not house his entire family, the Says moved to Villemomble, on the eastern side of the capital. Jean-Baptiste himself was now forty-five years old, and three of his five young children still lived at home.[1] Horace, working with Delaroche, lived in Nantes, and Adrienne was in the care of aunt Duvoisin in Geneva. In April 1813 the family moved to the Rue de l'Estrapade in Paris, where they would remain for three years. Say's return to the capital did not remain unnoticed by the imperial police. One year earlier, he had written to Delaroche that his ideas were directly contrary to those of the Master. Now an anonymous letter to the police minster signalled the arrival of one of the emperor's 'most violent enemies':

> Monsieur Say, a former member eliminated from the tribunat and presently domiciled at l'estrapade near the Panthéon and the rue d'enfer, is this criminal enemy. Nevertheless this perversely sly person is trying to slip into an administrative job and – who would believe it? – he sticks with a guilty tenacity to ridiculing the operations of the emperor, expressing himself almost always about him with the greatest contempt and the darkest maliciousness. When Monsieur Say believes that he is talking to individuals

he considers to be discontented about the government, and who *certainly do not have any relationship with the police,* he expresses himself not just with a guilty indecency, but as a truly furious person ...

Following Monsieur Say, a right understanding of the national interest requires that Bonaparte will succumb *by the sword* in order to deter the tyrants who might be tempted to imitate him, and although the emperor cares about his safety to the highest degree, Monsieur Say nevertheless thinks that *courageous people can beat him successfully.* Finally Monsieur Say pretends that for the coalition powers, one of the most effective and rapid means to put an end to the odious tyranny, is to *put a price on his head without delay,* adding that the streams of bloodshed he has caused and still is causing, have made him the object of public detestation; it is beyond doubt that a *well paid* small corps of tyrannicides would surely and rapidly deliver France from the cruel usurper oppressing it and robbing it without pity.[2]

On 4 November 1813, the police prefect made a note that these informations must be verified. This was less than one month after Napoleon's defeat at Leipzig. In these circumstances of course, rumours about a 'fifth column' stabbing Bonaparte in the back at home, were apt to find an eager audience.

In November 1812 Say recorded negotiations in his diary about a possible association with Mr Stone, 'of the Humbolt enterprise'. The German scholar and explorer Alexander von Humboldt lived in Paris since 1808.[3] However, no details or follow-up of this venture have been recorded, which means that Say was lucky enough not to get involved in Stone's bankruptcy. A letter of February 1813, to Michel Delaroche, is clear about the various uses of his capital. First, he told him to double his participation in a speculation – most probably in sugar – of his brother Louis. Second, he asked him to request some consideration with Horace's speculations from his American financial counterpart, Mr de Rham – a man of Swiss origin.[4] Finally he asked him to probe a man named Adrien (Delaroche?) about a possible business association with him.

For the time being his most urgent concern was to get his funds out of the hands of Grivel, who in 1812 paid small sums of about 500 F each, which were booked in the *Journal.* In June 1813 he paid 15,000 F. A few thousand were directly booked into the 'speculations account' of Horace Say, who had a free hand in doing business with Delaroche.

On paper, Say had lost more than 50,000 F when he split up with Grivel. As mentioned above, in 1813 almost two-thirds of his capital of 95,000 F consisted of Grivel's debt to him. About 26,500 F had been invested in French government paper, and Horace managed assets worth 7500 F.

Two years later, in March 1815, his portfolio had changed dramatically. The biggest assets were 'American funds' at 49,253 F. Next came Grivel with 20,000 F, Horace with 11,500 and government paper with 6000. 'American speculations' accounted for 3000 F. But Delaroche, Delessert & Cie in Le Havre had become creditors to the amount of 11,000 F. His capital had shrunk to 85,000 F, because of losses on the sale of French loans early in 1814. Also in 1814 he had transferred the remaining 50,000 F of Grivel's debt to Delaroche, 30,000 of which had been paid. Already two years earlier he had written that he completely trusted his relative, and given him a free hand in affairs and speculations. But soon after this bookkeeping operation he had to send an alarming letter to Le Havre, as Grivel had reported being unable to pay the last 20,000. As a consequence, Say remained Grivel's creditor for 20,000 F, and became a debtor of Delaroche for part of the amount spent on American funds.

He clearly lacked the talent of a Rothschild or a Ricardo for stock market operations. Later transactions were relatively small and concerned commodity markets. Early in 1813 he wrote to Delaroche about doubling his share in a speculation in funds and commodities. At the end of that year he asked Horace to spend 10,000 or 15,000 francs in a speculative transaction, 'depending on the greater or lesser risk of the operation'. In August 1814 he asked Delaroche to be allowed to participate in a speculative grain investment.

In 1812 Say had hinted at a possible move to the US. In February 1814 he asked Delaroche, seemingly on behalf of a third party ('a family you know'), to inquire with his overseas business relations about the possibilities for settling in England:

> *A family of French manufacturers, going to settle in England with its skills and capitals, would it be well received and could it found its establishment without suffering from barriers and delays of a 'here-bill' or any other law, which puts foreigners under the rule of a special legislation?*
>
> *Could it bring a patent of invention or importation of new processes? For how long does such a patent guarantee the exclusive right upon these processes, and by what criteria is the price for it determined? Will the process have to be made public at the expiration of the patent?*

If he asked this question for himself, a letter asking precise informations from his brother Louis in July gives an idea of what he might have had in mind:

1. *How long does one need, following the old method (which is probably the one used in England) from the moment one puts into operation raw islands sugar until one can put it up for sale as refined lumps?*
2. *How long does this take when one follows the last improved processes of Louis Say?*
3. *At what sum do you value your costs in Nantes for every operation resulting in a certain number of pounds of refined sugar?*
4. *Are there necessary intervals between the operations, I mean just after one has utilised a furnace, a boiling kettle, drilling engines, can one use them continuously, and work without interruption? Just to have an idea of the quantity every run can produce in a year.*
5. *Can a certain part of the process be kept a secret, or must one fear that the workers – and through them the other refiners – can get hold of our processes before we have been able to harvest a good revenue?*

6. *What is the percentage of production loss from the raw sugar, and do the profits offset this loss?*

It seems that by the middle of 1814, the roles of the brothers had been reversed. The younger, Louis, was no longer in a position where he needed Jean-Baptiste's advice and financial assistance. It was the latter who had trouble in making ends meet. With interest rates of 5 or 6 per cent, Say's capital of about 100,000 F which he extracted from Auchy in 1812, was inadequate to procure him a living. The loss of 10,000 in 1814, and the status of Grivel as a dubious debtor for 20,000 in the same year, might be called alarming. He badly needed an extra source of income, which was to arrive with the governmental commission for an economic reporting journey around England and Scotland, and the publishing of the second edition of the *Traité*.

Remarkably little attention is given in the *Acta* to the developments of 1813 and 1814 on the battlefield. Only the entry in Paris of the allied armies on 31 March 1814 was recorded. In June he sent flowers worth 12 F to aunt Duvoisin and noted that they had been 'confiscated by the enemy'. Clearly most of his attention went to the preparation of his second edition, which was delivered to the printers immediately after the defeat of Napoleon.

Finally: the *Traité*'s second edition

Already one year after the printing of the first edition, its success required a second one. From Maubuisson Say wrote to Duval in the middle of 1804: *My book will be sold out and it is one of my worries that I have no time to prepare a second edition, which will be necessary.*

But Teilhac reports that the *Direction de la Librairie* had explicitly forbidden the printing of a second edition to the publisher, and Say confirmed to the book-seller Paschoud that Bonaparte himself was behind this decision.[5] The precise date of the measure may have been unknown to Say when he wrote to Duval. The latter remained his confidant and sounding board, for eight years later, residing in Villemomble in 1812, Say asked him to send any books on political economy he might come across. Steiner quotes letters from the years 1805–1809 to Sismondi and other correspondents, in which Say complained about not being able to decently prepare a second edition. He envied Sismondi, who had time to write while he had neither the time nor the peace of mind for it: 'Once you have reached the age of forty, you start to have no more confidence in the future, and unfortunately I am in that position.' In 1807 he wrote to Frossard, a Swiss who had settled in Lyon, and had been one of the founders of the Society of Friends of the Blacks, about his prospects for publishing again:

Alas! The wind which is blowing dries out all germs, and for as long as this will last I will certainly not publish a single sentence again. My book on political economy is sold out. I would like to prepare a second, much less imperfect edition. I have collected the materials; they will stay where they are. Letters and commerce are in a sorry state.[6]

Seven years later, the wind blew from another direction. The printing history of Say's second edition is well documented. On 6 April 1814, one week after the allied troops entered Paris, he started to deliver his manuscript to the printer. On 30 May he noted the completion of his *Economie Politique*, as he consequently called the *Traité* in his *Acta* and *Journal*. Although the title page mentions Renouard as the publisher, Say carried the commercial risk. Already during the printing he was concerned with the international marketing of his book, as he wrote in May to the bookseller and publisher Paschoud in Geneva:

> *At present I have in the press a Second edition of my Traité d'économie politique, completely rewritten, of which Bonaparte prohibited a reprint. 2 Vol. in 8°, beautiful paper, beautiful print. I am the owner of this edition but for private reasons I have entrusted the selling to Renouard Librairie. However I would like you to have the sales for Geneva, Switzerland and surrounding countries.*[7]

And indeed Paschoud ordered a few dozen; with every dozen one free copy was delivered. Paschoud was also asked to send around a number of books to Milan and in Switzerland, and to deliver a complimentary copy to Etienne Dumont in Geneva.

All expenses were recorded in his *Journal*, from the first 1000 F paid for paper to the printer Crapelet, to the wages of binder and 'satineur', and the 6 F 'pour boire' given to the apprentices of the printer. Fifteen hundred copies were printed. A cost price of about 3.50 F can be reconstructed from Say's administration. Counting backwards from the stock remaining after one year, in March 1815, which Say valued at 2450 F, this corresponds to 700 copies still left. At Say's selling price of 8 F, cash sales of the first year corresponded to a number of 300 copies, and cheque payments from Renouard to 350 (not counting the discount copies).[8] Judging by the many letters thanking Say for his book, a fair number of complimentary copies must have been sent around as well. In August 1814 he even asked the bookseller Paul Ustery in Zürich to distribute on his behalf a dozen copies to journals and learned societies in Switzerland and Germany. His letter demonstrated an interest in translations of his work:

> *If, as I believe, it was you who procured to my friend Mr. La Harpe a copy of my book translated into German by professor Ludder, I beg you to have this reimbursed to you. I also beg you, Monsieur, whenever you hear people speak of a translation of this new edition, to buy a copy on my behalf and send it to me immediately.*[9]

Of course this was before the days of decent international agreements on copyrights, and lots of money could be made by printing robber editions of successful textbooks. During and after Say's lifetime, this would even happen with clandestine French editions of the *Traité* and *Cours Complet*. In the month of printing of his second edition, April 1814, he wrote to an Englishman staying in Paris, Mr Blake, asking him to contact a bookseller in London about selling an English translation:

> *... a translation which I have started to be made under my eyes by an Englishman kept prisoner in France against the law of nations and all principles of humanity ...*
>
> *The second edition is completely rewritten, much better organised, a lot more complete and enriched with several revelations about Bonaparte's administration. Judging by the success of the first edition and the interest for present circumstances, it will make some noise ...*
>
> *The first edition, however imperfect, has been translated into Italian and German, and is serving as a textbook for the chairs of political economy of universities in Germany and in St Petersburg.*

He proposed him to contact the French bookseller DeBoffe for information about the success of the first edition, but not to make a proposal on the translation to him as it might hurt his interest in the French original.[10] How desperately Say was trying to promote his second edition is shown by a letter to Duval, also written in August 1814 and apparently accompanying a review or abstract he had written himself:

> *You will understand how essential it is that my name does not figure in this. If you could arrange to have a few hundred copies sold, that would result in a public as well as a private benefit.*
>
> *Don't you believe that every Préfecture and perhaps even every Sous-préfecture should have a copy in their libraries? Also, the auditors at the Council of State would find something in it to their advantage, and would at least be a little bit informed about the elements constituting the prosperity of the nation they are being taught to administrate.*

Say also asked Duval for suggestions to improve his self-promotion text. Whatever the outcome of this action was, the final commercial result of the second edition was substantial. In November 1817, when the third edition had already come off the press, he stated the total revenue of the second as 7786 F. Not enough for a living, but after the fall of Bonaparte there seemed to be other opportunities for a true liberal, who optimistically dedicated his second edition to the Russian Tsar Alexander.

The original Say of 1814

In many respects the second edition is a completely new book. Not just in composition, but in content as well. The first edition is a Smithian treatise of classical economics. The second is still classical, but much more subjectivist in its value theory. In 1803, the still unknown economist J.-B. Say must have considered it safe conduct not to move himself too far away from his master, although he had already voiced some criticisms in his manuscript notes.

In 1814 he had come to regret this behaviour, which had earned him the reputation of being just a vulgariser of Adam Smith. In a manuscript note, which seems to have been occasioned by a review of the second edition in a British journal, labelling him as no more than a Smithian, he wrote:

> *Those who have accused me of having done no more than stating more clearly the principles of Smith, have thereby given me praise which I value highly, but they have not rendered me justice. I believe I have studied Smith just as much as they have, and yet I have not found an explanation of the phenomenon of production and consumption, which is the foundation of all political economy. Once the principles upon which this phenomenon is founded, the development of their relations with the various professions, and the laws and customs of a society have been well understood, only then it is possible to resolve the problems which present themselves when one wishes to govern well one's family or a state.*[11]
>
> *Although Smith's book on The Wealth of Nations contains a substantial number of elements of this science, and while it has been immensely useful to me in this respect, he constitutes the science so little that although he has been read and studied for thirty years, by very capable men, he has not solved one question on which there is agreement today, which I attribute to the fact that he has not integrated them in a complete system, and that he had no such system, whatever merit I recognise in his work.*[12]

These are not the words of a modest man. Two centuries hence, most scholars are convinced that Smith had developed a system of social science, and his pupil at best a skeleton of one. Still, Say's tripartite division of economics as the production, distribution and consumption of wealth was immensely successful. His specification of immaterial production – 'services' – was an improvement upon Smith. And by contrast to his first edition, he presented his own subjectivist theory of value.

In 1803, Say's *Traité* was divided into five 'books' in two volumes. The discussion of value and price was relegated to Book III, 'On the value of goods'. Its first chapter went under the Smithian title 'On the natural value of products, and their value in exchange, or current price'. In Say's treatment, the three factors of production – nature, labour and capital – determine the 'natural value' of a product on the supply side. In money terms, this is Adam Smith's 'natural price'; it is not the same as 'market price'. On the demand side, the essential property for a good to have any value, is to possess utility. This utility – or capacity to satisfy wants – can vary between individuals, as well as between climate zones and social environments. An individual's demand is determined by the ranking of his wants and by his purchasing power. The market mechanism will create an equilibrium with a market price somewhere around the 'natural price' of the sum of the costs of the factors of production. This is the equilibrium in the long run.

In shorter periods, relative price changes can occur, which however leave the value of total output unchanged.

When technical change is introduced, an absolute lowering of the price of certain goods can result (and total output will rise). Not surprisingly for a former cotton spinner, Say mentions the example of machine-woven stockings. Stockings used to be a luxury article, but mechanical weaving has brought them within reach of the masses. As a consequence, vastly bigger quantities of labour and capital are being employed in their production, and national income will rise. To Say, this means progress. For him, lower prices are always a feature of this development.[13]

The *Traité*'s second edition of 1814 is divided into three 'books' in two volumes: Production, Distribution and Consumption. Value and price are discussed at the beginning of Book II, 'Distribution of wealth'. But already in his introduction, Say has distanced himself from Smith in a wording reminiscent of what he had written in the margin of his own copy of *The Wealth of Nations*: '[Smith] attributes the power of producing value to the work of man only. This is an error.' The introduction also makes clear that Say had read a lot more since 1803, and wished to comment upon predecessors such as Verri and Galiani, who according to Say had hinted on connections and relations that had afterwards been proved by Smith.[14]

In 1814, he felt the need to justify the new composition of his second edition, and to describe the phenomenon of production – as the *creation* of value – before analysing the *nature* of value. Still, chapter one of Book I discusses human wants, utility and value. Say the subjectivist tells us that 'what seems useful to one person, may seem completely superfluous to another'.[15] But instead of going deeper into individual differences, and how to combine these into one demand schedule, he rapidly switches to 'that generally accepted estimation of utility' which Smith calls 'value in exchange', Turgot labels as 'appreciative value' and Say simply names 'value'.

In chapter one of Book II, 'On the foundations of the value of things', utility is the first foundation. Useful goods will satisfy human wants (which are considered as 'given quantities'). Remarkably, Say includes institutions in his examples of useful things: 'the courts of justice in Europe are considered to be one of the strongest connecting ties of society; while the indigenous inhabitants of America, and the Tartars and Arabs, can very well do without these'.[16]

Then he turns to the supply side: air, water and the heat of the sun are useful and free. Political economy occupies itself with utility added by the three factors of production. In the second as in the first edition, Say argues that, normally, supply and demand will lead to market prices around cost price level. Sudden variations in supply or demand may cause prices to fall below *value* or *cost price*, but only for a short period.

On the other side, fixing prices above cost price level is only possible if a government lets itself be paid too much for its services, or if it awards a monopoly to a private supplier. This is a political rather than an economic problem. And in the next chapter, on 'merchandise in circulation', Say argues against fixed and maximum prices which can only lead to speculation, or bring production to a standstill (and thus create a welfare loss).

As compared to the *Traité*'s first edition (1803), Say's treatment of value in the second (1814) brings out the real Say, who dares to be critical of Adam Smith and other predecessors. But it would not take long before his insights were challenged by his most formidable opponent in this matter, David Ricardo, whom he was to meet soon in England. It is possible to speak of two Great Debates between Say and other economists. The first being the Say–Ricardo debate on value; and the second the Say–Malthus (and to some extent Say–Sismondi) debate on Say's Law, or the Law of Markets. More will be said about the value debate in Chapter 7, in relation to Say's meeting with Ricardo.

As noted above, Say had proudly sent a version of his new chapter on *Débouchés* (or Say's Law) to Michel Delaroche in May 1812. In a letter of June 1814, accompanying the presentation copy for De Candolle, he wrote: 'It is an altogether new work, reworked during eleven years.'[17]

After the first and essentially microeconomic version of the law in the *Traité* of 1803, Say presented a long-term, macroeconomic version in 1814. William Baumol, in his classic article on *Say's (at least) eight Laws*, has plausibly argued that this version can be rightly called Say's own law.[18] Say's Law will be discussed below in Chapter 8, in the context of Say's *Letters to Malthus*.

Say's entrepreneur in 1814

We have seen what difficulties Say had to surmount in founding and running his factory. How did these experiences influence his theoretical notions? In 1814 the subject of entrepreneurship is discussed in Book II, *De la Distribution des Richesses*. Chapter VII, 'Of the incomes of [human] industry', first discusses industrial 'profits' (incomes) in general; then follow the profits of the scholar, the profits of the industrial entrepreneur and the profits of the worker.

Say starts with the observation that in countries with an *abundance of capital*, generally wages are high. And in those countries man's well-being is higher because the income of labour is supplemented by the revenue of capital and land. Then he lists five causes determining the level of wages, from 'dangerous and disagreeable working conditions' to the required 'degree of ability'. This last cause is explained by a human capital reasoning: when this ability is the fruit of a long and costly study, its salary includes 'the interest of the advances required for this study'.

Then the contribution of the scientist is described: 'The scholar, the man who knows how one can take advantage of the laws of nature for the utility of man, receives only a small part of the fruits of industry, although the knowledge he stores and expands is so prodigiously useful to it.'

This knowledge is often the product of scientific study and experiment. But practical knowledge can also be the fruit of a practical discovery by a manufacturer, which gives him an advantage over his competitors. In that case he is rewarded both as a discoverer and as an entrepreneur. This distinguishing of two processes of innovation is a new element in the second edition. In 1803, regarding the application of a given technology, the entrepreneur was just the intermediary 'between the man of science and the worker'. In 1814 Say explicitly mentions the process of innovation on the shop floor, by trial and error or just serendipity.

He also remarks that fortunately there are only a few trades where new industrial processes can be kept secret for a long time. Such monopolies are contrary to the public interest as they keep prices at a higher than natural rate (and thereby the possible number of consumers at a lower than natural rate).

The discussion of the entrepreneur's income starts with the same arguments as in the first edition. First the capitalist's and the entrepreneur's income are distinguished from each other. Then the two conditions limiting the number of entrepreneurs are mentioned:

1. The capacity to find the necessary capital;
2. The other entrepreneurial capacities.

The latter are specified in a way different from the wording of 1803:

Secondly this kind of work demands a number of moral qualities, the combination of which is uncommon. He needs judgment, constancy and a knowledge of men and affairs. The matter is to assess rightly the importance of a certain production, the demand for the product and the means to acquire it; it is also about activating sometimes very large numbers of people; it is necessary to buy or to let buy the raw materials, to get the workers together, to look for consumers, and have an orderly and economical mind; in one word the talent of administration. In the course of so many operations there are obstacles to surmount, uncertainties to conquer, technical troubles to repair, practical solutions to invent. Those persons in whom these necessary qualities are not united, run their enterprises with little success; these firms will not survive, and their labour will soon fall out of circulation. By consequence only he will stay in business who is successful, that means capable. In this way the requirement of capacity limits the number of people who can supply the work of an entrepreneur.

This is not all: a certain risk always accompanies the industrial enterprises; however well run we suppose they are, they can go bankrupt; the entrepreneur can risk losing his fortune even without deserving blame, and even losing his honour to a certain extent. One more reason which limits from another angle the quantity of this kind of service offered, and therefore makes it even more expensive.[19]

Then he gets back to the already familiar distinction between the routine capacities necessary for being a farmer, and the more entrepreneurial ones required for commercial and industrial entrepreneurs. But in comparison with the rather academic summing-up of entrepreneurs' tasks in his first edition, Say gives a much livelier one in the second. It reflects the breakdown and repair of the waterwheel in Auchy, the problems in finding raw cotton under the barriers of the Milan Decree, the quarrels with his partner Grivel and the trouble of getting his capital out of the joint venture. The close relationship of risk, uncertainty and profit is all there.

In an original contribution, Philipppe Steiner has drawn attention to Say's treatment of production as an essential element for understanding his theory of value as well as his law of markets.[20] He notes the seemingly irrelevant paragraphs on production at the beginning of Say's treatment of value. But these were essential for Say's approach of the subject, and especially for his distinguishing himself from Smith on this topic, beginning with his second edition (1814):

> So Smith did not build a complete notion of the grand phenomenon of pro-
> duction; which makes him err into some false consequences, like when he
> attributes an enormous influence to the division of labour, or rather to the
> separation of professions; this influence is certainly not nought, or even
> mediocre, but the greatest miracles of this kind are not caused by the nature
> of labour; they are due to the use man makes of the forces of nature. The
> misjudgment of this principle prevents him from establishing the true theory
> of machines with regard to the production of wealth.[21]

Steiner has linked this to the observation that 'the intellectual division of labour is an important element, introduced by Say in ranking the productive service of the scholar among the component parts of industry'.[22] One might also state this conclusion as: while Smith praised the effects of the division of labour under a (largely and implicitly) given production function, Say explicitly specified the big and combined results of the division of labour and technical progress. In other words, he expected the effects of (labour-saving) technical change to be at least equal to those of the division of labour in a changing production function.

Steiner continues by pointing to Say's observation that not only the inventions of scholars, but also the entrepreneurial innovations on the shop floor contribute to the greater efficiency of production. And he quotes a paragraph from the *Cours Complet* on the supervising capacities, necessary for being a successful entrepreneur. Published in 1828, these still reflect Say's own experiences in his Auchy mill:

> He must often suppose to be cheated, but never let this be noticed; he must
> let the interest of his staff coincide with his own; make it impossible for
> them to be illoyal; expose them to unannounced inspections; never mistake
> the result of an employee for that of another, in order to praise where this is
> due; to have them practice mutual control, without encouraging spying
> which is a reason for contempt.[23]

As a beginning economist, Say already had an original theory of entrepreneurship in 1803. Further supplemented by his experiences in Auchy in later editions of the *Traité* and *Cours Complet*, his ideas on the subject are still worth studying.

In 1971, when Say's status seemed to have been reduced to 'a minor figure in the history of economic thought', Koolman had already rehabilitated him with respect to his theory of the entrepreneur.[24] He pointed to Say's description of the qualities, necessary for being a successful entrepreneur, and to his distinguishing between the interest on capital and the income of the entrepreneur. He too has noted that Say nowhere mentioned the work of Cantillon as a possible influence. In his opinion, Say's weaknesses were the little attention paid to the role of the entrepreneur in capital accumulation, and the little insistence on his role in innovation. To the former objection we can agree, but it has been argued above that Say not only credited the entrepreneur for applying new scientific insights in the production process, but also for bringing about practical innovations on the shop floor. Yet we can agree with Koolman that 'judged by the standards of his own age, Say's ideas were highly sophisticated'.[25]

The Third Class of the Institut

With an undated letter, probably written in June 1814, Say presented a copy of his second edition to the President of the Third Class of the Institut, the one of History and Ancient Literature. Considering his later efforts to become a member of the Académie Française, it is quite probable that he hoped to be considered for membership of the Institut. Napoleon had abolished the *Classe des Sciences Morales et Politiques*, therefore Say had to choose between approaching the second class, of French literature, or the third, of history and ancient literature:

> *Please allow me to presently dedicate to it* [the Institut] *by way of your class, a copy of the second edition of this work, entirely recomposed and perhaps less unworthy of its attention. Although this kind of research is not specifically promoted by the Institut, I could not believe that it would wish to neglect any branch of the human sciences, certainly if more stubborn researches and more reliable methods will succeed in drawing these from the domain of conjectures, to found them upon the solid base of observation and experience. And if the first learned society of Europe does not exclude Political Economy from the sphere of its considerations, which class would be more appropriate to occupy itself with it than the one which carries the torch of criticism amidst the uncertainties of history.*
>
> *It seems truly difficult to conceive of correct ideas about the commerce and industry of the ancients, about the effects of their operations upon taxes and money, about the causes of prosperity and decline of their colonies, etc. when one does not seek the counsel of Political Economy, which reveals the march of wealth in relation to geography, to the laws and to customs.*[26]

He continued his letter by pointing to the importance, even with regard to ancient history, of making correct calculations of values and prices in the past. For that purpose, a special chapter had been written in the *Traité*. And he concluded by expressing his respect for the members of the Third Class, 'some of which are paying me the honour of a personal friendship'.

One of these personal friends, his former *Décade* colleague Ginguené, presented his report on Say's treatise to the Third Class in August; it was also printed in the *Mercure de France*.[27] Ginguené explained why he had neither chosen to just summarise Say's book, nor to sketch the improvements of the second edition upon the first. He preferred to concentrate on those parts of it that were of direct interest to the studies of the Third Class. But he did not fail to mention that the second edition had had to wait ten years before it could be published:

> The fall of a government *based upon lies, of which every measure was a calamity*, and the re-establishment of a power which can only reap its glory by healing the evils caused by the tyranny, and by reintroducing the good measures destroyed by it, have given the signal to the truth to reappear, and to the principles underlaying public happiness to show up again.

Before commenting on Say's relevance for the Third Class, Ginguené found it necessary to state that the Moral and Political Sciences (including economics and philosophy), although formally abolished as a separate class of the Institut, were indeed an integral part of the domain of this class. 'The man who grabbed power on 18 brumaire' had declared war on philosophy. The ideas and vocabulary of Condorcet and of the Idéologie were still alive in the mind of Ginguené, heaping wrath on the ideas and deeds of Bonaparte:

> Philosophy, which enlightens the minds by purifying and elevating the spirits, was the natural enemy of the degrading reign he installed; he declared a war on it.
>
> He came to repair all that was wrong; philosophy and the philosophers were the cause of it all.
>
> Who had covered France with ruins and prisons? The philosophers.
> . . .
> A whole class of the Institut was dedicated to philosophy, especially with regard to the needs of society; the class of moral and political sciences was suppressed.
>
> And effectively, of the six sections composing this useful class, those of *history* and *geography* could be transferred elsewhere; but what a danger was the *analysis of sensations and ideas*, i.e. *the idéologie*, for him who wished to overturn all ideas; morals, for him who wished no other morals, public or private, than passive obedience? What a dark shadow was the science of *legislation*, for him who wished no other law but his own will, and *political economy*, which to him counted for nothing; and he prepared himself to completely overturn, from top to bottom, the entire construction of public prosperity, which this science teaches to found, to build-up and to conserve in its entirety and for all classes?

After continuing on Bonaparte's bridling of the press, and his hiring of corruptible journalists, Ginguené finally came around to quoting useful examples from Say's text. And he concluded on his relevance for the study of economic history: 'The method suggested by Mr. Say, applied to historical studies, would result for all these examples in conclusions which, if not precisely exact, would be much nearer to the truth.'

It is clear that Say had hoped to be considered for membership of the Third Class. But for the time being, the Institut was still a bridge too far for him. Scientific homages and membership of academies were to come sooner for him abroad than at home.

6 Spying in Britain

A secret mission

On 19 September 1814 Say departed from Paris on his way to England. His personal diary of the journey gives no clue what may have been the purpose of this visit. But he clearly went on an official governmental commission, as already stated by his first biographer Charles Comte in 1834. After mentioning the interruption of regular contacts between France and England for twenty-three years, Comte writes about the commercial and industrial progress of Britain in that period. According to him, the French government, wishing to promote an industrial and commercial spirit in France, charged Say with a commission to examine as far as possible the progress made in England since the interruption of all contacts between the two countries.

In the letter of April 1814 to Dupont de Nemours, already quoted above, Say's primary objective was to offer his services to the provisional government under Talleyrand, as he urgently needed a job with a fixed income:

> ...the benevolent manner in which you have mentioned me in your precious collection of Turgot's works, gives me enough confidence to beg you to bring my name under the attention of Monsieur de Talleyrand, if you believe that I might cooperate usefully to the regeneration of France.
> ...
> My work [the *Traité*] was rapidly sold out and could not be reprinted. It was directly opposed to the doings of a savage government, and the press was no longer free. But German, English and Italian translations have established my name abroad. Please tell me, Monsieur, if my self-esteem is misleading me; but it seems to me that it would produce no favourable result if I would be left aside by the government which is generally well appreciated. I am addressing myself to you, Monsieur, and to your friend the Prince, for jobs that might well be entrusted to me, under the condition that they would be compatible with the positions I have held already. If the ministry of commerce and manufactures might be reduced to a division of the ministry of the interior, I would very much appreciate to be at the head of this division, or that of the Post, or at the head of public works or customs, even if as a

good disciple of the Economistes, I hardly like customs; but well, we are not yet ready for laissez faire and laissez passer.[1]

There existed no English translation as yet; and Say – for once – was opportunistic enough to pose as a true follower of the Physiocrats, although he had accused them of unfounded system-building in his introduction to the *Traité*. Whether or not the commission for Say's British venture was the result of this intervention, it was granted rapidly after Say wrote this letter. Already in May he wrote to the publisher and bookseller Crapelet, thanking him for 'offering his services for London', and asking him for a general introductory work on English public finance, as well as a number of specific titles on money and finance.[2]

Say himself was very careful not to record any formal statement on his commission in his *Acta* or *Journal*. And when writing from England, he urged his correspondents to avoid any allusion to the real purpose of his visit. The payments he received were made through the intermediary of a Monsieur Becquey. This must have been Louis Becquey, the director general of commerce.[3] And although a manuscript diary of his trip has survived, the formal report of his commission has not surfaced from the public archives. The only reference to the existence of such a document is Say's note on page 29 of his British diary, that he has glued the two preceding pages into his 'minute'. The little book he published in 1815, *De l'Angleterre et des Anglais*, is of a more general nature than just a report on industrial progress. But when he prepared his trip, he wrote a four-page *Study on the situation of English Commerce*, in which he summarised the ideas of unnamed authors – most probably Bosanquet and others – on the future of the British pound's exchange rate.[4]

Of course he was an excellent choice for the job, with his English apprenticeship, his theoretical background in economics and his practical experience as an entrepreneur. All these are reflected in his *Journal Anglais*. However this does not read like a spy story, as Say generally obtained easy access to mines and factories of all kinds. His entire journey lasted from 19 September 1814 till 4 January 1815. The first and the last month were spent in London. Between 23 October and 29 November he travelled to Edinburgh and Glasgow, going by way of York and Newcastle and coming back by way of Liverpool, Manchester and Birmingham. In December he spent one week on a trip to Gatcomb Park, Bath, Bristol and Ford Abbey, meeting David Ricardo and Jeremy Bentham.

One of his first visits was a sentimental journey to Fulham where he had lived with his brother Horace almost thirty years earlier:

> *Thirty years later, after twenty-five years of war and revolution, I went back to see the place again. I could find back almost nothing. I hardly recognised the house where we had lived. It had perhaps changed owners four or five times, and tenants twenty times, and everyone had made some small change to it. The village and its surroundings had changed even more, in a country with houses of simple construction. A lovely meadow where I had often walked with delight, had become a street filled with shops.*

Other places I had seen inhabited and well kept were unrecognisable because their maintenance had been neglected. I walked on a promenade along the Thames we often visited, only separated by a canal from the park of the Bishop of London, which was the most beautiful spot of the village. I found the place back as I had known it. But the sentiments it evoked were sad and painful. All those old trees had witnessed my brother and myself so often, as we always did our shopping together; now they saw me back alone, like a section of a wall remaining upright after a fire, looking for souvenirs and only finding the walls of Akkon where he had been taken away from me.

A young lady, arm in arm with her husband and with a child at her hand, walked a little distance ahead of us ... perhaps she was one of the demoiselles Wyburn, or mademoiselle Green, and I doubled my steps to overtake them. Stupid fellow! These young demoiselles you are looking for, are now perhaps grandmothers![5]

Say's *Journal Anglais* was of a much more practical nature. He was greatly impressed by the scale of application of coal, iron and steel. This was reflected in his first impressions of Glasgow:

Approaching Glasgow, many exploitations of coal. Abundant availability of combustion material favourable to industry, as heat is one of the most powerful and most productive agents of nature. Cooking, melting, spraying, distilling &c. I arrive in Glasgow. Many children, proof that people have the opportunity to employ them and to let them earn a living. The main street, beautiful and lively. The riversides well cleared, something I had not seen before in England. One Steam boat leaving and another arriving; new and interesting spectacle. From the outside I watch a spinning factory driven by steam and lit by gas.

In most cases he was allowed to inspect the inside of mines and mills as well. Under way between York and Newcastle he visited the coal mines of Kenton and Leaton. He described in detail the use of steam in pumping up water, and in transporting coal. His critical eye noticed the way the cables hoisting up the coal bins had been twisted or braided. Being flat instead of round, this made them better suited to rolling over pulleys with a heavy load attached. He noted this as an example to be followed. In Glasgow he saw a steam factory rasping wood, and visited a steam sawmill of staves for casks, as well as a steam farm. Here straw was being cut, butter churned and liquid manure pumped, all by steam power.

A detailed description of a steam engine was given by Say in his notes about the steamers on board of which he sailed from Glasgow to Greenock and back; from the size and form of the boilers, to the working of the cams moving the valves, and the transmission of power to the paddle wheels by means of cogwheels. He was amazed by their small size, which he estimated at a diameter of thirty inches, and twelve to fifteen inches wide. The sides of the paddle boards were hollow-cast, and were fixed to the axis at a slight angle, so as to have a better grip on the water surface.

In Birmingham he visited an iron foundry where machine parts were produced, from twenty feet fly-wheels to the very smallest pinions. The foundry process, with a thick layer of sand in double casting moulds, reminded him of a copper mill he had seen in Fontenay-aux-Roses. Waste iron was melted again with coke in blast furnaces; Say believed that chalk was added to the coke. This was also the combustible for the melting pot; he was told that the bituminous parts in coal might harm the pot. He noted the detail that the sand was removed while the iron was still red hot, to ease its shrinking in cooling off.

It can be questioned whether his French commissioners were really interested in these remarks of an interested amateur – even if he had the background of a factory owner. But it has been remarked by David Landes that the early melting foremen worked by instinct, and invented improvements by trial and error.[6] So all comments on industrial processes and suggestions for imitation from Say must have been welcome.

In the same factory, iron bars of various thickness were produced not by casting or forging, but in a rolling machine. This process was still in its infancy. The same was true for the production of steel which he observed in another Birmingham mill. There Swedish ore was melted by coke twice: the first time into *blistered steel*, and the second into various qualities.

The Industrial Revolution was not just a phenomenon of the capital goods industry. In the nineteenth century, the British were the greatest per capita consumers of metal household objects. Say also examined the production of consumer goods. In Birmingham he went to see the Thomasson factory, where silver-plated goods were made on a steel base. He had already visited another one where silver plate was put on a copper base. At Thomasson's, other products were copper wire and tubes of any thickness between eyeglass frames and balusters. In case of the latter, a steel kernel was solded inside. Thomasson seems to have been one of the dynamic entrepreneurs of the period, always trying out something new. Say was allowed to visit his warehouses – a privilege he shared with his new sovereign Louis XVIII. There he witnessed 'an astonishing variety of ironmongery, jewellery, medals, vases as well as objects of leather, of pasteboard &c'. In other Birmingham factories he saw the production of tea urns, of swords and of nails. The latter were stamped and hammered from metal plates.

Say seemed to be less impressed by the textile mills he visited than by the British lead in iron and steam. In Manchester he went to see a large cotton-spinning mill in a building of seven floors, where he noticed no difference with the techniques used in France, and a smaller one reminding him of a second rate French mill.

In Glasgow he visited a steam-powered mill weaving cotton fabrics. He had been introduced there by a Member of Parliament named Finlay, probably the owner.[7] This man radiated lots of confidence, and was very open about his methods of production:

How could the people of France steal our manufacturing processes, if even the people of Manchester cannot achieve this? Every country has its specific industry in which it excels and in which all other countries are at a disadvantage.

Say considered this formulation of an absolute advantage theory important enough to underline these observations in his diary. He also visited factories producing glass, crystal and papier-mâché, and one sugar refinery which he found rather dirty. The only place where he was confronted with strict secrecy was the London Mint.[8] He was neither allowed to see the steam-driven engine minting the coins, nor the one for the milling process. Boulton and Watt had built the machine, and had negotiated its trade secret. This evoked Say's scorn:

Although I have generally felt many reasons to admire the talents of Watt and Boulton for large machinery, I have also had twenty occasions to become convinced of their illiberality of mind. They are just clever factory workers who have become rich. They have nothing but contempt of France and of its products, yet they are afraid of them; which seems contradictory.

Spy, tourist and scholar

Say did not fail to notice that the Industrial Revolution was accompanied by revolutionary developments in agriculture and transport. He described the mechanisation of farms, like that of the one he saw in Glasgow, where all cows remained permanently in the stables. At the farm in Penrith of the older Buchanan (the economist's father), threshing went by machine, but the 4 HP required were still provided by four horses. At this farm, cows from Scotland were fattened up. Say wondered at the large beets they were fed, and at the fact that potatoes were not grown from seeds but by planting potatoes.

Say's interest in steamboats was already mentioned. He also admired the new waterways. In Glasgow he described the Clyde–Forth channel, with a fifty feet high aquaduct, where ships on their way from the Antilles to Petersburg could pass under full sail. In Liverpool he described the digging of the new docks. Respectfully he recorded that the Duke of Bridgewater received 30,000 pounds annually from his channel as well as from his dock.

The visits he paid to schools, prisons and theatres were probably outside his official commission. Also in his touristic capacity he went to see Kensington Gardens, Holyrood House and Blenheim Palace. At the palace he preferred the park, with its continuously mowed lawns, to the building. He contemplated why the British would not imitate more the designs of classical Greece and Rome and – of course – France. But in Oxford he admired the perfect maintenance of the medieval buildings.

Say may not have been impressed with all industrial achievements he saw, yet he was generally full of respect for the technical progress he witnessed, and at least as much for the entrepreneurial mentality which people like Thomasson and Finlay in Glasgow were expressing. He also noticed this quality in the owner of the Cooper Works in Glasgow, where casks of all sizes were produced. He called him 'an extremely active man who is continuously busy to use his steam-power for all kinds of useful ends'. In Liverpool the wealth heaped up in ware-houses, and the speed of business in that city, aroused a philosophical observation: 'He who grows rich does well, but enjoys alone.'

With some awe he described the so-called Lancaster Schools in Newcastle, where 500 children were being taught by one man. Here the children learned to write on slates after they had first been writing in sand. As an economist, he noticed the aspect of cost:

> *Almost no expenses for paper, ink and pens. An organisation by command, like the army ... They have organised everything in an industrial manner, even education.*

Joseph Lancaster had started his educational experiments in 1798. In 1808 these had been formally organised in the Royal Lancasterian Institution, embracing 95 schools with 30,000 pupils. The older children were engaged in teaching ele-mentary skills to the younger ones.

It was noted already that Say's official report of his trip is still missing. Therefore the only (surviving) letter he wrote from England to his contact person – most probably Becquey – is all the more interesting, as it contains very specific information on products and professional journals. The tone of secrecy is almost funny: Say does not write about England, but about 'the country where I am', and then continues about the English and British products.[9] The letter of seven densely written pages was sent after his first two weeks in London:

> It was your desire, Monsieur, that I would share my impressions with you of the country where I am. These are still quite superficial, as the English are not very communicative; one needs some time before gaining their confi-dence; and this is never unlimited, which is due to national pride and pecu-niary interests. Yet I do not wish to let a perfectly secure occasion which presents itself, go by without giving you some of my news.

Say described his journey, by way of Rouen and Dieppe, and reported that he had seen improvements in the local French industries as a consequence of the 'new order', and had observed a growing confidence with industrials and trades-men. A Monsieur Ricard had bought a beautiful cotton-spinning mill for 124,000 F after its owner deceased, and sold it eight days later to another private investor with a profit of 100,000 F. Returning to his English observations, he mentioned the enormous growth of trade: twenty years ago between 1000 and 1500 ships were moored in the London docks, and now almost 3000. New docks had been dug, including drydocks, and enormous warehouses surrounded these. The docks and warehouses functioned as free ports: the very high import duties were only due when the cargo had been sold and the goods were transported from the warehouses. Apart from this, two causes had enormously promoted British trade: the safety of the seas, and ('less observed') the exemption from taxation of trade, while agriculture and manufacturing were heavily taxed. Goods re-exported from bonded warehouses hardly had to pay any taxes.

According to Say, the English were largely unaware of this uneven distribution of burdens. The working class and the entrepreneurs were begging the government to allow imports of corn, in order to lower prices. And the government believed that lower grain prices would endanger future harvests. To his letter, Say added printed copies of the debates in parliament on this matter.

He argued that these problems had been responsible for the small advancement – and even retrogression in parts – of English manufacturing in the past twenty years. The quality of leatherwork had gone down, and the cotton industry as well. Silk had badly degraded, so smuggled Fench silk was tremendously popular. Say sketched a downward spiral of economising on labour and quality by manufacturers, a process undone by ever higher taxes. For the consumer this meant lower quality at a higher price.

But Say also reported a 'paradoxical' effect of these developments: an incentive for innovation – both product and process innovation. He had seen cotton tablecloth that was cheaper than linen. As a sample he sent a napkin with his letter, plus another sample of cotton yarn of enormous strength, as an example for the French cotton manufacturers. (Say surely was an expert in these matters.) He also sent a piece of pottery with 'metallic varnish' – most probably 'gold lustre' stoneware. While he had complained about high prices in general, he now wrote admiringly about its low price of 1 shilling 3 pence (between 27 and 30 French sous). A dozen little blue dishes cost only 3 shillings (1 franc and a few sous). Considering the taxes for the manufacturer, and the necessity of a profit of the shopkeeper, Say concluded that the production costs must be very low. Yet it was of a better quality than the French stoneware called 'fayence anglaise', and the only tableware used by the 'classe mitoyenne'. Say suggested that his samples be shown to the directors of the Sèvres porcelain works: by breaking these cheap articles, they might be able to analyse their composition. He further sent a sample of a leaden tube, produced by a drawing process, a piece of a new wool-and-silk cloth called 'Bombazine', and another called 'Popline'.

Finally, Say came back to his commisioner's request of obtaining periodicals with price lists, and professional journals. As these hardly took foreign subscriptions, Say had purchased a number of recent ones, and would have others sent to France by the services of booksellers. As titles he mentioned the *Repertory of arts*, and the *Retrospect of philosophical and mechanical discourses*.[10] Say noted that these also contained articles on French manufacturing. The *Tradesman* (or *Commercial Magazine*) was the last title he reported. And he sent two 'scandalously expensive' books on taxes and tariffs.

Say concluded by asking that new instructions or questions be sent to him by way of his family members, who would always be able to trace him. He requested the utmost discretion: 'By all means no printed matter – you understand how harmful that would be for me in this country.'

Whatever may have been the precise wording of Say's governmental commission, this letter makes clear that he gave a broad interpretation to it: from detailed reports on process and product innovations to comments on trade and tax policies. We may guess that his final report was more or less composed in the same way. In his pamphlet *De l'Angleterre et des Anglais* he would put the accent more on the general economic climate, the threat of a large public debt and the social disadvantages of industrial society.

Among economists and philosophers

From London, Say went north to the Midlands and Scotland. After coming back, he travelled to Ricardo at Gatcomb Park, and to Bentham at Ford Abbey. In the long run, the most important dividend of this trip consisted of his long-lasting contacts with Francis Place, James Mill, Jeremy Bentham and David Ricardo. In Say's pamphlet *De l'Angleterre et des Anglais* (1815), Ricardo is the only one of these economists and philosophers who is mentioned (in a footnote). But Say's correspondence with all of them testifies to a warm personal relationship as well as a shared economic and political interest.

Before his English journey, Say was already familiar with the work of Bentham and Ricardo. Yet they did not figure prominently on his list of people to visit. On 7 October, William Godwin had written a letter of introduction for Say to Francis Place.[11] One week later, Say paid a visit to the 'radical tailor', which was the start of a lasting relationship.[12] A scientific interest they shared was the problem of population.

It was only through the insistence of Place that Say finally paid a visit to Ricardo, Mill and Bentham. Perhaps he had seen enough of British mail coaches after his visit to Scotland. Anyway, early in December Place wrote to Mill that Say did not feel like making any more excursions outside London in the winter season. At first Place expected that a meeting with Mill could still take place in London, but as Say's return to France came nearer, he made a desperate effort to get him to Gatcomb Park and Ford Abbey. To Mill he wrote:

> *I was resolved to take no denial, I said all I believed of you, of Mr. Bentham, and of Mr. Ricardo – and I took the journey with him upon my maps – and the result is he goes to Gatcomb on Saturday by the coach. … He really feels himself honoured by the notice you have taken of him and but for this I should not have prevailed upon him.*

It is tempting to believe that this 'notice' would have regarded the subject of Say's Law, which had also been formulated in Mill's *Commerce Defended* of 1808. Mill himself wrote to Ricardo about the proposed visit:

> On mentioning to Mr. Bentham my project of bringing together you and Mons. Say, he started an idea which is perfection itself. If you can prevail upon M. Say, said he, to go to Mr. Ricardo's, perhaps we may prevail upon

both Mr. Say and Mr. Ricardo to come here. I am persuaded *you* will not think much of the journey. It is little more than 50 miles hither from Bath; and if Mr. Say should here leave you to go to London, the Bath and Exeter Stage passes at a few miles distance every day, so that you can return any way that you chuse. It would be a high treat to me to see you here, and to see you along with Say. To him I have no doubt it will be an object to meet with Mr. Bentham; and I am sure you will be gratified to be made acquainted with him.[13]

Say had set strict conditions for the trip: no more than one day with Ricardo at Gatcomb Park, and the same for Bentham and Mill at Ford Abbey, plus a visit to the glass houses and potteries of Bristol. The practical Place had already thought of a solution to this last request: 'A Bristol guide price 2 shillings sixpence will point them out and save time.' Place also considered the possibility that Say's visit would take more time, and he asked Mill to reserve some extra time, for otherwise he would keep 'a store of regret'. And indeed Say stayed at Ford Abbey (see Figure 6.1) from 14 December to 16 December.

Ricardo recorded his impression of his French colleague in a letter to Malthus:

He intends seeing you before he quits this country. He does not appear ready to me in conversation on the subject on which he has very ably written … yet he is an unaffected agreeable man, and I found him an instructive companion.

Figure 6.1 In December 1814, a memorable meeting took place at Ford Abbey between Jeremy Bentham, James Mill, David Ricardo and Jean-Baptiste Say. This engraving was made after a sketch by Lady Romilly, the wife of Sir Samuel Romilly.

Bentham wrote to Koe about the visit:

> Ricardo and Say came here yesterday at dinner unexpected; whether they
> go, however, or no, tomorrow, I know not. Both very intelligent and pleas-
> ant men, and both seem highly pleased.[14]

The opinion of the French visitor was transmitted to Mill by Francis Place:

> He spoke with rapture of you all, Mr. Bentham's Philosophy, and, as Mr.
> Say expressed it, 'his heart full of benevolence in every thing' made his
> eyes sparkle as he pronounced the words. You and Mr. Ricardo are, he says,
> profound economists, from both of you, he says, he has learnt much that
> will be useful.

From this visit on, Ricardo's ideas on value and price remained a continuing
challenge for Say, as is apparent from the subsequent editions of his *Traité* and
Cours Complet. Their correspondence is well known by the Sraffa edition of
Ricardo's *Works and Correspondence*. Bentham's influence is clear in print
from Say's reviews in the *Censeur Européen*, and from his essay on the Principle of Utility. Their direct and indirect communication is documented in Say's
correspondence with Bentham and Place.[15] The meeting with Malthus which Say
had in mind probably never took place. It is not mentioned in Say's *Journal
Anglais*. But later they met in Paris and entertained a correspondence.

In Scotland Say had met MacVey Napier by the mediation of Thomas Brown,
who shared the chair of moral philosophy with Dugald Stewart at the University
of Edinburgh; he just missed meeting the latter.[16] A letter of introduction for
him, written by Walter Buchanan, had been sent to Glasgow instead of Edinburgh. Stewart wrote back that he was 'no stranger to Mr. Say's excellent work
on Political Economy', and regretted having missed his visit. In Glasgow Adam
Smith's successor James Milne showed him the room where Smith had lectured;
Say noted in his journal: 'I sit down in his chair.'

Also his good introductions (or his good judgement) led him to a number of
other important people, like the Protestant lawyer and politician (of Huguenot
descent) Sir Samuel Romilly, the Scottish scientist Dr Brewster, Dr Roget (of
the *Thesaurus*) in London and the Baring bankers. Altogether he reaped an
invaluable intellectual capital during his visit to England and Scotland.

De l'Angleterre et des Anglais

In the short run, Say's remuneration for the entire journey was a very welcome
supplement to his not altogether healthy finances. The intermediary, Monsieur
Becquey, paid him 8000 F immediately upon his return, in January 1815, as well
as 4922.70 F for his own expenses and 1512.30 F for private purchases on Becquey's behalf. The last booking in March 1815 was one of 17,688.80 F as
'profits and remuneration' of the English journey. A nice sum, more than twice

the earnings from the second edition of his textbook, and equivalent to one-fifth of his entire capital. Now he was in need of a more permanent income to support his family. This could not be provided by the earnings from his *Traité*, nor from another offspin of his journey, his pamphlet *De l'Angleterre et des Anglais*.

This pamphlet of just thirty pages is a curious document among Say's writings for several reasons. Whereas the tone of his *Journal Anglais* is full of curiosity and admiration for the British people and their lead in steam and innovation, the main message of the pamphlet is extremely critical about the British monetary system, British public finance and the negative social effects of industrial society. This marked difference makes one curious about the message that Say transmitted in his official report to the French government about his findings in Britain. His letter written from London, quoted above, gives the impression that very probably he did not confine himself to observations from the shop floor in his assessment of the British economy.

The first ten pages of the pamphlet reflect on the consequences of the Napoleonic wars, which gave England its supremacy at sea and in international trade. The construction of docks and warehouses, combined with tax facilities, had been a favourable condition. But another development turned out to be even more important:

> Since the rise of Napoleon, the prodigious activity of this prince and his enormous talents, aided by the 'bravoure' of the French, threatened the independence of Europe; but Europe, already exhausted by stubborn wars and by contributions imposed by the Republic, could not support all the costs of these difficult expenditures. England, by its subsidies, covered a part of these costs.[17]

According to Say, England partly paid for the war through the effective depreciation of the pound sterling. (Without mentioning it here, he followed the Ricardian analysis of *The high price of bullion*.) On the continent, the British pound could be purchased at a discount from its bullion value. The British export goods purchased with these pounds were therefore subsidised in real terms, although the demand for these goods resulted in a vastly bigger output of British industry. The British people did not profit by these developments, as their gains were skimmed by taxes and loans, and they had to pay for their daily bread twice the amount of twenty years earlier.

The wars also resulted in an enormous public debt, as the cost of war was 'bigger for England than for any other nation'.[18] To these expenses, the costs of running a world-wide empire and the scandalous abuses of public spending at home could be added. With this classification of facts, Say called the tune for his critical assessment of the British economy.

The middle part of Say's argument switches from monetary and macroeconomic developments to the microeconomic effects for producers and consumers: 'The enormous charges levied on the English people, have made all products of their soil and industry exorbitantly costly.'[19] This observation is of course directly contrary to Say's idea, voiced clearly in his *Traité*, that economic growth and progress go hand in hand with lower prices. His theories did not provide a framework for a satisfactory analysis of the phenomenon of growth-cum-inflation.

But as a clever observer, Say noted the harmful effects of the Industrial Revolution on the losers of this process: 'the great distress of the class of just simply workmen'.[20] He reported that even highly skilled workers often earned no more than half or three-quarters of their basic expenses, and had to be supported by the charity of the churches. Say believed that one-third of the British population was dependent on this assistance. He even reported that former middle-class people, the owners of small business or small property, could no longer support themselves. On the other side of the spectrum he saw 'these great capitalists who may cross their arms and pursue no other business than their pleasures'.[21] In other words, thirty years before Benjamin Disraeli wrote about England's 'two nations', the Rich and the Poor, Say had identified them.

One may wonder how he came to change the positive attitude from his diary to the gloomy perspective of his pamphlet. He quoted Morris Birkbeck's report of his travels in France, in which the author showed his amazement that the French workers could earn a decent living.[22] In England Say had met people like Henry Brougham and Samuel Romilly, who were both involved in matters of poor relief. Certainly the subject had come up as well in conversations with Francis Place, who was an accomplished population theorist.

But it remains paradoxical that one of the prophets of nineteenth century capitalism and growth watched with wonder the accompanying social changes. With some amazement he wrote about the hectic pace of everyday life:

> In England, you don't see any professional idlers; you attract people's attention as soon as you demonstrate an attitude of not being occupied in some way, and as you are just looking around you. There exists nothing like those café's filled with idlers from dawn to dusk, and the sidewalks are absolutely empty except on Sundays; everybody is running, in total concentration upon his affairs. Those who slow down only slightly in the execution of their duties, are promptly struck by ruin.[23]

In *Olbie* (1800), Say had depicted the British middle class, with its 'comfortable' existence, as an example for his fellow countrymen. In his pamphlet of fifteen years later, it is the other way around. It is almost funny to read about the hardships the British have to suffer as a consequence of the unmitigated forces of competition, coupled with the extractions of a merciless government. For example, higher prices can only be afforded by a smaller number of consumers, which in turn is harmful for the suppliers. These react by embellishing their shops extravagantly, in order to attract the consumer's attention, and even offer products at prices below cost level:

> To notify the public of a new enterprise, or even of a simple move of domicile, a poster fixed to a wall is not enough, and people move around as

walking banners, amidst the busy crowd of Londoners, as promenading posters which the pedestrians can read without losing a minute.[24]

Despite higher prices, the quality of many consumption goods has declined, even that of textiles and leather in which the English used to excel. A triple amount of the Port wine imported is sold in the shops, so it must be heavily diluted.

Say's *classe mitoyenne*, for him always the central pillar of the economy as well as of civilisation, is having a hard time in Britain. As the economy is declining, so are *les lumières*. People are reading less: they don't have time for it, and books have become too expensive:

> That small amount which people of the world still are reading is, generally speaking, never of the best kind: truly useful reading demands a diligence they find burdening; and when, incidentally, they do read good books, it is a seed which falls on barren ground, where no good fruits could flourish. The *classe mitoyenne* is the only one studying usefully for society, and very soon it will no longer study in England.[25]

The examples of sinking quality of certain products are familiar from his letter written from London. Therein he also described the 'paradox' of the invention of superior and cheaper products, such as strong yarns and new textiles, and the cheap and superior tableware of the middle class. Here the theoretical economist Say, with a clear insight in the relationship of innovation, lower costs and prices, and economic growth, for once failed to correctly diagnose these developments when he observed them.

Positive observations: steam and scale

Seemingly in contradiction with this gloom and doom, Say continued on a number of positive economic developments he had observed. He noted the economies of scale he had witnessed in agriculture, in education and in industry, occasioned by 'the necessity to economise on all costs of production'. In Glasgow he had visited a farm of 300 cows, where milk was cheap. He described the Lancaster Schools, already mentioned in his diary. But above all, the introduction of machines in every kind of productive activity had made these processes more economical:

> In practically every large farm in England, for example, threshing machines are used for beating the corn, and by these means, in large-scale exploitation, more work is done in one hour than by the traditional method in one month.
>
> Finally human labour, which has become so expensive because of the dearness of consumption goods, is nowhere replaced to greater advantage than by *steam engines*.[26]

As an illustration, Say enumerated a number of industries where he had seen steam engines at work; here a clear parallel between his pamphlet and his diary is present.[27] Some descriptions are echoing the surprise he felt when he first observed a totally new spectacle, like the long convoys in the countryside 'advancing by themselves, and without the help of any living creature'. He noticed that the number of these engines had vastly increased over the past thirty years – without mentioning that he had been an eye-witness himself in the 1780s. Then there were two or three steam engines in London, and now there were thousands. In all big manufacturing cities there were hundreds, and even in the countryside one could see many of them.

In the last part of his pamphlet, Say is switching again to the big picture of the British economy. After a number of very critical remarks on the design and quality of English export products, he discusses the need for reform of the British economic system. He is noting that this discussion also takes place in parliament, and that advocates of change, though still a minority, have big names, great minds and powerful arguments. Change is urgently needed with respect to the Corn Laws and the English monetary system (especially the problem of paper money). Undoubtedly these remarks reflect the conversations he had entertained with Bentham, Ricardo, Mill, Place and many others. In a footnote, Ricardo's pamphlet *The high price of bullion* is approvingly mentioned.

After a fairly long digression on paper money, Say refers his readers to the *Traité* for a more fundamental treatment of money: 'These monetary phenomena, entirely new, are throwing light on the general theory of money, and will consequently produce some extraordinary facts.'[28] However, he only refers to the first of his monetary chapters, where the functions of money as medium of exchange, unit of account and means of hoarding are explained. His readers would in vain have searched there for new insights with respect to recent developments regarding the circulation of paper money.

The last subject discussed is the British rule in India. Say produces a lot of data on the costliness of running this colony. Most of his figures are borrowed from the work of Colquhoun. (Say's friend James Mill had started writing his *History of British India* in 1806, but it was not published till 1818.) Here of course, Say wished to repeat his prophecy of the end of European colonial rule:

> The old colonial system will fall everywhere in the course of the nineteenth century. People will renounce to the foolish pretension of governing countries situated at two, three, six thousand miles distance; and when these will be independent, people will entertain a profitable trade with them, and the expense of all military and maritime establishments, resembling costly supporting buttresses – yet not enough to sustain a collapsing structure – will be saved.[29]

In the concluding paragraph, Say hopes for the best with regard to the British, as well as the French economy. Implicitly he sketches a picture of international trade as a positive sum game between nations. As to his own analysis and foresight, he is certainly not a modest man:

For the simple-minded person, one event is following upon another: for the thinker, they form a chain. Sometimes it is even permitted to the latter to foresee the shackles which are linking the present to the future; then he knows all about the times to come that is possible to predict, since fortune-tellers and legal astrology have gone out of fashion.[30]

We have dwelt at some length upon Say's pamphlet on England, as it is revealing for several reasons. It shows the positive economist, who wishes to prove his theories by referring to facts. The clever observer Say is present with a number of his own findings. He is impressed by the British advances in industry and agriculture, through the application of steam engines and the effects of scale. He notes the harmful effects upon the condition of the working man. And he seems to be shrinking back at the consequences of industrial progress for society at large, and for the quality of life.

His argument, judged by his own standards, is not always consistent. Arriving in Glasgow in 1814, he wrote in his diary: 'Many children, proof that people have the opportunity to employ them and to let them earn a living.' And in his pamphlet he statistically documented the growth of population in the cities. In his *Traité* and other economic writings, Say drew a parallel between population growth and economic progress. But as an observer in 1814 of England for the French government, he did not follow this interpretation but reported on the large numbers of poor workers dependent on the charity of the churches. Regarding money, he negatively assessed the increase of paper money in circulation. And in his opinion, the quality of industrial output was often poor.

The different perspective of Say's English diary of 1814 on the one hand, and his letter from London and his pamphlet of 1815 on the other, remains enigmatic. Perhaps he wished to please his patrons, and therefore sketched a gloomier picture of the British economy than he had really observed. If this would indeed have received a favourable reception, Say might have painted a black-and-white picture for a broader audience in *De l'Angleterre et des Anglais*.

On the other hand, the journalist Say, the political author of *Olbie* and the economist of the *Traité* are all clearly present. The irreversible rise of steam and the economies of scale are well described. The menacing aspects of the Industrial Revolution for the middle and lower classes – at least in the short run – are acutely signalled. And his prediction of the end of colonialism has come true – albeit with only a delay of over one century.

7 A dissident under the *Restauration*

The enticement of the United States

For Say there were financial as well as intellectual considerations to think again about a possible emigration, this time to the United States. Already in 1803 he had sent a copy of his *Traité* to President Jefferson, praising the United States as an example for Europe:

> The happiness enjoyed by your country, and greatly enhanced under your administration, is enough to arouse the envy of the nations of Europe; your prosperity may be the source of theirs. They will see the degree of happinss attainable by a human society that practices common sense in its legislation, economy in its expenditures, and morality in its politics. It will no longer be possible to represent wise counsels as mere impractical theories.[1]

When his second edition had been published in 1814, he sent a copy to Jefferson in June; in the accompanying letter he described the 'savage tyranny that has set back France for several centuries' and his own career as a cotton manufacturer. He continued about his son Horace's travels in the United States, and his own plans for following him:

> I will admit that I am thinking seriously of settling there myself with my wife and four younger children. I would be deterred only by the uncertainty of being able to make a living by using my assets, which are not great, to purchase and develop a tract of land.
>
> In this situation, and feeling the need to breathe the air of a free country, and with nothing but hope that France may be well governed, I would regard it as a great favour on your part if you could be so good as to give me, or have given to me, a reply to the following questions to help in my decisions.
>
> Is there, in the neighbourhood of Charlottesville in Virginia, land available that is already cleared, or at least partly cleared, and with already enough buildings for both housing and exploitation?
>
> How many acres would be needed for the purchaser who develops it to live with a family of seven or eight persons?[2]

In August 1814, just before his departure for England, he wrote again to Jefferson:

> As for myself, if I remain in France, it would be because of the difficulty of moving with a numerous family and only a moderate fortune. I would rather live in a free country, and can hardly flatter myself that this country will become such. Not that the present government is strong enough or intelligent enough to be oppressive, but the people are too uneducated to escape oppression. They imagine in France that they defend their rights by attacking authority, and keep government within proper bounds by being undisciplined, and so the fear of disorders plunges us into servitude. Hence, if with 60,000 francs at my disposal I could become a farmer in your country and subsist comfortably with my family, I think I might so decide.[3]

Jefferson's answer was delayed till March 1815. It was a long letter, full of details on land prices, crop yields, transport facilities and weather statistics. Jefferson suggested that, if Say was still considering emigration, he might well try to combine a farm with a cotton mill, as the market for cotton spun was favourable, and for cotton cloth even more. After some time he could then decide which of the two undertakings was the most profitable. However, there was another dimension to such a project:

> Most of the hired labor here is of people of color, either slaves or free. An able-bodied man has sixty dollars a year, and is clothed and fed by the employer; a woman half that. White laborers may be had, but they are less subordinate, their wages higher, and their nourishment more expensive.
>   That it may be for the benefit of your children and their descendants to remove to a country where, for enterprise and talents, so many avenues are open to fortune and fame, I have little doubt. But I should be afraid to affirm that, at your time of life, and with habits formed on the state of society in France, a change for one so entirely different would be for your personal happiness. Fearful, therefore, to persuade, I shall add with sincere truth, that I shall very highly estimate the addition of such a neighbor to our society, and that there is no service within my power which I shall not render with pleasure and promptitude.[4]

We must guess whether the possible prospect of becoming a slave-owner, or Jefferson's cultural counsel, or French political developments finally made Say decide to stay where he was. As Jefferson's letter was written, Napoleon escaped from Elba, and his Hundred Days reign began. Say was approached on the emperor's behalf, with a request to provide a report proving that Napoleonic finance was more sound and creditworthy than that of the British government. Say replied that interest of British loans was at five per cent, while France had to pay almost nine: 'French finances would be in a better position if political economy were a little better understood among us.'[5]

But in his correspondence a letter from Lazare Carnot, Bonaparte's Minister of the Interior, thanking him for a copy of the *Traité*, offers slight evidence of a willingness to accommodate to the circumstances. At the end of March the latter wrote about Say's book: 'I believe, with good reason, that it fully deserves the reputation it enjoys, and that it is superior to everything we know in this genre.'[6]

Before the Hundred Days, thanking Say for a complimentary copy of the *Traité*, Count Marbois had written in February 1815 that he 'could not understand why people would deprive themselves of the services you might be able to render'.[7] He promised to express these feelings on every possible occasion. But Say's fortune remained insecure, even after Waterloo and the Bourbon Restauration.

In search of a job

Having been an early opponent of Bonaparte might have been considered a positive qualification after the latter's final defeat at Waterloo. But being a republican and a liberal far outweighed this on the negative side. With regard to political acceptance, Say was condemned to remain an outsider for many more years. From 1815 on, he taught political economy courses to an adult audience at the Parisian Athénée, for which he received between 600 and 800 francs annually.[8] His report on his British economic spying mission had not brought him enough recognition to receive another governmental commission. Say wrote to Ricardo that he envied his life of quietly studying political economy 'in your beautiful residence of Gatcomb Park'. There is some evidence that he tried in vain to get a job as a civil servant. In July 1815, after the second Bourbon Restauration, Talleyrand himself, thanking for a copy of Say's *Catéchisme d'Économie Politique*, wrote that he would read it with all the respect 'to which the subject and its author were entitled'. It would be a pleasure for him to bring Say's viewpoints to the attention of the Minister of the Interior. This seems like a fairly cynical remark, as its author was one of those reponsible for a political climate in which Say and other true liberals were regarded with suspicion – and accordingly Say's request was rejected.[9] In government circles, political economy was not seen as the science of modernity, but rather as a subversive discipline. Liberal political economy was interpreted as being almost synonymous with political liberalism. For this reason, the institution of chairs in the subject was delayed in countries like France and Italy.[10]

For the time being, Say's pen was his only and meagre means of existence, beside his small fortune and the Athénée fee. After *De l'Angleterre et des Anglais* in April 1815, he published the popularising, questions-and-answers booklet *Catéchisme d'Economie Politique* in July, with 1500 printed copies. The author noted in his *Acta* that Napoleon's Hundred Days retarded its distribution by a few weeks.

No figures are known about the earnings from the pamphlet in England. He wrote to the bookseller Delauney that the rights belonged to one Arthur Bertrand.[11] The *Catéchisme* had brought him 626.80 F after two years. The rights of the *Traité*'s third edition, published early in 1817, were sold to the publisher-bookseller Déterville for 5000 F. In November of the same year his private capital had shrunk to 55,000 F, as the result of a last, unsuccessful venture as an entrepreneur.

In March 1816 he associated himself with Nicolas Clément and Samuel Widmer to set up an alcohol distillery.[12] Say and Clément were the managing partners providing 10,000 F each, Widmer was a sleeping partner for 30,000 F. Say was exclusively authorised to sign on behalf of the company; Clément would be responsible for the distilling process. Already at the end of 1817, Say booked off as losses his initial 10,000 F plus another 5000 F he had provided later. Earlier in the same year, an annoying correspondence had been entertained between the two managing partners. Say reproached Clément that he had sketched a far too rosy prospect for their enterprise. Clément retaliated that Say had spent most of his working life in his study, while he himself had worked in factories. This had given to Say an attitude of 'generalising', and to himself one of 'particularising'. In his opinion, this was the cause of their disagreements.

On 31 March 1818, Clément wrote that he had managed to restructure the company, which was dissolved on the following day. Say was left with a claim of 34,000 F on his former partner.[13] In 1820, Clément was still in his books for almost 10,000 F, and only in 1824 did he disappear from them. Ironically, late in 1819 both former business partners had become colleagues again, as professors at the Conservatoire des Arts et Métiers.[14]

This had been Say's second joint venture which ended in quarrels and losses. Yet he had started it with lots of enthusiasm, as Ricardo reported to Malthus on his visit to Paris in 1817. In a letter written to Ricardo at the end of that year, Say was already trying to belittle his involvement:

> The incertitude of the fermenting process has kept me from spending great attention to my distillery. By an arrangement I made with my partner, he works for his own account and only pays me an interest for the capital which almost entirely belongs to me.[15]

A last – and again unsuccessful – commercial venture was Say's speculative dealing in potato flour, in the years 1817–1819. During Ricardo's stay in Paris in 1817, Say tried to convince him to participate in his investment. In July he wrote:

> I expect to count upon your discretion not to speak of my plans for a speculation in potato flour. If you have any interest in placing funds in France in this way, I would appreciate it if you do this on a fifty-fifty basis with me. I consider it a very safe investment. A third, friendly party will confirm the presence of the purchased quantities in the warehouse. The merchandise does not deteriorate. Its price cannot fall below that of quality flour because it can be mixed into it without altering its price; and all costs of transport, storage &c. can be easily calculated. I may give you more precise details on all this.[16]

Ricardo's reply has not survived, but it must have been quite reserved, and perhaps dressed-up as a request for further information. In December Say wrote back enthusiastically, reporting that all bakers in Paris mixed the stuff in their dough, and giving his expectation that it would rise in price between 30 and 80 per cent within the next nine months. He would invest a sum of 20,000 F, and asked Ricardo to participate with an amount between 30,000 and 40,000 – forgetting about his earlier fifty-fifty proposal. But Ricardo explained at length that he had slowly been withdrawing from business since Say's visit of 1814. That he had put most of his money in land, and recently – because of the low rate – had invested in French francs. Therefore it was impossible for him to participate as Say had proposed: 'My life has been one of success, but of anxiety, and I am endeavouring so to arrange my affairs, that I shall have no cares for the future, respecting pecuniary matters.' Once again he showed himself to be cleverer in business than Say, who after two years had to book a loss of 5000 F in this venture.

A French liberal among Philosophical Radicals

At the age of fifty, Say still did not have a regular and safe income. His books brought in some money, but not enough. If he had seen any possibility of making a living in Geneva, he wrote to Dumont in 1817, he would have preferred to move there. And in 1818 he failed to be appointed as director general of an insurance company, despite the circulation of a printed letter of application stating his career, publications and references.[17]

Things must not have been made easier by the stance he took as a supporter of the journal *Le Censeur*, founded in 1814, which defended freedom of the press – the subject of Say's earliest publication in 1789 – and advocated parliamentary reform. In 1817 its name was changed into *Le Censeur Européen*. Its editors were the lawyer Charles Comte, who was to marry Say's daughter Adrienne in 1818, and the liberal economist Charles Dunoyer. The periodical's motto was 'Peace and Liberty', and liberalism and anticlericalism were its leading concerns. In 1817 the two editors were arrested for publishing a piece (first printed in London) called *Manuscript coming from the island of St Helena, in a manner unknown.*[18] To their request to be released, they added a list with the names of seventeen well-known citizens who pledged a guarantee for them; it included the banker Lafitte, the general Lafayette, Benjamin Constant and the economists Destutt de Tracy and J.-B. Say.

The latter was one of the journal's contributors as well. Very probably he wrote a review of Dumont's translation of Bentham's article on parliamentary tactics; and certainly that of Bentham's *Plan of Parliamentary Reform*. This review was also published as a pamphlet with the title *De l'influence ministerielle sur les élections en Angleterre.*[19] In a letter to Place he wrote that he considered this publication as a contribution to the popularising of the ideas of 'our friend at Ford Abbey':

*The service which his friends might render, would be to extract from his works all that is directly **useful**, and to translate this into common language. Being available in less bulky volumes, easier to read, and cheaper to purchase, that would circulate more easily and have more direct effects. If that excellent man lived more in the real world, he would notice that people, being carried away by the hustle and bustle of interests (public and private) of the moment, hardly have the time to read and to reflect. So it is necessary to facilitate them for this activity.*[20]

Together with this letter he sent two French pamphlets of a certain Schoeffer. The first, on England, at Place's request; the second, on the state of liberty in France, at his own initiative, with a second copy for Jeremy Bentham added. This publication had been confiscated, and its author arrested. That makes it understandable that Say chose to publish his Bentham pamphlet anonymously. In 1819 he wrote to his lifelong friend and correspondent Amaury Duval whether he was sure to have an article – possibly for *Le Censeur Européen* – published under his own name: 'I do not want to compromise you in any way.'[21]

The freedom of the press had been the subject of Say's earliest pamphlet. Under Napoleon, he had been muzzled himself. And in 1820, his son-in-law Charles Comte had to flee from his country as a consequence of his publications. Because of this climate of censorship, Say operated cautiously and wrapped his opinions in the guise of foreign examples. He published the pamphlet on Bentham's 'Parliamentary Reform'. And he read his memorial lecture on Sir Samuel Romilly before the French 'Society of friends of the freedom of the press', by 'his own special request' as he noted on the manuscript of thirty pages. The materials for this lecture had been largely provided by Jeremy Bentham, and were written down by Francis Place junior. Say thanked Place senior for them and promised him a copy of the printed version of the *Éloge funèbre*, which however never came off the press.[22] In the lecture Say drew a parallel between the present (of 1818) and the age of the French Revolution, during which the French had also honoured famous foreigners such as Franklin and Washington. (Alas, they were rewarded with a Cromwell instead of a Washington, Say commented.)

Romilly was credited by Say for his penal reform activities, and for the fact that in his capacity of solicitor general, he had never prosecuted anyone for libel. France owed him a great debt of honour, for in 1814, while Wellington's troops were still on French soil, he had questioned in parliament the prosecutions of Protestants in the Languedoc. As a consequence of his intervention these came to a halt. Romilly suffered a tragic death when, exhausted by an election campaign and severely hit by the loss of his wife, he committed suicide.

Say continued to give vent to his feelings about the illiberal French Restoration climate to Francis Place from time to time. At the end of 1818 he even foresaw the possibility that a coup might altogether silence the liberal opposition, 'in which case you will no longer be informed about our situation by the press'. He added that falling share prices contributed to the government's problems. The next letter preserved partly confirms these feelings as it reports the flight of Charles Comte, together with his wife A(n)drienne Say and their young child, to Switzerland in order to escape imprisonment on a libel charge: 'They have fled the persecutions of our infamous tribunals and have been received with lots of attention by the friends of liberty.'[23]

But even there the Comtes were threatened by the Bourbon government. In 1823 Say asked Place's advice about the possibility of their moving to England, as the French government had demanded the expulsion from Switzerland of all French refugees:

> *I have come to ask your friendly advice. You will have learned from the papers that the French government has demanded from the Swiss cantons the expulsion of all the French who have fled to Switzerland. Mr. Comte my son-in-law is involved in this exiling. He has withdrawn from the unfair condemnations which his writings have provoked, and he had accepted a chair as a law professor in the Canton Vaud. Obliged to flee again, he can only find asylum in England.*[24]

Place promptly replied and proved to be of great help to the Comte family, who could only return to France at the end of 1825. Earlier that year, Say and his wife paid a visit to them in London.

The value riddle

Say found a number of good and long-lasting friendships in England. But he also came across two formidable adversaries in his own discipline. With Ricardo he fought a battle on the nature of value, which kept him busy even after the British economist's death. And still more famous is his debate with Malthus on the subject of 'Say's Law' – on the (im)possibility of gluts and overproduction. After Say's first meeting with Ricardo, the latter wrote about him:

> He does not appear to me to be ready in conversation on the subject on which he has very ably written, and indeed in his book there are many points which I think are very far from being satisfactorily established, – yet he is an unaffected agreeable man, and I found him an instructive companion.[25]

Say himself was not entirely happy about the fluency of his conversation. He met Ricardo again in Paris in 1817 and in 1822. As an economist, Ricardo considered himself superior to his French colleague, as he wrote to McCulloch in 1821 about Say: 'He is certainly very far behind in his knowledge of the present state of the science.' To Hutches Trower he wrote in 1822:

> At Paris I saw M. Say several times, but never found him much inclined to talk on the points of difference between us. I believe M. Say finds it difficult to converse on these sujects; his ideas do not flow in a sufficiently rapid flow for conversation.[26]

On the other hand, in 1814 he had written to Malthus that Say, in the second edition of his treatise, had very well demonstrated 'the doctrine that demand is regulated by production'.[27] Regarding Say's Law, there was always agreement between Ricardo and Say on its validity. Regarding value, it is clear that Ricardo made Say reconsider his theories. In the Say papers, two dossiers with many dated and undated notes illustrate his struggle with the subject, which is already evident from the subsequent editions of the *Traité*.[28]

The letter with which he presented a copy of his third edition to Ricardo in 1817, is clear about the credits given to him for making Say reconsider his argument:

> Accept, my dear Sir, a copy of my 3d edition in which you will find several corrections, some of which have been suggested by my conversations with you. Following editions will offer many more for which I will be indebted to your works. My theory of value is already worth more than the one you have criticised.[29]

What precisely were their differences of opinion? The simplest summary of their conflicting views is to say that Ricardo was an objectivist regarding value, and Say a subjectivist. In the market process determining prices, Say always gave more attention to the demand side than his opponent. But in defending his position, he sometimes included arguments that seem decidedly irrelevant. For example, in the third edition of the *Traité* Say established an unfortunate link between the value of a good and its ownership. As a positive economist he wished to measure values by market prices; sale or exchange implied a change of ownership, so he added the dimension of 'possession' to his theory of value.

In 1819 the fourth edition came out, shortly after the Constancio translation of Ricardo's *Principles*, annotated by Say. A long footnote comments upon the conclusion of Ricardo's chapter XXX, that prices (with the exception of monopoly prices) do not depend on supply and demand, but on cost of production.[30] Say brings forward the role of supply and demand, and analyses the connection between factor markets and product markets. Ricardo's labour theory of value was part of a paradigm that was altogether alien to Say. But instead of recognising this himself, for the rest of his life he kept seeking convulsively for a common ground with his opponent. His notes on the Constancio translation summarise his points of disagreement with Ricardo: 1. value is essentially variable; 2. corn may be a reasonable long-term measure of value, but Ricardo has not explained why; 3. the value of an 'average' Ricardian product is no less variable than the value of labour itself.[31]

In the *Traité*'s fourth edition, Say moved a little in Ricardo's direction. Utility is still a first condition of value, but he no longer asks the question how to measure this. (The notion of marginal utility would never be introduced in his reasoning.) The market price is the ultimate measure of value:

> In the first editions of this work, I said that the measure of value was the value of another product. This expression was not precise. The measure of

value is the quantity of another product. The result of this error was a vagueness in several examples. This is what various critics, even unfair ones, have made me discover. Fas est ab hoste doceri.[32]

Then Say explains again the relationship between product markets and factor markets. It is *not* the value of productive services that determines the value of products, but the other way around: the values of many products compared between them, do determine the factor prices.[33] Thus he seems to have arrived at a simple general equilibrium model, composed of factor markets and product markets, where the demand side of the product markets is analysed more deeply than the supply side. But Ricardo's criticisms continued to haunt him, as many of his manuscript notes reveal.

The Englishman reacted to the fourth edition of the *Traité* by explaining his labour theory of value not as a measure of absolute, but of relative value. Say's answer made it clear that they were indeed on different planets:

> I must confess that I do not quite understand the distinction you make between the value of labour which does not determine the value of products, and the amount of labour, necessary for production, which determines the value of products.[34]

Another proof that labour theories of value did not appeal to him is an undated manuscript note, commenting on Adam Smith's labour theory, *withdrawn as being too metaphysical* from his lectures.[35] Already in his handwritten notes in his copy of *The Wealth of Nations*, he had criticised Smith's ideas on a labour measure: *So it is not an invariable value susceptible of being compared to variable values.*[36]

Of Say's many notes on value in his manuscript papers, two can be dated with certainty to 1821 or later. The first because Say labelled it *Solution of 22 October 1821*, and the second, *Ricardo and Say in agreement*, because it reacted to Ricardo's third edition of 1821 – the edition of his *Principles* to which he added the famous chapter 'On Machinery' with the conclusion that the introduction of machines might be harmful to employment.[37]

In the first, Say repeats his linking of value and ownership: *A useful good is only an object of wealth when one is obliged to buy it: either by productive services, or by products (which are nothing but productive services by another name).*

In the second, he writes about the role of rent in determining prices: *Ricardo agrees that the costs of production are not the foundation of prices. Say agrees that rent is not a part of price.*

In the fifth edition of the *Traité* (1826) and in the *Cours Complet* (1828–1829), Say returned to his more familiar subjectivist approach. In 1826, the legacy of Ricardo is exonerated from the use of 'algebraic formulas too evidently not applicable to political economy', but found guilty of an 'argumentation resting upon abstractions', with the consequence that his conclusions are often falsified by the facts.[38] In September 1826, just before this edition came out, Say paid a visit to Sismondi, who noted his comment on Ricardo:

> I had this morning a visit from Say, who said to me that his friendship for M. Ricardo and his school has very often cramped him, but that in truth he finds that they have injured the science by the abstractions into which they have thrown it, and that he shall be obliged, in the new edition he is preparing, absolutely to oppose them.[39]

In 1826, the demand schedule is derived from a ranking of individual preferences, and the possibility of substitution of one good by another is explicitly stated. Preferences plus purchasing power determine market demand. Supply is determined by cost of production. Say's explanation serves Ricardians and non-Ricardians alike:

> Those who, like Ricardo and others, are of the opinion that labour (and not the cooperation of labour, capital and nature) is the only component of value, may replace *productive services* by the word *labour* in that explanation; it will lead to the same conclusion.[40]

After Ricardo's death in 1823, Say planned to publish their correspondence in English. Ricardo's ghost was still haunting him. He had written his obituary for the *Tablettes Universelles*; it was posthumously reprinted in Say's *Mélanges et Correspondance*. This was the *pretty little éloge* for which Bentham thanked him.[41]

Sraffa, as the editor of Ricardo's *Works and Correspondence*, was the last person to have seen Ricardo's original letters. A little note was attached to them, telling that the public could consult these at the office of the *Revue Encyclopédique*. The publication in the *Revue* of Say's article on McCulloch would have been the occasion of this public viewing. However, Sraffa had his doubts whether this really took place as, very soon after, the plan was made for publication of the correspondence. But Say was not pleased with the quality of Place's translation of his letters, and he did not wish to offend Ricardo's family, so nothing came of it.[42] Sraffa has given a benevolent interpretation of a number of differences between the original letters and the printed versions in the *Mélanges*, as the possible result of miscopying. But this cannot explain the paragraph in the letter of 19 July 1821, with the jibe on Ricardo's fortune, which is altogether different from the manuscript.[43] We may just as well guess that Say felt the need to embellish his part of the discussion, for his letter of 2 December 1815 was never posted (if Sraffa was right), yet included in the *Mélanges*. Elsewhere, he changed a few words as well: 'scabrous word' (*mot scabreux*) as Ricardo's epithet for value, is no more than 'difficult word' in his original letter.

Philippe Steiner has written an insightful contribution on the question of Say's 'embellishment' of his published letters to Ricardo, as compared with the original ones.[44] His explanation for the omission of a number of letters, and the alterations in some others in the posthumous editions by Ch. Comte, and later by E. Daire and Horace Say, is Say's explicit wish to only have published those texts 'which can provide instruction and enjoyment to the public'.[45] This may be phrased a little too benevolently, in view of Say's repeatedly expressed antagonism with Ricardo. But we can agree with Steiner in his rejection of Hollander's interpretation that Say and Ricardo were fundamentally in agreement.[46] Their starting points in value theory from utility (Say) and from a labour measure (Ricardo) were essentially opposed.

Finally, in the *Cours Complet*, Ricardo is credited for observations that have made Say reconsider his argument. In a footnote to an overview of 'productive funds', he writes:

> I have felt the necessity to draw this schedule, as the consequence of very long discussions that took place between David Ricardo and myself, in conversation and in correspondence, after he had, in his *Principles of Political Economy and of Taxation*, blamed the definition I gave of the word 'value'. The same discussions, by obliging me to reconsider these first principles, have given me the opportunity to present them with more clarity than perhaps has ever been done.[47]

A complete discussion of 'Say on Value' could easily fill a complete chapter. In the summary presented here, the accent has been laid upon Say's subjectivism and his long struggle regarding this subject with Ricardo, beginning with their first meeting in 1814, and lasting well after the latter's death in 1823. The full story of this debate has been presented by Kurz and Gehrke (from a Ricardian partisan viewpoint) and by Steiner (in a more objective and detached manner).[48] In the final chapter below, we shall return to the subject in the context of these assessments.

Household affairs

Say's private correspondence from the years 1815–1819, between his trip to Britain and his appointment at the Conservatoire, makes it abundantly clear that he had to watch closely over the management of his capital, and even of the smallest returns from the sale of his books. There still was the debt of his former partner in Auchy, Isaac Louis Grivel, which was only paid in small instalments. One of the last letters he wrote in September 1814, before leaving for England, as well as the very first one after his return in January 1815, concerned the last few thousand francs of the regular debt, and the 20,000 F which had been transferred to Say's account with Delaroche, Delessert & Cie as unpaid bills of exchange. The first 6000 of these were paid in March 1815. One year later, Say reminded Grivel of a sum of 5400 F, due in April. This was his last letter to him on this subject.[49]

Less problematic was the splitting-up with his distillery partner Clément, who still owed him 9894 F in 1819. One year later, they had become colleagues as

Conservatoire professors, and Clément's debt was redeemed in regular instalments. In 1824 it had been completely repaid.

With regard to the sale of his books, Say followed various practices. In June
and July 1815, he was active in promoting the sales of the first edition of the
Catéchisme and of *De l'Angleterre et des Anglais.* To his financial agent de
Rham in New York he suggested selling *De l'Angleterre* and the *Traité* in New
York and other big cities on the American East coast. And indeed he sent him
fifty-four copies of *De l'Angleterre* in August. To the Parisian bookseller Delaunay he sent sixty-two copies of the *Catéchisme.* To Paschoud in Geneva he sent
twelve copies stitched (plus one free) and twelve copies bound (plus one free) of
the *Catéchisme*, for a total sum of 37.80 F minus 10 per cent commission. To
Treuttel & Wurtz (in Paris and Strasbourg) he sent another thirteen copies of the
same work in August, asking them to promote it as well in Germany, Holland
and Switzerland. In the same letter, Say suggested that one English bookseller
had purchased ninety-six copies of it.[50] De Rham and the continental booksellers
only had to pay after selling the publications; so the commercial risk remained
with the author.

But from the London bookseller and publisher John Murray he expected
direct payment of 144 F for the eight dozen (plus eight free) copies of the *Catéchisme* which he had delivered for him – upon Murray's request – at the *Hôtel
des Etrangers* in Paris. These were the copies referred to in his letter to Treuttel
& Wurtz. However, one week later he was informed by the Parisian bookseller
Delaunay that Murray had left the hotel without taking the books with him.
Politely Say wrote to Murray in London whether he had charged one of his
Parisian correspondents to ship the books for him, or that he wished Say to do so
by way of Calais. Apparently Murray did not react after the books had effectively been sent, so after three months Say asked Francis Place junior, who was
staying in Paris with the Say family, to send Say's procuration to his father in
London, in order to cash the sum of 6 pounds 8 shillings from Murray on his
behalf. If Place senior would purchase for him a copy of the English translation
of Say's *De l'Angleterre et des Anglais*, he could deduct its price from this
sum.[51]

Another two months later, in January 1816, he wrote again to Murray,
reminding him of his explicit order for *purchasing* the books, and not taking
them in consignment:

> *If the shipment would have been for my account, I would have sent it to the
> bookshops selling my other works in London. Instead, I have refrained from
> sending any to them because you had taken them already.*
>
> *As I cannot believe that you would wish to ruin your reputation of trim-
> ness for such a small affair, I am sending again a bill of exchange on you to
> my friends in London, and I am asking you to settle it.*

The affair dragged on. In October 1822, the entire consignment came back from
London, shipped by Murray to the booksellers Treuttel & Wurtz. Say took the

trouble to explain its complete history to this firm, how he had met Murray at the house of friends, how the Englishman had explicitly ordered ninety-six copies (and received eight bonus copies on top), etc., etc. In his conclusion he reserved the right to sue Murray for his debt, and asked Treuttel & Wurtz to keep the books as a security.[52] Of this deal, no final settlement can be reconstructed from Say's papers.

We have seen that the second edition of the *Traité* had resulted in a revenue of 7786 F. Say himself carried the risk of this printing, with Renouard as publisher. For the third edition of 1817 he returned to the publisher of the first edition of 1803, Déterville. To him he sold the rights of the third edition for 5000 F, and those of the fourth edition in 1819 for 10,000 F. This was the highest sum he ever received for one of his books (with the possible exception of the *Cours Complet*, of which no figures have survived). Say expected this edition to sell as quickly as the third, and therefore the printing was raised to 3200 copies. But in February 1825 Déterville still had 531 copies in stock. Already in 1819 there had been some irritation between author and publisher, as is evident from one of Say's letters:

> *You are, my dear fellow citizen, a bit too much what is called a tyrant in business, and you count a little too much upon the disinterestedness of the authors. The limit of what I can accept albeit with great regret, is the number of 3,200 copies, and five copies at my expense which we are obliged to give to the direction de la libairie. This is my ultimatum: As to the terms of payment, we will change nothing*
>
> 1. *because you are rich and an advance payment troubles you less than anybody else,*
> 2. *because the terms are the same as in our last deal, except for the price which should not change anything in the terms,*
> 3. *because in the present circumstances I can flatter myself that the 4th edition, although more numerous, will not take longer to be sold out than the third.*[53]

This last expectation turned out to be false. In 1826, regarding the fifth edition of that year, Say wrote to Déterville that the latter had induced him to look around for better conditions than he could offer. And indeed he had spontaneously received an offer 'which is a little more advantageous and will, I believe, stimulate the sale by bringing it into the quarter of the exchange and the bankers'.[54] However, from his new publisher Rapilly he only received 5000 F, for a printing of 3000 copies.

In 1821, the publisher Bossange bought the rights of the second edition of Say's *Catéchisme d'Economie politique* for 750 F. On top of the 2000 copies of this printing, Say asked another eighty for himself, as he would have to send his work 'to scholars spread over all parts of Europe' and as a member of seventeen learned academies he must send a copy to all of these as well. Then he specified his other conditions:

You will print at your risk and peril, and on beautiful paper, and sell for your account, the second edition of my Catéchisme d'Economie politique, 2d edition entirely reworked and augmented, *in a number of Two thousand copies; I will charge myself with the correction of the proofs. As the fee, for this second edition only, you will pay me the sum of 750 F as soon as the printing will be completed, and you will give me 80 sewn copies, in a pretty paper cover. I engage myself only to let this work be reprinted again when this 2d edition has been sold out. You will sell it with the usual facilities and discounts, and when it is fully sold, I shall be re-established in all my author's rights, and shall be able to dispose of my manuscript as will please me.*

In another letter, he asked Bossange to sell for his (Say's) account a number of remaining copies of his pamphlets on the canals of France, and on England. He wrote that he was pretty sure of getting announcements for the *Catéchisme* in the *Courrier*, the *Journal du Commerce*, the *Revue Encyclopédique* and perhaps the *Constitutionnel*. But for that purpose he would need two extra copies for each journal.[55]

Other business managed by Say himself and mentioned in his letters concerned the rent of the few remaining Normandy possessions of his wife, as well as purchases of wine and provisions. In November 1815 he personally ordered 'between 50 and 70 pounds' of butter from dealers in Isigny in the Calvados area (Normandy).[56] In May 1816 he wrote about the quality of the two tuns of butter he had received: one excellent, the other detestable. Nevertheless he ordered another 50 or 60 pounds, of the first quality.

In 1822 he sold a meadow from his wife's heritage near Falaise in Normandy for 5000 F. The largest sum recorded for food and drink was 285 F for Malaga wine purchased from Delaroche, Delessert & Cie in le Havre. In 1825 he wrote to his former Auchy bookkeeper Perturon, asking for information on the prices of his Bordeaux wines, as he was 'forced by reasons of health to prefer this quality above my *ordinaire*'. And indeed he ordered two casks of *Bordeaux bon ordinaire* and one year later another two, of the year 1825.

In 1816 the Say family had moved from the Rue de l'Estrapade to the Rue du Faubourg St Martin, just outside the Porte St Martin. In September of that year he invited Etienne Dumont to see him there on a next visit to Paris: 'I have now more agreeable lodgings, easier to reach rue du faubourg St.Martin N° 92.'[57]

In the 1820s, when Say held the chair of Economie Industrielle at the Conservatoire in the Rue St Martin, it was just a straight and short walk for him from home to work.

Altogether, the copies of Say's letters convey the impression that, certainly in the years 1815–1819, he had to give a disproportionally large amount of his time to managing the sale of his books and the collection of debts. His Conservatoire professorship was to bring him relief from the worst of these concerns.

A last echo – at least in print – of Say's literary and philosophical interest was his *Petit Volume* which came out in 1817.[58] In seemingly simple but sometimes biting comments he wrote down aphorisms on religion, human vices, politics and sometimes even economics. A few examples:

> You are complaining that children have wrong ideas; but you have transmitted these. I heard a child ask: To whom do the clouds belong? And the mother answered: To the good god.
>
> *
>
> In England, the countryside offers wonderful landscapes; one can see clean and well-kept dwellings, nice gardens, beautiful trees and flowers; however the total impression is sad, like the smile of an unhappy person. In this country, pleasure meetings, popular feasts, and even comedy performances are sad.
>
> *
>
> One should not judge princes by their words. A well chosen word is often a spirited character's charlatanism. When Bonaparte answered an academy member who wished that a title of nobility must be a condition for being admitted to the Institut: *Ah, monsieur de Fontanes, let us at least have a republic of letters*, was there a single person equipped with enough benevolence to imagine that Napoleon would let exist any more liberty, even in the Académie?
>
> *
>
> In literature, in order to choose certain subjects, one must be a fool; in order to choose some others, one must be vulgar.
>
> *
>
> The public interest is always the pretext, and the private interest the true motive for action of the common man.

Jeremy Bentham, after receiving his copy of the *Petit Volume*, soon took the trouble to read it, and he wrote to Say that 'small as it is, [it] has been an occasion of a cruel and exorcising tax imposed upon my weak and disordered eyes for the entertainment of my mind'.[59] And he added the qualification *multum in parvo* – much in little.

Praise abroad

To the publisher Bossange, Say wrote about his membership of seventeen academies. The title pages of the subsequent editions of the *Traité* listed the most important of these. In 1803 Say could call himself a member of the Tribunat. In 1814 he was only an 'ex-membre du Tribunat'. But in the third edition of 1817, he was 'Chevalier de Saint-Wolodimir, membre de l'Académie impériale des Sciences de Saint-Pétersbourg, de celle de Zurich, etc; Professeur d'Economie politique à l'Athénée de Paris'. In 1819 the Royal Academies of Naples, Madrid and Avila were added to this list. And in 1826 the Academies of Stockholm and Cordoba followed, and his professorship had changed to that of the Conservatoire chair.

The St Petersburg academy diploma was sent to Say in 1816 by his colleague K.H. Storch, who had already sent him a copy of his textbook.[60] He also praised Say's *De l'Angleterre et des Anglais*, and asked him to publish his positive appraisal of his textbook in a scholarly journal. In 1818 King Charles XIV of Sweden wrote to him, thanking for a copy of the third edition of the *Traité*:

> *With pleasure I learned that we will have a translation of your work into Swedish; I hope that the propagation of the sound principles it contains, will prepare the nation I govern for the improvement I wish to carry through in its administrative system, and which my son will be able to acquire more easily if I am not destined to complete this myself.*[61]

An impressive number of translations (and subsequent editions) of Say's works appeared already during his lifetime. Of the *Traité* alone, this comprised six in Spanish (from 1804), five in German (from 1807), six in English (from 1821), as well as an Italian (1817), a Danish (1818), a Polish (1821), a Swedish (1823–1824) and a Russian one (1828).[62]

Say's *Letters to Malthus* (1820) were an immediate success, and were very soon translated into English and German. The German title referred to the 'causes of the present stagnation in trade'.[63] In Say's correspondence, many instances reveal his interest in the number and quality of his works in translation. With some of his translators he entertained a correspondence. His Spanish translator, Don Manuel Gutierrez, wrote three letters in 1817, beginning in January:

> *I did not know if you had already published your new traité d'économie politique, when I was asked to examine the translations into Spanish of the abstract of this work, and of your Catéchisme, translations which I cannot possibly approve as they seem to me hardly worthy of their original author.*[64]

He continued on the substantial differences between the first and the second edition of the *Traité*. He apologised for omitting in his translation a number of papagraphs as being too sensitive in the Spanish political climate, like those on inalienability of territories, and on the difficulty of teaching morals by means of books. He also explained that – also for political reasons – the translation of Say's *Catéchisme* had been published under another name, and that of the *Traité* under the names of Rodriguez and himself, although the former had only translated the beginning. Finally he asked Say for a copy of his introductory lecture pronounced at the Athénée, the announcement of which he had read in the *Journal des Débats*.

In his second letter he reacted to Say's reply, regretting that his translation of the *Traité* had been made from its second instead of its third edition. He told Say that in his opinion the Spanish government 'protects more and more every day the chairs of political economy where the science is taught from your traité'.

Still there were a few people believing in the doctrines of physiocrats and mercantilists ('the agricultural system, the unimportance of trade, the fiscal rule and their chimerical balance of trade'). He mentioned the trading company of Aguirre as a depository of his translation, and regretted that, although this was a correspondent of Delaroche & Delessert in le Havre, it was difficult to ship copies to them. He expressed thanks for a copy of Say's *De l'Angleterre et des Anglais*, and concluded by telling Say that he had proposed him for membership of the Economic Society of Madrid. And indeed in July he confirmed that Say had been unanimously admitted by this society as a corresponding member.

His Italian translator Chitti wrote to him in 1818, sending a copy of his translation:

> *The first edition of your Traité in Italian is completely sold-out. Before publishing a second, and apart from* [correcting] *the mistakes which had slipped into the first, I wish to refute the criticism of an Italian scholar (Mr. Gioja) who by isolating some of your expressions, and presenting them in another light than where they find themselves in your work, inverts their meaning, and ascribes to you ideas you never had, and which are even at odds with your doctrines.*[65]

Four letters were written by Say's second German translator, the Heidelberg professor of law Morstadt, in 1818, 1820 and 1821.[66] The first accompanied a complimentary copy of the first volume of Morstadt's *Traité* translation, in which he cautiously announced a number of 'light doubts' concerning some of Say's ideas, to be forwarded in a second letter. In that letter he expounded four questions, two of which concerned the functioning of markets. And he asked Say the favour of providing him with his portrait, either as an engraving or 'sketched by an able draughtsman'. In his little private museum, this would be placed next to that of Montesquieu, 'your worthy predecessor'. In the third letter, of October 1820, Morstadt apologised profusely about his delay in answering Say's question for a list of and comment on German economics textbooks. He thanked Say for a copy of his fourth edition, and presented him with a copy of the second volume of his own translation. He praised highly Say's works on England and on the French canals, and further announced that he planned to write an article on Say's refutation of Ricardo, 'in which you have carried a triumph over him'. In his last letter, of 1821, he praised again the 'penetrating and victorious sagacity of the author [Say] of the notes accompanying the Constancio translation [of Ricardo]', and reported that 'a certain Mr. Rau, professor of economics in Erlangen' had produced a German translation of Say's *Letters to Malthus*. Say noted on the letter that he must 'thank him for the second volume of his translation of Destutt de Tracy's Commentary on Montesquieu'.

While Gutierrez had made a few understated references to the illiberal Spanish political climate, Morstadt was quite explicit in his references to the murder of the Duc de Berry (1820), after which 'even the German professors had been subject to controls and to the espionage of the postal agents', and in mentioning the German laws of censorship.[67]

Karl Heinrich Rau, the 'certain Mr. Rau' mentioned by Morstadt, wrote to Say in 1820.[68] Perhaps Say had asked him the same question he had put to Morstadt, about the state of economics in Germany, as he sketched the institution of political economy chairs between 1790 and 1800, 'where the system of Adam Smith was taught'. Without mentioning Ricardo, Rau continued on 'Smith and the followers of his sect' as being too objectivist, and 'plunging into abstractions'. The need for an institutional approach, combined with the need for a common German customs system, had promoted the specifically German approach of *Volkswirtschaftslehre*, following the Italian economists:

> *In spite of the perfect harmony in most of its content, and in spite of the high esteem which the striking clarity of your demonstrations and explanations obtains everywhere, there is a number of points, for example on machinery, and on the complete liberty of trade, on which the german school could not completely agree with You. The* nouveaux principes *of Mr. de Sismondi more or less express his manner of thought, which is dominant among a part of our scholars, of which I have sketched You a picture, because the others have nothing special, and because I share the views of the first mentioned.*

What Rau meant by these 'first mentioned' became clear in his communication that he had obtained a chair of Cameral Science (the descriptive and institutionalist German school), where he would teach agriculture, technology, commerce, national and financial economy, and statistics.

Thus from Say's international correspondence the picture emerges that in most European countries the main competing schools of economic thought were represented by the objectivist Ricardian and the subjectivist Saysian heirs of Adam Smith, and in Spain a number of mercantilists and physiocrats survived, while in Germany – and to some extent in Italy – a cameralist-institutionalist approach dominated.

Say was not very happy with the English translation of the *Traité* by C.R. Prinsep, made from the fourth edition of 1819. He particularly disliked Prinsep's comments in his footnotes, and his omitting of the original Introduction. On a letter from Prinsep of 1821 he wrote: 'This letter of Mr. Prinsep does not seem interesting enough to me to be printed. It's just babble. He answers to nothing.'[69] Much better he liked the American edition of Clement Biddle, who presented it to him in 1824.[70] This was already the second American edition – Biddle referred to having sent the first as well, which apparently had not arrived. Say must have been pleased that Biddle called Prinsep's notes 'useless controversies'. And he must have been flattered when Biddle told him that the first edition was rapidly sold out, and the second was highly in demand as a textbook in prominent schools. Regarding legislation on economic matters, liberal principles were 'slowly but constantly' gaining ground in the United States, and Biddle seemed to borrow Say's vocabulary in a plea for observing facts, and founding theories upon the nature of things, instead of following 'systems', which could only result in barriers to development. Biddle did not specify whether he hinted at the physiocratic or at the Ricardian school, but it is clear – as also proved by the correspondence with Gutierrez and Rau – that economic insiders of the period were well aware who were their theoretical friends and foes.

8   Late recognition

Conservatoire professor

Between 1815 and 1820, while his international reputation was growing, Say seems to have operated in a certain political isolation at home. This was clearly reflected in his correspondence with Francis Place. His son-in-law Charles Comte, one of the editors of the *Censeur Européen*, even had to flee from his country for 'abusing' the freedom of the press. In 1817 he wrote to Dumont in Geneva that he would prefer to move to that city, but that his scarce means of existence tied him to Paris.

Of course the success of his textbooks, the *Traité* and the *Catéchisme*, firmly established his scholarly reputation. And in 1818, when his letters to Place and to Jeremy Bentham became more and more desperate, two pamphlets on practical matters brought him closer to influential people. In February, he published *De l'Importance du Port de la Villette*; and in April *Des Canaux de Navigation*.[1] These pamphlets reflect his interest in waterways, which had been aroused in Britain; the canal through Scotland is mentioned in both. In the first, Say held a plea for a port – preferably an entrepôt harbour – in the La Villette basin. He expected this would be an important stimulus for trade and industry in the Paris region, and would greatly facilitate the provisioning of the capital. The problems of 1816, when a bad harvest had caused high grain prices, had demonstrated the urgency of this matter. Say had become involved in the economic and political discussion on the subject.

In January 1821 he wrote a letter on the same subject to the banker Laffitte, suggesting a private undertaking of the construction of canals, and pleading for a kind of public-private cooperation in the funding and exploitation: 'Here a company negociating with the government, and contracting a clause to share a part of the profit, is the most interested to obtain guarantees.'[2] However, as Horace Say wrote in an editorial footnote: 'People would not listen to his voice, and the public interest was sacrificed.'

In 1817 Horace had joined the firm of the very rich industrial entrepreneur, Guillaume Louis Ternaux 'the older'.[3] In 1818 Ternaux published a plan for a *Compagnie de Prévoyance*, which would improve the grain provisioning of Paris by the creation of buffer stocks of grain and flour, to be brought on to the market when prices rose above a fixed threshold. It included a long letter of approval by Say.[4] But even if Ternaux ranked him among 'the most distinguished authors' of political economy, Say's reputation was no guarantee for publication of all of his writings. In a letter to the editors of an unnamed journal, he had to beg for restitution of his manuscript review of Ternaux' pamphlet. Apparently they had first promised to publish the review, and then rejected it, as Say wrote: 'The bearer of this [letter] has been charged to ask it back from you for the fifth time.'[5]

Ternaux had been a member of the Conseil de Perfectionnement du Conservatoire Royal des Arts et Métiers, from its founding in 1817. The Conservatoire had developed from an eighteenth century private collection of machinery into an educational establishment for the textile industry in 1794. Say himself had set his first steps as a spinning apprentice here in 1804. In 1818 he wrote a letter to – and upon the request of – the chemist Baron Thénard, a colleague of Ternaux in the school's Conseil de perfectionnement, suggesting to include the subject of *Economie commerciale et manufacturière* in the Conservatoire's curriculum.[6] This was undergoing a fundamental revision, triggered – among other causes – by a report of the engineer Dupin on higher technical education for the navy, and on Scottish construction practices of roads and bridges. It is not clear who invented the label of 'industrial economy', instead of the – at least to government circles – more subversive-sounding 'political economy'. Say phrased the following question:

> *How and wherein do practical techniques* ['arts'] *contribute to the formation of values, which are the true substance of riches. The entrepreneur of any commerce or manufacture must be instructed on this matter, for it is him who combines the efforts with the results, the means with the goal, the investments* ['avances'] *with the products.*

The argument of Say's letter to Thénard revolved around the necessity for businessmen to be informed about the political economy 'of the new school', *Economie politique expérimentale*. He pointed to the success of the Scottish economy, which owed a lot to the teaching of economics at the universities of Edinburgh and Glasgow; in this last city the subject was taught by Adam Smith, 'the father of modern political economy, as it is presently being taught'.

One year later, on 25 November 1819, the decision was taken to establish 'a public and free education for the application of the sciences to industrial practices' at the Conservatoire. Dupin was nominated to the professorship of mechanical engineering, Say's former business associate Clément (calling himself Clément-Desormes after marrying his business partner's daughter) to that of chemistry and Say to the one of industrial economy.[7] It took another year before he would first lecture on 2 December 1820.

He was now fifty-three years old, and beginning to show signs of physical deterioration. Three days before his official appointment, on 22 November 1819, he noted in his *Acta*: 'I fall and lose conscience in the rue neuve des petits champs.' But it took another four and a half years before he suffered the second of these attacks of 'apoplexy', as he called them. Then they returned more frequently, with fits in 1824, 1827, 1828, 1830 (three times) and 1832 (twice). In 1824 he noted that there were reasons to believe that these were 'only nervous attacks'. His description of the symptoms does not allow for a reliable diagnosis in modern medical terms; the complaints might well have been of a cardiological character, or alternatively of an epileptic nature. His doctor treated him with blood-lettings, which in 1830 caused hallucinations, nightmares and a painful foot even one month later. But in the first years of his professorship he could work quietly, with the certainty of a basic income.

However Say's Conservatoire salary of 480 F was not sufficient to cover all of his monthly spending of around 1000 F. (For a comparison of these figures: his housekeeper earned 300 F annually, and the kitchen help 250 F.) For 1820, the first year of his appointment, he had to wait till April 1821 before his salary of 2642.40 F was paid. From then on it was paid monthly. His additional income consisted of the interest of government loans, payments by Clément, participations in Horace's ventures and the sales of his books. Nevertheless, his *fonds capital* was shrinking from 50,000 to 37,500 F in 1820, to 34,000 F in 1821 and to 28,500 F in 1822. The last time these figures were consolidated was on 31 December 1823, at 26,000 F. From September 1824, all substantial receipts and payments were channelled through H.E. Say & Cie.[8]

National and international reputation

If Say's financial capital was going down, his reputation still was going upward. The number of his correspondents, of the letters preserved in his private papers, is higher for the last twelve years of his life than for the three preceding decades: in a total of 120 names, seventy appear for the first time in the years 1820–1832 (not counting the thirty-odd letters from his students).

Say's lectures were always fully written-down. This made it possible that they were read by other people; in his later years, his health problems sometimes made this necessary. In his first Conservatoire year, December 1820 to July 1821, he taught a total of thirty-one weekly sessions. From January till June, 1822, he lectured twice a week, totalling forty-seven sessions. From the survey of his lectures in the Say papers, it is clear that he adapted the order of subjects from that of the *Traité* to that of the *Cours Complet*, the publication of which would only come about in 1828–1829. But already in March 1820 he noted in his *Acta* that he started working on his *grand cours*. In 1822 he annotated lecture number 13 with the remark that some of its sheets were 'the short version of the elaboration that can wait till the printing of the *Cours*'. André Liesse, who described Say's Conservatoire professorship in 1901, was mistaken in his hypothesis that Say still followed the order of chapters from the *Traité* in his lectures.[9] This was only true for 1821 and 1822. In his second year he still started with part I of the *Traité, Production des Richesses*; in thirty-six lectures he treated thirty-five chapters. In the first half year of 1823 he noted many *suppressions* in his programme of lectures. From December 1823 he slowly worked up to the sequence that would be the ordering of the *Cours Complet.*

In his programme survey he then started to write down the chapter titles as well as their numbers, which clarifies the transition to the *Cours.* The years 1823–1826 were transition years, and for 1827–1828 Say noted: 'I have started here to use the new division of chapters which will be followed in print.'[10]

We may guess that Say's professorship had given him the peace of mind necessary to concentrate on another long-term project. After the six volumes of the *Cours Complet* had been printed in 1828–1829, Say used parts of the printed text in his lectures at the Collège de France in 1831–1832. These cut-outs were glued on paper, and intersected by pieces of manuscript text, as well as annotations for presentation; these were mostly of the kind: 'pause' (*repos*).

There were substantial differences in the length of Say's teaching semesters. In 1821 and 1822 he went on till early July and late June, and in 1823 he last lectured on 7 May. In 1824 he halted altogether by mid-April, for reasons of health. In 1826, 1827 and 1828 he continued respectively till early May, the middle and the end of April.[11] In 1822 he taught forty-seven lectures, and in most other years between twenty-nine and thirty-three. His student numbers at the beginning of the course have not been recorded, but in 1827 and 1828 he wrote that the last lectures were still attended by around fifty people. The way he prepared his fully written lectures does not suggest that his presentation was very sparkling. An exception must have been his lecture of 24 March 1827, about which he noted: 'This lecture has caused amusement because of the denouncing remarks I have put into it.'

In spite of his respectable position, he was still not trusted by everybody. Someone who had been suspected by Napoleon's police was not automatically a trusted citizen to the Bourbons. Say's liberal protégés Ch. Dunoyer and Ch. Comte – the latter his son-in-law – had been driven out of the country on a libel charge. And, in the cautious words of Liesse, 'It is certain that the economic doctrines taught at the Conservatoire, were not precisely in complete harmony with those practiced by the Restauration.' Therefore, Say 'could hardly be *persona grata* with a government so suspicious and full of mistrust, especially against education'.[12] Liesse quotes the revolutionary Auguste Blanqui, whose brother Adolphe was to succeed Say in the Conservatoire chair. Auguste went to school with Say's son Alfred and recalled visiting his family around 1820: 'Jean-Baptiste Say had very revolutionary ideas for that period. He equally detested the Bourbons and Bonaparte, an apparent contradiction which filled me with amazement.'[13]

John Stuart Mill, who stayed with the Says in Paris in 1820, in his *Autobiography* recalled Say as

> a man of the later period of the French Revolution, a fine specimen of the best kind of French Republican, one of those who had never bent the knee to Bonaparte though courted by him to do so; a truly upright, brave, and enlightened man.[14]

In his lectures, Say did not hesitate to speak up against certain vested interests that wished to reestablish the former guilds, although he noted in 1819 that 'for reasons of prudence' he had refrained from pronouncing a statement on a certain kind of education from which only tyrants would benefit.[15] In 1822 he was targeted in the journal *Le Constitutionnel* for his explanation of 'consumption of services'. Say prepared a biting comment which however he did not pronounce in one of his lessons, not wishing to provide a pretext for a possible campaign against his teaching. Two years later, only a few months after Charles X's accession to the throne and his abolishment of censorship, the Parisian police prefect found it necessary to scrutinise the lecture rooms of the Conservatoire. Strangely enough, he started with the audience of Dupin, the professor of mechanical engineering, in December 1824. But in his letter of 17 December 1824, he reported to the Minister of the Interior:

> The agents charged with this investigation have penetrated as well into the lecture rooms where the chemistry course of Mr. Clément Desormes took place, and the one of industrial economy of which Mr. Say is the professor, and judging by the reports given to me, these courses would deserve the attention of the authorities.
>
> The listeners there are indeed much less serious than those following the course of Mr. Dupin; they frequently walk in and out, and circulate in all corners of the lecture rooms, forming groups that can create an opportunity for malevolent people to spread the germs of ill thoughts.
>
> I have ordered that these courses must be subject to special surveillance, and if this will occasion specific remarks, I will immediately communicate these to Your Excellency.[16]

Already by 28 December, he reported again on the courses of the three professors. Without specifically alluding to anyone of them in particular, he signalled 'numerous groups of workmen and strangers, among which several Spaniards were recognised', visitors of 'literary cabinets of the worst reputation in the capital', and 'minor authors who qualify themselves as men of letters'. As to the professors, without alluding directly to anyone in particular, the letter suggested that they always found an occasion to 'slip into their lectures a few critical remarks about some of our institutions and about certain measures adopted by the Government'. However, Liesse finds it improbable that Say or his colleagues would have been aware of the presence of police officers in their audience.[17]

Say's international reputation is confirmed by the number of correspondents from other countries, and by his membership of foreign academies. In 1820 the London newspaper owner James Perry wrote about his 'high authority' and in 1822 he was the first overseas member to be admitted to the British Political Economy Club.[18] The Danish crown prince had been among his students.[19] His lectures were not only attended by the suspicious Spaniards reported by the police prefect, but by a number of other foreign students who took the trouble to write down their questions and comments. Some of these will be quoted in Chapter 10.[20]

The *Letters to Malthus*

The second (1814) and third (1819) edition of the *Traité* had firmly established Say's scholarly reputation. His *Catéchisme d'Economie politique* was aimed at the general public. But his *Lettres à Malthus* (1820) were an astounding success among economists and the public at large.[21] It is unclear whether Say's planned meeting with Malthus effectively took place in 1814, but they met at least once, in Paris in the summer of 1820.

In a letter of August to Sismondi, Say wrote:

> *I saw Mr. Malthus in Paris recently, and I was much happier with his conversation than with his book. He is a respectable man and he gave the impression of not being too displeased with me, in spite of our disagreements. I wish you would say the same about me, my dear Monsieur.*[22]

Malthus wrote to Ricardo that during this visit of about five weeks he had seen most people he wished to see – without explicitly mentioning Say.[23]

Of the two 'great debates' in which Say was a protagonist, the value debate was a discussion for economic insiders and connoisseurs. But the practical side of the debate on Say's Law, the General Glut Controversy regarding the post-Napoleonic depression, was of a very practical interest to any citizen, whether he was an involved businessman or just an interested layman. Say was aware of this, and he widely circulated copies of the *Letters*. One of his addressees was James Perry, the owner of the London newspaper *The Morning Chronicle*.[24] Say's English friends must have directed him to this radical paper (on which John Stuart Mill was to be employed later). Perry did not hesitate to write back, in September 1820:

> *I have read it with attention and pleasure. Your doctrine is unanswerable and must make a strong and lasting impression on every liberal and thinking mind. In my Journal, The Morning Chronicle, I have made it my duty to announce the Work to the English public, with such an extract as will make its principles known in opposition to the inconsiderate notions of your opponent. At no moment could your most useful Work come more opportunely before the public. Committees by both Houses of Parliament have made Reports on the erroneous system of our commercial restrictions and your high authority confirms, and even goes beyond their opinions on the policy of free and unshackled interchange of produce among nations. I fondly trust that your noble efforts will tend to deliver us from the thraldom of our Customs House Laws. In the present oppressed condition of the French press, I beg leave to assure you, that the columns of my Journal shall be devoted to the course which you so ably support, and any Article in favour of your own constitutional regimen which your vile Censure would suppress, shall certainly be made public if transmitted to me.*

The transmitter to Paris of Perry's letter was the former colonial administrator John Crawfurd.[25] Perry introduced him as a congenial mind to Say, 'not only in regard to commercial but to civil and religious freedom'.[26] The newspaper owner himself had been imprisoned himself for libel, so his remark about the 'oppressed condition of the French press' was more than a polite reference. His letter demonstrates that the authority of Say was invoked in the British Corn Laws debate. But let us first examine the theoretical discussion around Say's Law, or the *Loi des Débouchés.*

The notion that 'supply creates its own demand', or more precisely that in order to be a demander, one must be a supplier, was known in economic theory before Jean-Baptiste Say. It can be found in physiocratic literature and in Adam Smith. In its simplest wording, it is no more than a tautology. It can just as easily be said that this proposition is always true as that it is always false – more or less like vulgar versions of the Quantity Theory of Money.[27] Regarding its more sophisticated versions, the real question is not whether the law is true or false, but rather under what conditions it holds. This question gave occasion to much debate among the classical economists. In the post-Napoleonic stagnation, the practical side of the debate was known as the General Glut Controversy. Later in the nineteenth and early twentieth century the law went into relative oblivion, but was revived by Keynes who in his *General Theory* (1936) presented Say's Law as a summary of all that was wrong with classical (or perhaps even all pre-Keynesian) economics. Keynes probably never went deeply into Say himself, but came to the law in a roundabout way through his biographical study of Malthus. It has been said that both of them rebelled against doctrines of macro-economic self-adjustment and self-equilibration. An excellent overview has already been given by Schumpeter.[28] Thomas Sowell has written an authoritative book on the subject, which is especially useful on the versions of the law before J.-B. Say.[29]

In a barter economy without hoarding, it is clear that the law must hold: when you cannot produce anything, you cannot be a demander of anything else. This version of the law is commonly called Say's Identity. When hoarding is possible, or money is introduced, it is clear that you can be a demander in a later period than the one in which you were a producer. So why should markets clear?

Adam Smith and Say believed that the market would solve this problem: why should anyone leave any resources – including money – idle? He who has more money than he actually wants to spend, will lend it on the capital market where it will find borrowers for the purpose of consumption, but more probably – and more profitably – of investment. On this point, there was some disagreement among the classical economists. Smith and Say had no doubts about the profitability of every new investment, where others saw problems of decreasing returns.

Baumol (1977) has fully rehabilitated Say as the true author of the law. Not however because of the wording in the first edition of the *Traité* (1803), which still presents a tautological version of it. Only in the second edition (1814) a true 'law' emerges, stating that 'in the long run, demand is able to keep up with enormous increases in output'.[30] From Say's letter of 1812 to Michel Delaroche, quoted above, it is also clear that he considered his version in the second edition of the *Traité* far superior to the elementary wording of the first.

Say's Law was fully accepted by Ricardo. Sismondi and Malthus were Say's fiercest critics among his contemporaries. Their debates concentrated upon 1. the mobility of production factors (capital *and* labour) in the short and in the long run, and 2. the role of population as a demand and supply factor. Sismondi accentuated the immobility of factors of production, which gets in the way of the adjustment process between supply and demand. Malthus' propositions stressed the relative rigidity of monetary wages in a slump, as a barrier to employment of the idle part of the working population.

'It is one and the same thing'

The two 'Genevan' economists Say and Sismondi entertained a friendly relationship, but they disagreed fundamentally on the validity of Say's Law. In Say's letter to Sismondi of August 1820, after describing his meeting with Malthus, he continued about their points of disagreement:

> *All I can tell you with absolute certainty, is that I only have the progress of the science in mind, and if I have targeted you in particular, it is because I consider you as the most worthy interpreter of the opinions I do not share. I have the vanity of those ancient devout persons who only wished to compete with their peers. Why would you and I be interested in the opinions of Mr. So-and-So. To some of these you have already paid too much tribute by only naming them.*

In 1823, Sismondi wrote to Say as 'concitoyen', and explained that this label not only referred to their Genevan citizenship, but also to world citizenship and to the fact that 'liberty is a home country' and a 'sacred city'.[31] (Unfortunately the Genevan liberty was not sacred enough to prevent the expulsion, around that time, of Charles and Andrienne Comte, with other refugees, from that city upon threats of the Holy Alliance.)

Sismondi's *Nouveaux Principes* (1819) stated that in a commercial society, where producers work for unknown customers, 'all production has become speculation'. So the demand is uncertain, and sectoral overproduction is often the result. Unsold products mean: no income for their producers. On the other hand, Say always maintained that a reallocation of labour and capital would quite soon generate production – and thereby incomes – in other sectors of the economy, which would remedy the overproduction.

By contrast, Sismondi not only shared Ricardo's views that machines are too specialised to be transferred from one industry to another. But he saw the same problem for labour: after a long and costly apprenticeship, workers' skills are part of their 'capital' which cannot be used in another profession. As a consequence, the mobility of factors of production can only redress a disequilibrium after a long period of adjustment. While according to Say, if consumption falls short of output, this happens because elsewhere in the economy there is an insufficient production to generate enough effective demand. Say had more faith in the entrepreneurs to solve this problem by reallocating capital and labour. He remained vague however about the question whether they will employ idle factors of production, or reallocate between their present employment and another.

Say's *Letters to Malthus* marked an important step both in the theoretical debate and in the General Glut Controversy. As a remedy to the seeming 'overstocking of all markets of the universe', Say recommended an augmentation of production. And he took hold of Malthus the population economist, who in his *Essay on the Principle of Population* had demonstrated that there will always be enough consumers. To Say, this cannot be consistent with his pessimism in the question of gluts, where he predicts a shortage of them.

In defending his law against Malthus, Say seemed to exclude overproduction by simply refusing the name of *product* (and thus of income) to all unsold production. Schumpeter has interpreted this definition as a statement 'that overproduction is excluded by definition'.[32] This criticism seems a bit unfair, as Say's microeconomic definition of production is clear and consistent: it means adding value to a combination of production factors. The real problem here is of course macroeconomic (and eternal): it is all right to define unsold production as investment to make national accounts fit. If however this remains unsold, the accounts must be corrected and national product redefined. But this does not imply that Say accepted Sismondi's pessimistic views on the possible length of periods of adjustment. In the *Letters to Malthus*, the Genevan economist is almost as heavily attacked as the addressee, especially in the third and fourth (out of five) letters.

As to the flexibility of capital and labour, Say was prepared to admit to Sismondi that there are *natural* and *social* obstacles to unlimited factor mobility, and to unlimited economic growth as well. The very modern concept of *learning* is Say's example of a 'natural obstacle' as a cause of delay in establishing an optimal division of labour in an economy and between nations. Knowledge and skills – in Say's vocabulary taken together in one word: *Arts* – take years to acquire.[33] Here the analysis by Say and Sismondi of frictional barriers in the reallocation of labour runs parallel, but in the end the latter's conclusions are pessimistic and the former's optimistic.

With respect to the 'social obstacles' in the economic process, Say argued that the pressures of taxes and duties can form a burden to production, if a part of the value added is *devoured* by the tax authorities. And finally he wrote that another form of learning is necessary, namely to overcome the ignorance among businessmen about what to produce and where to find markets for their produce. This also implies that Say did not share Malthus' pessimism about a possible satiation of wants.

In September 1820, a few weeks before James Perry, Sismondi replied to Say thanking him for his copy of the *Letters to Malthus*:

*A thousand thanks, Sir, for your letters to Mr. Malthus and the polite manner in which you speak about me. It is truly a great question that we do not agree upon, and today perhaps the greatest of all in political economy. We are both too much animated by the same love of the happiness and liberty of our brothers, we seek in too good spirit the same goal, for the controversy to hurt us. It honours me when I find myself against an opponent like you. However, I do not consider myself vanquished and I believe that it is necessary to continue the discussion to clear up the question. When there are several people holding the same opinion, while each of them has his own version, they are exposed to the possibility that those who react to them do confuse their positions. Thus you reply page 20 to the [Sismondi's] accusation of considering merchandise as algebraic signs, which is certainly not addressed to you but to Mr. Ricardo, although you have been wrapped into it by a kind of politeness towards Mr. Ricardo, to soften the blow. I will also say that all your reasoning to prove that one only buys products with other products, is not addressed to me. For I am far away from denying this proposition. Indeed from a proportional increase of products demanded I do expect and I do hope for a re-establishment of universal well-being, but I do not at all believe that **demand** and **product** are interchangeable terms, as Mr. Mill has said I believe in the Edinb. Review. I do not believe that product and revenue are one and the same thing, although the revenue comes from the product.*

[Note by Say in the margin: It is one and the same thing.]

*Don't we agree to call **revenue** that part of riches which is annually reproduced, which can also annually be consumed, without its owner becoming poorer?*

[Say in the margin: Anything which does not diminish the fund.]

Don't we agree that if this revenue, instead of being definitively consumed, is reproductively consumed, it is in this way changed into capital or accumulated?

*But by calling these **annual product** and **revenue**, they are not identical, no more than **consumption** and **expense**. Where is the difference between them? You do not seem to me to have established, you have not demonstrated that what I had signalled is not true. That still seems to me to be the essential part of the question. Upon which we will have to come back.*

In less than a month I will have the honour to send you my answer to the article in the Edinb. Review on the same question, which I wrote at the same time when you wrote to Mr. Malthus, but it awaits the commodity of the editor who has to publish it. This reply is a pretty short piece, and one which is not addressed to you, for yor opinion regarding this question is not at all as absolute as the one of Mr. Ricardo, nor by consequence in my opinion subjected to the same errors. I am very much tempted to reply to your letters also for my part, but only after some time of rest, for the fear that the public will get tired of a pretty abstract question, which in spite of its extreme importance has perhaps never been examined with all the atten- tion it deserves. If I will do it, I do not need to say Monsieur that while I allow myself to attack some parts of your reasoning with all the force I have, I will above all feel the need to express the high esteem inspired by the talents and the character of a man which I am honoured to call my friend.

Sismondi's letter is extremely polite and friendly.[34] He is doing his very best to define the points on which there is agreement between Say and himself. And he clearly believed that the problem under consideration was so theoretical that it might soon start to annoy the general public.

His definitions are quite clear: the national income (or net value produced) can be spent in consumption and investment. But there is no guarantee that the propensity to consume and the propensity to invest will add up to 100 per cent of national income: he is 'hoping for an increase of demand' that will achieve this. Say's brief notes in the margin demonstrate that his analysis is formulated in real terms: production means income, income means spending or saving, savings will be invested – 'It is one and the same thing'.

In 1824, Sismondi and Say crossed swords again in the *Revue Ency- clopédique*, in two articles under identical titles: *Sur la Balance des Consomma- tions avec les Productions.* In the first, Sismondi's pessimism was not directed against the possibility of supply shocks in the economy: 'It is not against machines, against discoveries, it is not against civilisation that my objections are aimed; it is against the organisation of modern society.' In his reply, Say stressed the role of the entrepreneur in the equilibrating process of the *débouchés* – implicitly making giant steps from micro to macro reasoning: 'The interest of the entrepreneur guarantees that quantities created cannot permanently and con- tinuously exceed what is required.'[35] However he remained vague about the pos- sible duration of the adjustment process.

It is clear that Say found occasion in his discussions with Malthus and Sis- mondi to review his ideas about the long-term limits to growth. Thus in the fifth edition of the *Traité* he added the following lines to the *Débouchés* chapter:

One will perhaps wish to know what would be the term of a growing pro- duction, where every day a more considerable output of products would be exchanged against other ones; for finally there is only an infinite progression in abstract quantities, and in practice the nature of things puts a limit to all surpluses. Now it is practical political economy we discuss here.[36]

Already in the fourth edition he suggested (in a footnote) the possible necessity of public works to overcome the temporary unemployment effects caused by the introduction of new machinery.[37] He had taken seriously Sismondi's suggestion to correct 'the organisation of modern society'. And in 1827 he wrote to Malthus that his theory is *in fact subjected to some limitations*. This brought him Malthus' familiar objection – repeated by Schumpeter – that Say denies the name of production to products sold below cost price, to which the latter replied that *my theory of markets remains complete*.[38] In the same year, 1827, Say annotated his copy of the second edition of Sismondi's *Nouveaux Principes*:

> *M. de Sismondi does not wish to understand tha*[t I] *agree with him that it is necessary for the* [pro]*duction to be favourable, that the products are de*[manded]*, paid and consumed; so this is not at all the qu*[estion] *under discussion. The point on which we differ* [is] *to know what makes that people demand the product*[s which] *are overabundant. He pretends that this comes about by producing l*[ess] *that means by reducing what determines the prosperity* [of] *the state; and I pretend that it comes about by producing* [more] *which procures to new producers new incomes, which will make them new consum*[ers].[39]

Say's rephrasing of Sismondi's position clarifies the different reactions they expected from entrepreneurs in periods of gluts: Sismondi predicted a contraction, and Say an expansion of output. So on the whole it is clear that Say's optimism, and his belief in progress, were equally important elements as – if not more important than – his economic analysis in predicting the end of gluts. He shared Sismondi's hesitations about the flexibility of labour, but only in the short run. For the larger part Say, Malthus and Sismondi shared a common framework of analysis. Their discussion was less of a conflict of paradigms than Say's value debate with Ricardo. In the end, their conclusions about growth, stagnation, population and technological unemployment were determined by their value systems and their positions in society.

As a disciple of Condorcet, as a classical economist and as a former cotton-spinning manufacturer, Say was not pessimistic about the effects of the introduction of machines, which *produce and do not eat*, or at least can be had *cheaper than men*. Therefore he was an ardent pleader for saving and capital formation. In this respect he qualifies as a thoroughly classical economist for whom the issue of economic growth was one of the core topics.

Baumol points to the fact that Say's Law is consonant with his other ideas with respect to population and machinery. Say's (and Sismondi's) ideas on population are not Malthusian in the usual pessimistic sense. Say's ideas on population and gluts are more consistent than Malthus', as a growing population will always furnish enough consumers for a growing output. However, Say does not 'prove' that there will always be enough capital and flexible labour to allow rapid adjustments to an unbalanced composition of output. He needs optimistic assumptions, but then according to Baumol his reasoning is a 'support for the expanding spirit of capitalist enterprise that accompanied the young industrial revolution'.[40] And to Forget it is characteristic of the 'fundamental concern of the *ideologues* with social stability'.[41]

Regarding the value debate, lots of notes in the Say papers illustrate his struggle with the subject, and the evolution of his ideas in time. Nothing equivalent is to be found with respect to the law of markets. As the papers are clearly incomplete, one explanation could be that a dossier *Débouchés* has existed but not survived. Another might be that, although perhaps not a dogma or paradigm in Say's thought, the law was such a core element in his theories that an elaborate defence would be superfluous. This idea is consonant with Say's belief in spontaneous order and in progress.

Say's law and population

On population, Say was a Malthusian even before having read Malthus. In 1803 he wrote in the *Traité*:

> Whatever the limitations which are set upon the multiplication of humans by laws and by individuals, the attraction of the sexes is so powerful that the procreation of children will always rise above the means of a country to provide for their needs. It is an awful truth that in almost every country, and especially the densely populated ones, a part of the population is dying from hunger.[42]

A letter from Say to the Genevan philosopher and physicist Pierre Prévost (1751–1839), thanking him for his translation of Malthus' *Principles* in March 1810, gives the impression that this was the first time he learned about the latter's ideas: 'I will tell you that your translation of Malthus is one of the most useful books I know, and one of the most interesting a political philosopher may read.'[43]

In Say's second edition of 1814, Malthus' *Essay* was praised as being 'full of evidence and judicious reasoning', and proving convincingly 'the general thesis that the population of states is always proportioned to its total production'.[44] The population issue also was an important interest shared by Say and Francis Place. Their first meeting in 1814 had been brought about through the mediation of William Godwin.[45]

On this subject, Say never got engaged in the kind of long and serious debates that he had on value or *débouchés*. His discussion with the American diplomat and economist Alexander Everett has attracted little attention. Yet it was a remarkable interchange of thoughts, with important linkages to the question of *débouchés*. According to Schumpeter,

> A.H. Everett, an American diplomatist and newspaper editor, was perfectly right to call his book *New Ideas on Population* (1823). For his main point, viz. that increase in population means increased production of food and is likely to induce improvements in the methods of its production, was new in his day, much more so at any rate than Malthus ever said.[46]

Everett, working at the time at the American embassy in Brussels, sent a copy of his book to Say. In his reply of January 1824, the latter tried to explain his Malthusian position to him.[47] Everett reacted immediately and somewhat surprised:

> *I owe you, Sir, an apology for having sent you a tract controverting one of the opinions expressed in your very valuable treatise without alluding in my letter to this circumstance. The truth is that I was not at the time aware that you had adopted in your work the theory of Malthus. I purchased and read your work when I was at Paris in the year 1812. It was then scarce; and I remember that I paid 30 frs for a copy which I afterwards disposed of to a friend. Since that time I had not recurred to the work; and had no distinct recollection of your opinion on the subject of Population, which may perhaps not have been expressed in the First Edition.*[48]

In spite of his polite introduction, Everett did not hesitate to confront Say with the seeming inconsistencies in his argument. He admitted that his own thesis about the growth of population as a cause of wealth was not fundamentally at odds with the ideas of Malthus and Say, that population will always be proportioned to the means of subsistence:

> *If an excess of production is impossible, it seems to follow of course that an excess of producers – that is – of population must be equally so. Your discovery – as it may be justly called – furnishes therefore an indirect refutation of the principles of Malthus and a convincing proof of the correctness of the contrary by direct reasoning.*

He asked Say to reconsider his argument, and perhaps to replace Malthus' name by his own in the next edition of the *Traité*. In the fifth (1826) edition of the *Traité* Say omitted six pages of the first population paragraph, about the proportion between agrarian and industrial output, as well as the consequences for international trade. A manuscript note tells us as an explanation that 'Later obtained data have considerably changed my ideas on these matters.'[49] It seems no heroic assumption that Everett had something to do with this change of ideas.

He and Say corresponded again in 1829, but it seems that the latter did not agree to a proposed meeting. His excuse – health problems in his family – may well have been the illness of Mrs Say who died a few months later, in January 1830. Everett's letter said:

> *I pray you, my dear Sir, to keep the Review which I took from the depot here solely for your use. Accept my thanks for your polite expression of approbation in regard to some passages. I hope you did not understand the one, in which I remark that the science of Political Economy had made no material advances since the time of Adam Smith as intended to apply to your works. I had in mind merely the modern British school. No one is more disposed*

than I am to acknowledge the great services you have rendered to the science by methodising the principles of Smith & completing in several important particulars the system of which he laid the foundations. I have expressly stated in another work that you stand in public opinion at the head of the contemporary writers on the subject.[50]

The positions of Say and Sismondi with respect to population, and in relation to Malthus, have been nicely summarised by Guillaumont (1969).[51] He finds Say less Malthusian than he believes himself to be, and Sismondi exactly the opposite, while the difference between the two in matters of population is smaller than both of them believe. Guillaumont draws a comparison between the demographic ideas of Say and Sismondi, and the general optimism or pessimism in their economic analysis:

> The demographic theory of Say, in going further than Malthus, seemed to us like an essential element to explain Say's optimism. But Sismondi's theory, while analogous to Say's, far from introducing an optimistic element in Sismondi's thinking, seems to reinforce the pessimism of this author. And Sismondi's pessimism seems to come together with that of Malthus: 'The multiplication of population, caused by the marriages of the poor workers, is today a great calamity for the social order.' The reason why the theory of population in Sismondi's works brings about a different vision of society from Say's, must be found in the fact that this theory is linked with Sismondi's economic ideas, different from those of Say.

It is clear that for Say as well as for Sismondi, the link between population theory and the theory of *débouchés* was a fundamental part of their analysis. To a certain extent, both economists were 'Malthusians'. But if we follow Guillaumont in his perspective of 'different visions of society', we see in Malthus, Say and Sismondi respectively a conservative, a liberal and a radical view of gluts in classical economics.

Professional and private contacts

As his relationship with Sismondi demonstrates, for Say scholarly disagreement did not necessarily stand in the way of friendly contacts. The same was true for his understanding with Ricardo. And indeed in many cases there was a parallel between his scientific or business contacts, and close personal ties. From his *Décade* days, Andrieux and Amaury Duval remained lifelong friends. He kept in touch with his trusted bookkeeper from Auchy, Monsieur Perturon. As young men, Francis Place junior, John Stuart Mill and Eyton Tooke stayed with the Say family in Paris. In a wider perspective, Say belonged to a number of overlapping networks composed of Genevans, Huguenots, Utilitarians and Philosophical Radicals. In his political ideas he always remained a republican, a liberal and an Idéologue.

As his reputation grew, he was increasingly approached for membership of committees, or authorship of new publication projects. One of these plans was the idea of the Italian Marquess Arborio Gattinara de Brême (1754–1828), to organise a prize contest for a new elementary textbook of economics. This Italian diplomat and former Milanese minister of the interior fostered agricultural and educational studies. With the jurist and philosopher Baron de Gérando (1772–1842) as intermediary, he asked Say in 1819 to act as secretary of the Learned Committee with the long-winded purpose:

> *to finally determine the general opinion on certain cardinal points of political economy, in the hope of letting disappear prejudices and uncertainties forthcoming from ignorance, and still worse, paralogisms and sophisms resulting from vested interests, serving as pretext and shield for doctrines and dispositions fatally harmful to public happiness, which they attack in its most fertile source, the rural and commercial industry.*[52]

His praise of the 'rural industry' has a distinct physiocratic flavour. He continued by referring to 'our late immortal authors', who had left a vacuum with regard to political economy in most Italian universities. He probably had in mind Galiani and Verri, and it had not escaped his attention that in Italy perhaps even more than in France, liberal economics was seen as a subversive discipline, the teaching of which was not encouraged in academia. Other proposed members of de Brême's jury were Ganilh, Garnier, Le Sur, Sismondi, de Gérando and 'perhaps Hennet'. With some regret de Brême remarked that two of these – certainly Sismondi, and most probably Ganilh – held opinions divergent from Say's, but he expected the committee would reach a unanimous conclusion. Say annotated the second letter as 'replied' but did not keep a copy or abstract of his answer. However, an earlier letter from March 1819, unearthed by Hashimoto, proves that Say was seriously interested in organising and judging this contest.[53] To Baron de Gérando he wrote that he had spoken to Sismondi and that the latter had agreed to sit on the jury as well. Now the publicity had to be discussed; not only in the French journals, but also by a widely circulated, printed leaflet. The submission date envisaged by de Brême of 1 January 1821, seemed problematic to Say as it would take some time before the announcement had reached the farthest provinces of Italy and of Russia. So he suggested 31 December of the same year as the final date.

In the end, the plan probably underwent the same fate as the project of an economics textbook for women, proposed by the bookseller Audot from the Sorbonne quarter in Paris: *Political economy for the instruction of ladies*, or *Conversation between a father and his daughters on general and private Economy*. In December 1820, the month of his inaugural lecture at the Conservatoire, he wrote to Audot that his other occupations would suffer too much from such a project. He no longer needed to spread himself thinly over many small projects – even if these two would have fully served his purpose of teaching and popularising economics.

In this respect, a curious announcement in the January 1824 issue of the *Revue Encyclopédique*, on The Teaching of Political Economy, signed by 'Z.' must be mentioned.[54] It conveys the impression that it had either been written by Say himself, or composed by the editor Jullien upon his instigation. It started by stating that, although 'servile and liberal doctrines are splitting Europe and America', everyone agreed that the sources of public prosperity must be sought in political economy. Z continued that it was well known that the Danish crown prince corresponded with 'our great economist J.-B. Say':

> He has recently sent to this publicist a magnificently bound copy of the Danish translation of his *Traité d'Economie Politique*. (This work of Mr. Jean-Baptiste Say, the clearest and most complete work that has been written on this subject, is serving as the base of teaching in all universities except those of France, where people do not know what Political Economy is.)

Princes such as the Russian Emperor, and even the Spanish king Ferdinand VII (considered a sworn enemy of *les lumières*), according to Z are promoting the study of economics. In England the opposition and the government equally wish to abolish barriers to industry, and patriots have instituted a chair of political economy in honour of David Ricardo, 'equally deplored by the science and the country'. Z named McCulloch as the most probable occupant of this chair. We have seen already that Say was capable of writing self-promotional texts. This brief announcement decidedly has the flavour of having been another of these.

Say's political economy is not generally associated with the French mathematical approach, practiced in the famous circuit of the department of public works, the Ponts et Chaussées. Yet his interest in the French system of canals was evident from his pamphlet of 1818. Gérard Klotz has reconstructed his influence on the economic evaluation of roads and communications during his lifetime and briefly after.[55] In his *Cours Complet*, Say expressed a low opinion of public servants in charge of public works. Anticipating Niskanen's *Bureaucracy and Representative Government* (1971), he accused them of being 'interested in making the construction process last and in multiplying the expenses' as well as 'costing a lot and producing little'. Say preferred the British system of private constructions of waterways which he had observed already in 1814. This system produced profits, superior to those gained by the French engineers of public works and mines: 'among these [engineers], those who have real talent do prefer the system of liberty'.[56]

In measuring the utility of public works, Say's average (instead of marginal) utility approach was clearly deficient. Nevertheless he stood at the origin of the first French efforts at measurement of this utility. In a letter of 1832 he commented upon a first draft of an article by the engineer Charles Joseph Minard on the economics of public works:

> You have admirably well demonstrated, my dear monsieur, the applications one can make of the soundest principles to an important branch of public consumption, a consumption which is only a transformation of capital, a

transformation which if properly judged, can result in a true growth of national capital, and of public wealth.[57]

Minard only published his article eighteen years later, in 1850. By that time, Jules Dupuit had published his classic article on the measurement of the utility of public works in the *Annales des Ponts et Chaussées* (1844). Say's work represents a first step in France towards this measurement.

Privately Say continued to write to his aged aunt Duvoisin in Geneva, and to pay her the annual interest of 620 F. But her health was deteriorating, and in May 1825, just before his departure for London to visit the Comtes there, he was obliged to write to his brother Louis about the settlement of the estate of their late Genevan aunt. In the same letter he rejoiced about the prospect of the English journey:

> *My wife, Octavie and I will depart for London, and I did not wish to let the sea separate us without giving you a sign of life. This excursion gives lots of happiness to us and the Comtes, and the doctors are assuring me that the state of my nerves will allow it. I go there with confidence, as my health has constantly improved since the beginning of the year, and the symptoms which could worry me have become increasingly rare.*

It was already mentioned that Charles Comte had been arrested in 1817, together with his fellow editor of the *Censeur Européen* Charles Dunoyer, for publishing the *Manuscrit venu de Sainte-Hélène, d'une manière inconnue*. After his liberation, Comte was obliged to flee to Switzerland to escape from a libel lawsuit. And even there he was not at rest, as Say wrote to Bentham in 1823:

> *And again from there those man-eaters in the name of God, who call themselves* Holy Alliance, *have thrown him out. I hope England will offer him a safe refuge. He is one of your pupils, my worthy master; cover him with your wings; incite your influential friends to his favour. Liberty will smile at you from the high skies and I shall erect an altar for you in my heart. Comte is a particular friend of Lafayette who kept him hidden for months in his chateau de la Grange.*[58]

Writing to Bentham had clearly inspired Say to insert a few Benthamite metaphors into his letter.

The visit to London of the Says lasted three months. In his *Acta*, Say only recorded that he fell into the water while disembarking at night in Calais (see Figure 8.1). But Mrs Say kept a small diary.[59] She described their visit to an iron foundry, and two visits to private picture collections. At the Marquess of Stratford's she saw pictures by Constable, and with Lord Grosvenor she admired his Rembrandts. Some of her observations are an echo of her husband's opinions during his visit in 1814, and are illustrative of French feelings of superiority. Admiringly she noted some visits of parks and gardens, but only rarely she liked

Figure 8.1 Say was a prophet of the age of steam; he kept this leaflet in his papers. The General Steam Navigation Company was founded in 1824, so Say may have travelled to London in 1825 aboard one of its ships

buildings. At the annual *salon* for paintings she disliked most of them; she admired only the *mignatures* and the watercolours.

On the programme were a ball of the Lord Mayor, and – of course – a theatre performance in Drury Lane. The dinners they attended, with their countless toasts, she found 'lengthy and boring'. She was truly amazed that the ladies did not mind leaving the dining room well before the men. At the ball she noted the bad taste in dresses, and the crowding for the free ice creams irritated her. And like her husband in *De l'Angleterre et des Anglais*, she wondered at the British industrial mentality. After visiting the iron mill, she wrote: 'The masters of this establishment are working enormously. Wealth must be a first necessity for people who decide upon such a laborious existence.'

Say's own visits and contacts can be reconstructed from his correspondence. Of course he visited Francis Place and James Mill, and very probably Bentham as well. They must have been instrumental in introducing Say to a number of new friends and contacts, like the economists McCulloch and Tooke, the jurist and philosopher John Austin and his wife Sarah, and the banker and historian George Grote and his wife Harriet.

Together with Place, Say visited the House of Commons during the discussion on the *Combination Laws Bill*.[60] Place had been an active member of the committee pleading for abolition of the old laws, which made him decidedly unpopular with many MPs. Joseph Hume, one of the sympathisers, was speaking in favour of the committee and of Place's correct behaviour. But the atmosphere was hostile, as Place reported in his notes:

When the bill was reported I was again in the house, and Mons. J.B. Say was with me. On this occasion the most rancorous hostility was again shown; allusions to me were so particularly personal and graceless, that at length M. Say proposed that we should leave the House, as he observed that my friends were made uncomfortable, and we withdrew.[61]

Place was involved in Say's abortive plan to publish a pamphlet with the correspondence between himself and Ricardo, which he cancelled in November 1825, after returning from London. James Mill was also very active in proposing and organising visits for the Say family. On 28 May he wrote:

My dear Sir,
I have the pleasure of enclosing introductions to the several docks, which will procure you the means of seeing them to the best advantage. I have in my turn a favour to request, which is, that you and Miss Say will accompany me to Croydon on the 11th of June, where Mr. McCulloch has promised me that he will meet you. Saturdays and Sundays are the only days I have for Croydon, & both of these days on that occasion I hope you will spend with me. It is a great mortification to me, not to be able to invite M. & Mad. Comte at the same time – but my house is small and will not afford another bed. I must therefore hope to see them at another time. I have also

enclosed tickets for a meeting on account of certain schools; where several of the leading men in both houses of parliament will make speeches, which it may be interesting to Miss Say to hear.[62]

No further information is recorded about this visit to Croydon, where Say had acquired his first impressions of England exactly forty years earlier.

The economics of slavery

Already before becoming an economist, Say had been an abolitionist activist in the second Society of the Friends of the Blacks, and of the Colonies, in 1798–1799. In his later lectures and textbooks, he took a stance against slavery, and predicted the future bankruptcy of the colonial system. However, as a positive economist, he was open to considering the economic pros and cons of the slavery system, as distinct from its moral dimensions. In all six editions of his *Traité*, there is a discussion of the economics of slavery in the chapter on colonies.[63] After comparing the colonisation models of classical antiquity and of modern times, i.e. establishing trading posts versus creating emigration settlements, Say is asking the question: 'What is the effect of slavery with regard to production?' In the first edition (1803), the second sentence already makes quite clear what his conclusion will be: 'I have no doubt at all that it greatly augments this, or at least that in the work of a slave, the surplus of his output above his consumption is bigger than in the work of a free person.' In the second edition (1814), this statement was turned into an interrogative sentence: 'Is the surplus of value produced above value consumed bigger in the work of a free person than in that of a slave?'[64] Steuart, Turgot and Smith are then quoted by Say as believing that slave labour is less productive than free labour. Their argument is that a slave has no private interest in the result of his work, that his long working hours shorten his life (and thereby make his labour relatively more expensive), and that his living expenses are administered with less efficiency and economy than those of a free person who takes care of himself.

Say presents an arithmetical example of the contrary: a slave in the Antilles, purchased at 2000 F, and costing no more than 300 F a year for his living, is cheaper to employ than a free person. In the fifth edition of the *Traité* (1825) he added the sentence: 'Philanthropical authors have considered that the best way to turn people away from this shameful practice is to prove that it is contrary to their interests.'[65] Yet in all editions he maintained the concluding statement of his arithmetical sum: 'The simple reasoning indicates that the consumption of a slave must be less than that of a free worker.'[66]

But he seemed to hover between considering the possible economic rationality of slavery on the one hand, and condemning it on moral grounds on the other. In the third and fourth editions of the *Traité* (1817–1819) he wrote:

A number of travellers who have all my confidence, have told me that they believed any industrial progress in Brazil and the other American colonies to be impossible, as long as they will be infested by slavery. The States of northern America which are most rapidly marching towards prosperity, are those in the north where slavery is forbidden.

In the fifth (1826) and sixth (1841) editions, this observation was replaced by the following statement:

On top of this, it does not only matter to know at what price one can hire a working man, but at what price one can hire a worker without violating justice and humanity. Those who count on force before anything else, and on equity least of all, are powerless calculators.[67]

The subject of slavery was touched upon in a letter by Say from 1822, neglected so far among his published works by modern commentators. It was probably printed privately by the recipient, Polidore Martelly, a Frenchman trading in London, and later in Haiti.[68] Martelly had asked Say to comment upon a pamphlet by Pierre André, a local politician pleading for the expulsion of foreign tradesmen from all Haitian ports. Say had a clear answer: 'This question is the same for all monopolies and privileges.' And he explained that the privileged always only had their own interest in mind, and never that of the whole community:

What is the interest of Haiti? That every kind of economic acivity appropriate to this happy [*sic*] island, can comfortably develop itself; that its agriculture can grow, that manufacturing industries will be established; that its commerce creates relationships with all nations of the world.

The best way to reach this is ... to only show hostility towards those monsters in human guise who are still dreaming of the former slavery and the former ties of dependence. Furthermore all communications are favourable. These only will introduce in Haiti the economic activities still lacking, the needs of fully civilised nations, and reciprocal trade relations which satisfy its wants and provide the largest *débouchés* to the national output.

This paragraph is a nice concise summary of Say's Law and of Say's view of economics as a positive sum game: products are paid for with products, and the better the trade channels, the more this process is facilitated. In trade, the surplus of one nation is not another's loss, but all parties are gaining in the end. And slavery and colonial relationships are a thing of the past.

The US is an inspiring example: European immigrants have developed New York, Boston and Baltimore into front-ranking trade cities. And against André's argument that 'strangers have no interest in conserving the social structure', Say – as an institutionalist economist – stipulates that they have a special interest in conserving a social order which is beneficial to them. He waxes lyrical about the possible blessings of their commercial activities: 'Twenty directors of foreign houses will provide subsistence for another ten thousand Haitians.'

André's plea for individual trading permits, to be awarded by the Haitian president to Haitians only, in combination with a compulsory trading guild membership, receives Say's scorn:

> One cannot believe that this could be written down by someone representing the national interest; by a man who, by virtue of his colour alone, should be horrified by any kind of chains, whatever garlands these might be decorated with.

In Europe, compulsory associations are a thing of the past; they should not be allowed to cross the ocean.

At the end of his letter, Say remembered having met another coloured Haitian in the meetings of the Society of the Friends of the Blacks, and of the Colonies, Alexandre Pétion (the former Haitian president).[69] And he concluded by praising his successor, President Boyer, who like Washington never sought to enlarge his own political power, but only to consolidate the liberty of his country.

'Slavery is incompatible with productive industry'

It must have been a surprise to Say when, one year after the Letter to Martelly, the first edition came out of Adam Hodgson's pamphlet against slavery, and against its economic justification attributed to … J.-B. Say.[70] Hodgson was the son of a Liverpool slave-trader, and had become an active abolitionist. He was a member of the Liverpool Society for the Mitigation and Gradual Abolition of Slavery, to whose president and members the pamphlet was dedicated. Its first paragraphs were:

> Sir,
> It is with much concern that I observe, in your excellent and popular work on political economy, the sentiments you express on the subject of the comparative expense of free and slave labour. Accustomed to respect you highly as an enlightened advocate of liberal principles, and to admire the philanthropic spirit which pervades your writings, I cannot but regret that opinions so calculated to perpetuate slavery, should have the sanction of your authority; and that, while you denounce the slave system as unjustifiable, you admit, that, in a pecuniary point of view, it may be the most profitable.
>
> As this subject is of peculiar importance at the present moment, when efforts are making both in this country and in France, to effect the gradual abolition of slavery in the Colonies, I will not apologize for addressing you.

Hodgson politely asked Say to reconsider his argument that however objectionable slavery might be, it might also be possible that the slavery system was more profitable than free labour:

> The same regard to truth and candour which secured your reluctant assent to an opinion little in unison, I am sure, with your feelings, will lead you to

examine with impartiality any facts or arguments which I may adduce in my attempt to controvert it.

The larger part of these facts and arguments consisted of quotations from Adam Smith, the economist Storch, the British MPs Joseph Hume and Henry Brougham, Alexander von Humboldt, William Wilberforce, an anonymous Barbados planter and many others. From their findings, Hodgson drew the following conclusion:

> If slave labour were cheaper than free labour, we might reasonably infer, that in proportion as the circumstances of the cultivation rendered economy indispensable, either from the difficulty of obtaining slaves, or other causes, the peculiar features of slavery would be more favourably established, and that every approach to freedom would be more sedulously shunned in the system of culture. But it is found by the experience of both ancient and modern times, that nothing has tended more to assimilate the condition of the slave to that of the free labourer, or actually to effect his emancipation, than the necessity imposed by circumstances of adopting the most economical mode of cultivation.

Surely Hodgson must have considered that including Say's name in his title would be an extra selling point, certainly after the success of the latter's *Letters to Malthus*.[71] Say did not hesitate to write back as soon as he had received his complimentary copy of Hodgson's pamphlet, and his letter was included in the second edition of 1823:

> Sir,
> I have received, from the Baron de Stael, the letter with which you did me the honour to accompany the printed letter you have addressed to me.
> I thank you for the obliging expressions in both of them, and accord with your sentiments on all the main points of the question at issue. You have collected, in a small space, an accumulation of facts and arguments which it appears to me impossible to resist.
> You have probably read only one of the first editions of my Treatise on Political Economy, as in the later ones I have materially corrected what I said with respect to the labour of slaves, so as to arrive nearly at the same conclusion as you; but not having myself confined to that particular subject, and being unwilling to swell my book, I was only able to advert to it slightly. I approach still nearer to your sentiments in the works which I am preparing.
> Slavery is incompatible with productive industry, in a state of society moderately advanced. It is already verging towards its extermination among all people of European origin; and as the restlessness and intelligence of Europe will ultimately pervade the globe, we may affirm that slavery will one day be extinguished every-where.

I have communicated your valuable pamphlet to one of our literary journals (the Encyclopedical Magazine), in which I have been promised that some account of it will appear; it will probably be in the Number which will be published on the 1st of May. Perhaps this journal is to be met with in some of your literary institutions.

Accept the expression, &c. &c.

J.B. SAY
Paris, 25th March, 1823

When he wrote this, four editions of the *Traité* had been published. So when Say distinguished between the 'first editions' and 'later ones', he was speaking of editions 1 and 2 as the first, and 3 and 4 as the later ones. Yet in the third and fourth editions (1817–1819) he still only quoted the authority of 'travellers who have all my confidence' as a testimony of the economic superiority of free labour, and did not present it explicitly as his own opinion. Only in the fifth (1826) did he condemn the violation of 'justice and humanity' in the slavery system. We may guess with some reason that Hodgson's pamphlet was one of Say's considerations for this adaptation.

Another interesting choice of vocabulary in his letter is the 'restlessness and intelligence of Europe' that will 'ultimately pervade the globe'. This is reminiscent of what he said in his Athénée lectures in 1819. Speaking of population and emigration, he remarked:

> We start by noticing in the people of Europe, or those emigrating from Europe, a very special moral character, distinguishing them from all other inhabitants of the world. I mean a sort of restlessness which drives them to change their position, and a capacity which generally allows them to change it for the better, to improve it.[72]

He contrasted this with the character of the native people of America and Asia, who seem to have arrived 'at the limits of their intelligence since a long time'. According to Say, they have failed to innovate in their techniques of production for ages. So if his moral judgement pronounced itself against slavery, he still maintained a notion of racial superiority regarding the Europeans. (He did not include these considerations from his lectures in the later editions of the *Traité*, or in the *Cours Complet*.) But the abolition movement and the black remigration initiatives to Africa continued to have his attention, as shown by his comments in the *Revue Encyclopédique*.

9   The final years

The platform of *La Revue Encyclopédique*

There is a certain continuity in the periodicals to which Say was successively committed during his career. Republicanism, progress and the unity of the sciences, all were to some extent characteristic elements of the editorial policies of *La Décade* (1794–1807), *Le Censeur Européen* (1817–1819) and *La Revue Encyclopédique* (1819–1835). Under Say's editorship (1794–1800), the *Décade* could perhaps be labelled politically as middle of the road, in its later period it decidedly was left of centre; so were the *Censeur Européen*, edited by Charles Comte and Charles Dunoyer, and the *Revue Encyclopédique*. This monthly periodical was founded in 1819 by Marc Antoine Jullien.[1] Its tables of content demonstrate that 'économie politique' had been fully accepted as one of the 'sciences morales'. Both as an author and as a reviewer, Say was a regular contributor.[2] The discussion with Sismondi in the *Revue* has already been summarised above. Say's successor-to-be at the Conservatoire, Adolphe Blanqui, also published in the journal.

Already in 1820 the *Revue* had included an announcement of an American public funding campaign, launched with the support of the Haitian president Pétion, for the society for colonisation of former slaves in Africa. The journal continued to inform its readers about this movement, and in 1824 it published a letter in support of this society from Pétion's successor Boyer.[3] Earlier that year, Say had received from Jullien a copy of the *New York Observer* reporting about these developments, and as a reaction he proposed to write a comment on Boyer's letter, originally addressed to the American Society for Colonizing the Free People of Colour, and also – if this would suit Jullien – submit a piece on the development of the Liberian settlement.[4] This was published as the opening article in the *Revue*'s September issue of 1824. It just escaped the censorship of Louis XVIII, who had died on 16 September. His successor Charles X had softened the rules, with the result that Say's complete text could be printed in the issue dated 29 September.[5] Jullien did not fail to point out to his readers the originally censored passages. The first of these came right at the beginning: Say's denouncing of the economic profitability of slavery – he had learnt his lesson from Hodgson's interpretation of his analysis. The second came after his sketch of the sorry state of liberated but still discriminated people of colour in the United States. Say's argument was directly aimed at his own government: 'certain governments for which it seems impossible to rise to the level of their era, have only established settlements on the African coast with the clear objective to cover up the slave trade'.[6] Say continued by falsifying the arguments brought forward by opponents of the African colonisation idea, such as the unfertility of the soil, the health risks, the unwillingness of coloured Americans to move, etc. He mentioned the 'success' of the comparable British project in Sierra Leone as a positive example for the American one in Liberia. And he seemed to be hinting at the creation of a French colonisation society after the American model. Finally, the economist Say briefly sketched the perspective of an increased remigration of former slaves to Africa, facilitated by lower shipping fares, and resulting in a bright future for intercontinental trade:

> With regard to trade commodities, the United States will no longer carry chains and whips to Africa, but tissues, household articles and all the products of the manufacturing industry. 'America' will no longer bring back muscle power suffused with tears, but ivory, gums, feathers, perfumes, medicine, and perhaps many other objects still unknown to the European nations.[7]

Say's article drew the attention of the French Société de la Morale Chrétienne, which even reproduced it in its own journal; in 1822 this society had founded its own committee for the abolition of slavery. A last reference to the slavery issue in the Say papers is a long letter by Major Moody from 1828. Apparently Say had asked him for information on the British colonies in the West Indies, and Moody replied:

> *I should have been very happy to have answered your questions, respecting the termination of Slavery, and the cultivation of Sugar in the West Indies. But I find I could develop the result of my observations, without writing a book, for which I have neither the leisure, nor indeed the inclination, from the repulsive nature of the subject. As an Englishman I can only approach the Subject, under the condition of respecting the rights of private property of the White Capitalist and their claim to the fair physical exertion, obedience, and skill of their black labourers. If white labourers from Great Britain or Ireland could cultivate the West Indies, I am quite convinced, that the Slavery of the blacks would not be necessary, in order to protect the legal rights of the White Masters with respect to the Black Slaves.*[8]

The slavery and colonisation question is just one example of Say's engagement in the issues of the day. The near-censoring of his article offers another testimony to the fact that, despite his firmly established reputation as an economist, he still was not above political suspicion from the government. Of course this was true for many other authors for whom the *Revue Encyclopédique* was a platform. For Say, this journal was a forum where he could publish a number of his important later articles; his exchange with Sismondi on the validity of 'Say's Law' has already been discussed above.

Also as a simple reviewer, Say continued to contribute to the *Revue*. In the February issue of 1824 he inserted a brief summary of the annual report of the Royal Institute of Liverpool on technical advancements.[9] In cotton spinning, the use of steam had increased output by a hundredfold; in certain mills the length of the cotton thread spun in a year was equivalent to twice the circumference of the globe. Machine weaving had seen the same revolutionary development. In America a machine had been designed producing sixty pins per minute. Adam Smith's famous example of a pin factory only applied to the division of human labour, but this effect of mechanisation was even more spectacular. (This is consonant with what was remarked in Chapter 5 about the different approaches of Smith and Say, with the latter specifying a changing production function.)

In all of Britain, steam power was equivalent to that of one million manual labourers: 'It has multiplied time, like gas lighting has multiplied the daytime.' Even more spectacular was the invention of Babbage's difference engine: it executed tasks considered to be 'purely intellectual'. This machine even corrected its own mistakes! Upon recommendation of the Royal Institute, the British government had granted to Babbage £1500, a sum equal to 37,500 F, in order to encourage his further research.

In 1826, in the section on books from abroad, Say announced fourteen English publications in less than three full pages; thirteen pamphlets were related to the slavery issue. James Stephen's *England enslaved* (1826) was commented upon by a comparison to France:

> The zeal and the talent, relentlessly deployed by the English *abolitionists* against the slave trade and against slavery, are in contrast with the deplorable and guilty half-heartedness of other nations regarding these subjects. In France, it is true, they have some imitators; but the trade continues, and the infamous negro-carriers of Nantes, aided by their accomplices from other ports and from Paris, continue their business of man-eaters and go about every day in snatching victims from Africa in order to sell them to colonists of Guadeloupe, Martinique, Havana and other colonies, who feel no shame in being merchants of human flesh and executioners of their equals.[10]

The fourteenth publication was the 800-page *Parliamentary History and Review*, with the debates of both houses of Parliament in the year 1825. Say was particularly interested in the introduction:

> The authors have had the fortunate idea to let their *Parliamentary History* be preceded by an abstract, in the form of an introduction, of the excellent work of *Bentham* on *political sophisms*; which means, on the techniques employed every day to influence the convictions of deliberating assemblies in the direction of private interests, and opposed to the public interest.

Not all pamphlets sent for reviewing by Jullien were accepted by Say. In 1827 he bluntly refused to comment on four publications in which he could not discover a single new idea:

> On the one hand I do not wish to snub an author who has shown his good intentions; on the other I don't want to degrade the Revue by writing insincerities, not even when hiding my initials, as people know that I am consulted by it on works of political economy.[11]

The author's fee for these articles was no longer a very important issue for Say. In September 1825 he wrote to Jullien that Jeremy Bentham was staying in Paris, and offered his services as a possible intermediary. In the same letter he asked for fifty offprints of his big article *Economie politique*, offering to bear all the necessary expenses, and proposing to deduct these from his author's fees.[12]

Less than two months before his death, on 20 September 1832, Say replied to the director of the *Encyclopédie des Gens du Monde*, J.H. Schnitzler, who had asked him to write articles for this project.[13] Schnitzler's letter had been addressed to Say and to Charles Comte, who in the meantime had been elected to the Chambre des Députés. Say agreed to write the article *Economie politique*, at a fee of 300 F per printing leaf. He insisted on correcting the proofs himself. Also he offered Schnitzler permission, free of charge, to use the definitions from his *Epitome* for his encyclopaedia. But he would not arrive at completion of his article.

The British connections

Jean-Baptiste Say was a true cosmopolitan. As Huguenots, his great-grandfather and his grandfather had moved around Europe. In England he received part of his commercial education. He lived in an age where push and pull factors moved many people across national boundaries and even across continents. Changes of government, lack of freedom of religion, or of freedom of speech and of the press could be important incentives pushing people from one country to another. The enticement of the United States, as a great new republic of unlimitable possibilities, was seriously felt by Say himself. His uncle Daniel Delaroche, after his medical and botanic studies in Leyden and Edinburgh, for political reasons had to move several times between Geneva, Paris, England and Lausanne, before finally settling in Paris. Say's son-in-law Charles Comte first had to move to Switzerland, and then to England for several years on a libel charge. Say belonged to an international intellectual community, in which England occupied a dominant place.

As already noted by Schumpeter, 'Say's work grew from completely French sources'.[14] But his English apprenticeship of 1785–1787, and his visit of 1814, had given him a more than adequate schooling in British society and the British way of life. If the *Traité* of 1803 owed a lot to Adam Smith, the second edition of 1814 demonstrated that he had become much more versed in the international literature – not least the British contributions. And beginning with his visit of 1814, Say had met several of the leading English economic thinkers and philosophers in person. With some of them he just established friendly relations, with others he developed warm friendships. A number of new personal contacts were the result of his London visit in the summer of 1825.

Say's visit, together with Francis Place, to the House of Commons has already been mentioned. With Place he further discussed his plan for a pamphlet composed of 1. his article on McCulloch from the *Revue Encyclopédique*; 2. Say's letter to Robert Prinsep, the translator of the *Traité*; 3. his correspondence with Ricardo. After his return, on 11 November 1825, he was happy to note in a letter to Place that 'within a few days' the pamphlet would go to the printers. He insisted upon a precise correction of the proofs and had already composed a list of English names for the mailing of complimentary copies: Bentham, Mill, McCulloch, Tooke, Mrs Grote and Mrs Austin were among the envisaged recipients.[15] But on second thoughts, he was unhappy with the quality of the translations. On 27 November, he suggested to Place that Bentham's protégé Richard Doane, who in 1819 had stayed with Say in Paris, might be approached for help, or alternatively Mrs Austin or Thomas Tooke. Say believed that asking James Mill would not be a good idea, as he attacked some of his ideas in the pamphlet.

After these hesitations, he dropped the project altogether in January 1826 when he received the English translation of his article on McCulloch, probably made by Place. To the latter he wrote a letter beginning in French, and continuing in English:

> It reached me when I just began my public lessons which are delivered twice a week. However I compared your english with my french, but as I went on, some scruples got into my head. Is the nature of my pamphlet sufficiently interesting for the English nation? Is it not too late to attack M'Culloch's discourse? What will Ricardo's family think of publication? And so on. In short I was totally discouraged about the matter.[16]

Say concluded the letter with cancelling the plan, and asking for his manuscripts and articles back from Place. His harshest comment on its cover in his papers, that Place's translation was 'worth nothing', he kept to himself. The unexpected move to drop the project may have influenced his relationship with Place, but they continued to correspond till September 1827.

The new friendships with Thomas Tooke (qualified on Say's mailing list as *a Russia merchant*), George and Harriet Grote, and John and Sarah Austin, were probably promoted by James Mill and other utilitarians and Philosophical Radicals. Thomas' son Eyton Tooke was a friend of John Stuart Mill. The Comtes may also have played a role in establishing contact with the Austins. In 1831 Sarah Austin wrote about Comte that for her husband he had always been an exemplary 'courageous, highminded, consistent patriot'.[17] In the Say family, the contacts with George and Harriet Grote lasted for three generations. After the death of Jean-Baptiste, Harriet corresponded intermittently with Horace and

Léon Say until she died at the age of eighty-six in 1878. On the occasion of dramatic events, like the revolutions of 1830 and 1848, George took up his pen as well. In 1828 Harriet wrote to Say about his first volume of the *Cours Complet*. In one letter she combined her comments on the book with a reproach to Comte for not answering to her last letter, with a report on their private finances which would not allow a trip to the continent, and with a remark on the British capital market.[18]

The formidable character of Jeremy Bentham was in the background of many of Say's communications with British utilitarians and Philosophical Radicals. Since their first meeting in 1814, the two of them entertained a lifelong correspondence – they both died in 1832. It was more than a coincidence that the international utilitarian network extended itself to Geneva, where Etienne Dumont was Bentham's editor and translator. Generally Say was not prepared to recognise other minds as superior to his, but in the case of Bentham he was immediately converted to the ideas of the philosopher of Queen's Square Place. It has been noted above that in 1817, on the occasion of the publication of Bentham's parliamentary reform article in the *Censeur Européen*, he wrote to Place about the duty of Bentham's friends to popularise his ideas. Alas the philosopher himself did not notice that people hardly had time to read, so this must be facilitated for them.

On his side, Bentham completely took Say seriously. In 1817 he immediately read his complimentary copy of Say's *Petit Volume* of aphorisms; and he reported in his letters the names of admirers he did not let in, and of adepts he did not take seriously.[19]

Practical matters were often the subject of the Say–Bentham correspondence: books and articles were exchanged, and people introduced. A few times Say was helpful in conveying books and letters to General Sir Samuel Bentham, Jeremy's brother, residing in the South of France.

In Bentham's first letter he already wrote about his bad eyesight, and again in 1823 and 1824. Thereupon Say ordered a very thick piece of crystal glass from the St Gobain glassworks, from which a reading lens might be ground. The precise technical details in Say's letter accompanying it are reminiscent of his descriptions of factory visits in 1814: the grinding of convex or concave surfaces, the determination of focal distance, and the possible combination of the lens with reading glasses, a combination he used himself. This shared handicap probably made it a little easier for him to overcome his hesitation in asking Bentham to have his letters copied by a secretary. Already before this, he had asked Francis Place if he could discreetly clarify Bentham's illegible scribble.[20] It seems that Bentham found the lens helpful, as he came back to it in an undated note of a secretary on his behalf: 'Mr Bentham wishes to know what is the greatest thickness of the plate glass at present made in France.' The note refers to the glass which in 1825 'Mr Say was kind enough to beg a friend of his (name unknown, a great manufacturer of glass)'. This was 'of considerable use' to Bentham, who nevertheless hoped to order a lens of even greater magnifying power.[21]

In 1820 Bentham commented on the visits of two of his pupils, Richard Doane in 1819 and one year later John Stuart Mill, to Say in Paris. Both were under way to Sir Samuel Bentham. Richard Doane wrote a letter of thanks to Say in 1820, which was completed by Bentham:

> *Your young protégé being returned, I am going to send to my brother another boy to manufacture: the eldest of Mill's. R[ichard] D[oane] impoverished you: you may get rich by shewing J[ohn] M[ill] at 6 francs a piece. Fasten to his shoulder a pair of goose's wings. You shew him for an Angel, and you will meet with no unbeliever. Don't be angry with him or me: he understands political economy as well as you; but this is but a drop in the ocean of his intelligence. Amongst other things, he understands abundance that neither you nor I have any notion of. I send him to my brother that he may be dealt with as Joseph was dealt with by his brethren, and then be sold to the Algerines. I will send you by him a copy of a letter of his to my brother who was desirous of being informed of his progress since 1814. Farewell.*[22]

Some of Bentham's comments upon young protégés can be read as updates of the Benthamite membership list, or instructions for the utilitarian drilling class. Take for example this introduction of Peregrine Bingham:

> *This letter will be delivered to you by Mr Peregrine Bingham, a newly acquired and most valuable disciple of mine …*
>
> *Bingham is* homme de loi *having a wife and young child. He employs a profession the vices of which he had rather cure than profit by, in providing a supplement to the allowance he receives from his father. He is already in possession of most of my ideas respecting morals, politics and legislation, without efforts becomes master of everything as soon as he looks at it, and is in a condition to preach it, and apply it everywhere. He is perfectly acquainted with your great work, admiring it upon the whole, but finds two or three points on which he proposed to battle with you.*[23]

Bentham died less than six months before Say, in July 1832. A final proof of his respect and affection for Say was the ring with Bentham's profile which he – as one of twenty intimate contacts – received after the latter's death. Sarah Austin wrote to him about her impressions of Bentham's final days and, one month later, Bentham's secretary John Bowring sent the ring:

> *Here is the souvenir of our illustrious deceased. He has bequeathed this testimony to twenty people in the whole world – of which you are one. Will you please confirm to me the reception of this memento of his friendship and esteem.*[24]

Among Say's other British scholarly contacts, the Scottish statistician Sir John Sinclair wrote to him twice.[25] In 1821 he proposed: 'immediately commencing, and to carry on with unceasing energy, a great literary undertaking, to which I intend to give the name of "A Code of Political Economy".' He referred to his own *Statistical Account of Scotland*, and declared his intention to refer to 'the works of my old friend, Adam Smith (with whom I was particularly connected)', and promised that he would send an outline of his plan to Say. Apparently it escaped him that Say had deceased in 1832 as his next letter, with the plan and an introduction for his book, was dated 1834.

Henry James, classified by Dennis O'Brien among the 'monetary non-conformists', wrote a lengthy letter to Say in 1822 about the 'ruinous depreciation' in England 'in the value of almost all descriptions of property and productions'. He referred to his *Essays on Money, Exchanges etc.* which he had sent to Say in 1820. On eighteen points he asked Say for information: on France's silver standard, the switching from livres to francs, and changes in the prices of land and wheat etc. His purpose was to compare these data with their English counterparts, and to falsify Ricardo's views on monetary phenomena:

> *That the depression has been principally brought about by the operations upon our currency, since 1813, has been uniformly my opinion, and the opinion of many others also who have paid attention to this subject. There are those again who deny this, among whom Mr. Huskisson and Mr. Ricardo stand preeminent, but without assigning any other definite cause which can have produced such general and extraordinary effects, contenting themselves with asserting that the depression is not confined to England alone, but that the property and the productions had undergone a corresponding and a simultaneous reduction in value.*[26]

Say noted on the letter that it contained information on depreciation and paper money, but he seems not to have answered this letter. Another correspondent on monetary matters was Thomas Tooke who in 1825, the year in which they met in London, presented Say with a copy of his *Considerations of the state of the currency.* Say thanked him for improving his understanding of the English commercial crisis, and the monetary causes of this development as explained by Tooke.[27] He did not fail to praise Tooke for his method, as all his observations were founded upon facts: 'This practical philosophy is far superior to the obscure metaphysics to which some of your compatriots wish to reduce economic problems.' And he offered his apologies for having troubled Tooke by asking him for advice on the cancelled plan of publishing his correspondence with Ricardo.

Among Say's other English correspondents, John Cazenove was a remarkable character as a declared anti-Ricardian, while being a critic of Say's Law as well. In 1828 he wrote to Say (in French), commenting on the fifth (1826) edition of his *Traité*:

> *... in which I find a number of very correct and well explained remarks on the doctrine of the late Mr. Ricardo.*

Mr. Ricardo was a very amiable and gallant man, who also had a great mind, but he has founded a system upon pure abstractions. He has constantly argued upon imaginary data and not upon truthful foundations, and therefore his conclusions are almost always denied by experience.

His sectarians Messrs. Mill and McCulloch have carried his extraordinary opinions even further, without having directed these to any useful purpose. They do not represent the state of things as they are, but as they would have been if their data had been correct; *which is rarely the case.*

Cazenove continued by enumerating six 'wrong opinions' from Ricardo's labour theory of value, after which he concluded:

Nevertheless these are the opinions of the Professor who will occupy the Chair of Political Economy at the University of London and who unfortunately does not lack followers of his sect even in our society (Political Economy Club) which has the honour of counting you among its Members. But justice must be given to our Society. Everyday it becomes less Ricardian and little by little it returns to just principles.

It is much to be desired that those who adhere to the School of Adam Smith (like you, Mr. Malthus, Mr Sismondi etc.) unite as much as possible to bring forward the true principles, to reveal what is false and to prevent that a pure system will occupy the place of true philosophy.[28]

Of course the unnamed Ricardian professor was McCulloch. The letter ended with some critical and some laudatory remarks on Say's theory of value. For Cazenove, Say was 'essentially in agreement with Adam Smith'. His concluding sentence was: 'It is absolutely necessary to combat the Ricardian School, and I hope that your new work will not grant him any honour.'

Altogether Say's correspondence with English and Scottish economists of the first and second rank clearly proves that his was a household name to many if not all of them, both as an economist of great repute, and as a figurehead of the anti-Ricardian school.

Failed *Académicien*

From his *Décade* editorship till the end of his life, Say remained true to the Idéologie programme of the unity of sciences. He was aware of the recent advances in the natural sciences, and saw his own research as part of comparable steps ahead in social science. Membership of the Institut or of its most prominent successor, the Académie Française, seemed a logical consequence for someone with his reputation and network.

Of course it was a handicap for him that Napoleon had abolished the second class, of the moral and political sciences, of the Institut. But the literary merits of his writings were such that a membership of another class was certainly not impossible. For many years he had been moving in literary circles and salons, and a number of his friends belonged to the ranks of the Immortals.

Perhaps, in spite of his well-established reputation, he was socially and politically too controversial to be admitted into the highest academic circles. We have seen that the first letter demonstrating his interest in becoming a member of the Institut was written in 1814, accompanying a complimentary copy of the second edition of his *Traité*. Then he was still modest enough to aspire only to a membership of the Third Class, of History and Ancient Literature. In 1816, Louis XVIII officially reinstalled the Second Class, of French Literature, with its forty 'Immortal' members, as the Académie Française.

In the 1820s, with Say's national and international reputation firmly established, the time seemed ripe for another move in this direction. To Baron Cuvier, the famous naturalist and an Academy member since 1818, he sent a copy of his fifth edition in October 1826:

> If my style is noteworthy by a certain purity and lucidity, and a degree of elegance and warmth which comes with scientific matters, this is perhaps partly caused by studying your writings, as I found deeper thoughts in your eulogies than in those of [the Cartesian author] Fontenelle. These motives will be the foundation of my Discourse of acceptation, if ever I might experience the honour of being seated at your side.
>
> In soliciting election to the Academy, I have not addressed myself to any *cotterie*; in the academy I have only noticed eminent writers of various talents, and only members whom I suppose to be eager to augment the glory of the body they belong to, and to make choices that will be approved in France and abroad; my esteem of them is high enough to attribute to them the most perfect independence. On this title I am asking for your vote, if you find me worthy of it.[29]

Cuvier's reply to this quite hypocritical epistle is unknown. But a letter from his old colleague in the Tribunat, Pierre Daru (1767–1829), who as a general, politician and historian had shown a better political survival instinct than Say, gave him little hope as it was very clear about the influence of royal circles on the election of new members. Daru himself posed as an outsider:

> *We countrymen, we don't allow ourselves to get mixed up in politics ...*
>
> *But for the majority [of the voters], my answer is that it will be very compact, I mean very docile. That is one of the great advantages of the absolute monarchy, for which you authors perhaps do not demonstrate all the respect which it deserves. My conclusion therefore is that in order to reach your goal, you must put your energy into obtaining the votes of the high powers which distribute the seats.[30]*

Daru wrote in November 1826. Andrieux, himself a member since 1803, wrote to him in December, with thanks for a complimentary copy of the *Traité*'s fifth edition. He also mentioned the death of their old *Décade* colleague Toscan. Being of the same generation as the latter, he predicted that Say would soon receive his own notice of decease:

> *I would like that you would not just receive this as my friend, but even more as my confrère at the Académie. I don't know what we will do on Thursday. I would wish that our society would be inspired enough to feel that it needs names which confer honour to it, and that Literature is not just a frivolous art, but an instrument to be applied to all elevated and useful purposes.*[31]

Neither of Andrieux' expectations was fulfilled. Not only did he survive his friend by one year, but also his desire to see him elected as a fellow *Académicien* did not come true.

A last abortive effort by Say to join his friends in the Académie was launched with the publication of his *Cours Complet* in 1828–1830. As soon as Volume I had come out, he sent a copy of it to the Academy's secretary, and continued to do the same for the other five.[32] Judging by the number of letters thanking for complimentary copies, he must have sent the volumes to all or practically all Immortals, thus taking to heart Daru's advice about canvassing individual members.

How directly – not to say shamelessly – he applied for membership, is demonstrated by a copy of the letter he wrote to the *Académicien* F.J.M. Raynouard in November 1829, accompanying a copy of the fifth volume of the *Cours Complet*:

> *I have the honour to present specifically to you my Cours complet d'Economie politique which I have already presented to the Académie française as a body, in the order by which the volumes have been published. The printing of the sixth and last volume will be achieved before the end of this year, and I will have the privilege to present this to you as well.*
>
> *I will not hide from you, monsieur, that one of the principal driving forces of my labours has been the hope of obtaining, from the natural protectors of literature, a crown not less honourable for those who award it, than for him who obtains it. Perhaps they will judge that a book in which on every page the love of humanity, the necessity of order and the respect of property rights is taught, a book in which the author demonstrates that the interest properly understood of all peoples, in conformity with their duties, is not at all contrary to public morals, and can have an influence which other rules, however prizeworthy these may be elsewhere, cannot obtain. The work is important by its subject matter and by its scope, and in this respect at least worthy of the Body which is requested to judge it.*
>
> *After the honour of having been admitted into the ranks of so many illustrious académiciens, nothing can flatter the ambition of the author so much as the radiance of their rewards.*[33]

Apparently he could not wait to post this letter till the sixth and last volume was published. Raynouard wrote back promptly, assuring him that 'fully aware of the importance of the special subject to which you have devoted your life and your talent, I will not be among the last to pay full justice to your devotion and successes'.

In Say's correspondence, beside Andrieux', Daru's and Raynouard's letters, thanks for *Cours Complet* copies have been preserved from the Academy members Briffaut, Coquebert de Montbret, de Féletz, Lacretelle,[34] Lainé, the Duc de Levis and Royer-Collard. The *Académicien* Laplace thanked him in 1826 for a copy of the *Traité*. Guizot, who was to be Destutt de Tracy's Academy successor in 1836, received a copy of the *Cours Complet* in his capacity of founder and editor of the *Revue Française*, which promptly signalled the book as it came out.

In the years 1828–1829 his old friend Andrieux, as Permanent Secretary of the body of Immortals, became ever more apologising about the voting of his colleagues, and about his own modest role in this process. He kept repeating that literature was a *means* and not a *goal* by itself; that the talents of speaking and writing were nothing, if not applied to 'teach the people what is most important for them to know, and to combat easy pleasures and vulgar truths'. This he wrote early in 1828; in September of the following year, he wrote that Say's *Cours Complet* put him in a high rank 'among the Scholars of political economy'. (Unfortunately not among the literati, he seemed to imply.) In the same letter he told Say, who apparently had asked if he could share his loge in the Opera, that he was only occasionally invited to use the seats there of Alexandre Duval, Amaury Duval's brother, an Academy member and secretary to its reading jury. He concluded the letter by referring again to Say's possible membership:

> *The death of Mr. Daru is a great loss to the Academy. He was a man of rare merit. You have already been in the ranks to join us; you might still be seated there, and certainly I would with great pleasure see you* intrare in nostro corpore, *as some say. But I cannot tell you if you would have many supporters. By nature I am not a* leader; *I only wish that our Academy does not allow itself to be led, and certainly not to be thwarted.*

The implicit message was clear: the 'high powers' to which Daru had referred in 1826 still determined the vote three years later. In the revolutionary month of July 1830, Andrieux wrote that the selection committee was 'of the best disposition with regard to your work'. For reasons of health, Say had left Paris to stay in the countryside with his brother Louis. Andrieux did not expect the vote to take place before August, and advised that Say's attendance at the session might be useful.[35] Whether or not he effectively did attend this meeting, it was of no avail.

It would take two more years before the old Second Class of the Institut, abolished by Napoleon, would be revived as 'Académie des Sciences morales et politiques' in October 1832. Guizot, as minister of public instruction under the new King Louis Philippe, wrote in his advice for its new founding:

> The moral and political sciences directly influence among us the fate of society, they rapidly modify the laws and the manners. It may be said that since half a century, they have played a role in our history. For the first time they have acquired what they were always lacking, a truly scientific character.

The five sections of the new Académie were: (1) Philosophy; (2) Morals; (3) Legislation, public law and jurisprudence; (4) Political economy and statistics; and (5) General and philosophical history. For Say personally, its revival, one month before his death, came too late. If he had read Guizot's advice, he might wryly have.concluded that both as an Idéologue and as a political economist, he had contributed a lot to establishing the 'truly scientific character' of the moral and political sciences.

Collège de France

Towards the end of his life, one more academic mark of honour would be bestowed on Say. If the July Revolution of 1830 came too late for him to enable an Academy membership, it did create an atmosphere that would allow the establishing of a new political economy chair at the Collège de France.

With the publication of his six-volume *Cours Complet d'Economie Politique Pratique*, his economic legacy was completed. It was published by the bookseller-publisher Rapilly in an edition of 2300 copies, between April 1828 and December 1829. Within three months from the publication of Vol. 1, 700 copies had been sold.[36] But for December 1829, Say's only comment in his *Acta* concerned the illnes of his wife, who was nursed at home by a neighbour's wife. He was rightly worried about her condition, as she died on 10 January 1830. For once his beautiful round handwriting let him down as he noted almost illegibly: 'Saddest day of my life. I lose my wife.' Later he added in his normal hand: 'The sixth volume of my Cours Complet is published on December 31, and hereby my dear wife is visibly satisfied.'[37] She did not live to see the culminating point of her husband's career.

The July Revolution, which made John Stuart Mill travel to Paris in a hurry, was witnessed from a distance by Say and his daughter Octavie, who were staying with Louis Say in Nantes.[38] Already two months later, on 29 September, Say was invited to dinner by the new 'Citizen King'. And three days later he presented his *Cours Complet* to the crown prince.[39]

We do not know whether Say had been effectively lobbying with the king for the institution of a new political economy chair at the Collège de France. This institution, founded in 1530, was – and still is – primarily a research institute, where the professors also read public lectures. At any rate, the dossier at the ministry about the new chair contains a reference to a royal comment on the teaching of political economy in France and other European countries. However, the earliest mention of such an initiative is a letter by three Parisian law students, named Gros, Lombard and Lacombe, dated 11 November 1830. Pretending to speak on behalf of their fellow students, they asked for the institution of an economics chair at the Collège 'in view of the future promised to the French by our beautiful July revolution'. In a letter of 3 December, they were told that the matter was already under consideration with the professors of the Collège. On 16 November, the ministerial letter asking the professorial advice had been dispatched:

A number of persons, choosing for their argument a paragraph from a Royal speech with respect to the teaching of political economy in France, and otherwise referring to the development this science receives in England, in Germany, in Russia, in Poland, and even in Spain, have proposed to me the creation of a chair of political economy at the Collège Royal de France.[40]

The committee of professors reported on 6 December: 'Today there is no longer any doubt about the usefulness which the teaching of political economy can deliver.' Its advice was that economics and law must be taught in the programme of the 'second degree', after mathematics and physics. According to the professors, the Collège was eminently equipped for this purpose, as it was the highest institute of public instruction, not subjected to conditions from outside, in the service of the young and the elderly, of private persons and civil servants alike.[41]

The professors did not suggest the name of a candidate for the new chair. A draft note bearing the name of Adolphe Blanqui as a potential candidate is among the papers in the ministerial files, but the Royal Decree of 3 March 1831, was clear in its first article: 'A chair of Political Economy is created at the Collège de France. Mr. Jean-Baptiste Say is nominated as Professor of this science.'[42]

Say himself mentioned his appointment in his *Acta* on 16 March, the day it was published in the newspapers. One week later he experienced again one of his fits of 'apoplexy'; in 1830 he had suffered three of them. Already on 31 March he attended the first meeting of Collège professors; his old *Décade* colleague Andrieux was one of them. Also among his twenty-five colleagues were Cuvier, Ampère and Champollion. Say's annual salary was 5000 F, the same as at the Conservatoire. The first monthly payment came in December, so in total he received exactly one year's salary. But already in June 1831 he had given his first lecture, 'well attended and well applauded'.[43]

He still occupied his chair at the Conservatoire. He noted that as from 6 December 1831, his lectures there were read from his notes by a Monsieur de Mersand. This conveys the impression that he no longer cared much about this job. But as late as November 1830 he had still acted as a prophet of the age of steam, by recommending the purchase of models of steamships and 'of iron tracks along which steam engines move forward with great rapidity'. In February 1832 he was one of the authors of a report on *Ecoles d'Arts et Métiers*, in which the founding of ten professional schools in the French provinces was proposed for the education of manufacturing foremen (*chefs-ouvriers*). On 5 November he attended a session of the Conservatoire's Conseil de Perfectionnement. He intended to resume his course on 4 December 1832.

Say's last comment in his *Acta* concerned the death of Madame Ginguené, on 14 October. Exactly one month later he suffered a fit of apoplexy, the third one of 1832. In the evening his son Horace came to see him, while he underwent a blood-letting. Then he had already lost conscience, and he died at half past one in the afternoon of 15 November. The last sentences in his *Acta* were written by

Horace: *He had been aware that he commenced to feel unwell, but otherwise he had no premonition that his passing away was near.*

Say was buried in the Père Lachaise cemetery, where his modest tombstone and the one of his wife were later integrated into the massive monument of his grandson, the colourful French member of parliament, Edgar Raoul-Duval (the son of Octavie Say). The friendly family relationships – and the small amount of Say's fortune to be divided – enabled a rapid handling of the inheritance. This was settled within a month, and signed on 14 December 1832. Say did not own the house he lived in. His furniture was split in four *à l'amiable* among his two sons and two daughters. A Colombian loan was administrated in London by George Grote, who sold it on behalf of the heirs. The firm of Horace Say managed securities worth around 17,000 F. The bridal trousseaus and dowries of Andrienne and Octavie had been worth 11,000 F each. Half of this sum had been compensated to their brothers after the death of Mme Say, so now they both received another 5500 F. A final payment of 1547.93 F was made to all four children.[44] Just this meagre sum had remained as the estate of the greatest French classical economist.

The four heirs appointed Andrienne Say's husband, Charles Comte, as executor of Say's writings, *in their own interest as well as in obeyance of the often and expressly formulated intentions of their father and father-in-law.* He would be free to decide about possible reprints of Say's books and new editions of his manuscripts. Of the latter he was to receive half of the revenue, and of the former one-fifth.

The nomination of the successors to his chairs took a much longer period. One applicant for the Conservatoire chair was Monsieur Demersant – most probably the de Mersand who had been reading his lectures for Say towards the end of his life. But the successful candidate was Adolphe Blanqui, who first attended a meeting of the Conseil de Perfectionnement in May 1834.

At the Collège de France, the council of professors proposed the installation of Pellegrino Rossi in July 1833. But the minister of public education also asked the advice of the Académie des Sciences Morales et Politiques, which suggested the name of Charles Comte on 12 August. Two days later, Rossi was appointed. Already before this date Comte had asked for annulment of Rossi's candidature, on the grounds of his Genevan citizenship, of his membership of the cantonal council, and of numerous articles of the law. His objections were of no avail, and he had to content himself with treading in the footsteps of his father-in-law as the editor of his posthumous works only.[45]

As an introduction to the posthumous edition of the *Cours Complet*, Comte wrote a historical report on the life and works of his father-in-law, which he concluded with the following remarks on his character:

Monsieur Say, who has ever since 1789 pronounced himself in favour of the cause of liberty, and who served it by all means within his powers, has remained faithful to his principles till the very end of his career; nothing in the world could have let him decide to associate his name with measures disapproved by his conscience ...

A stranger to all cliques, he occupied himself with his science and lived enclosed in a circle composed of a small number of friends and of his family members.

These statements of an admiring son-in-law of course have the somewhat hagiographic flavour of an obituary written not long after the passing away of its subject. In view however of Jean-Baptiste Say's documented legacy, his appraisals of other people, and the many sympathetic comments on his character by others, we may rightly conclude that Comte's praising assessment has stood the test of two centuries.

An unfinished agenda

As an economist, Say had said all he wanted to say. But he had not yet completed his research agenda. In the introduction to his *Catéchisme*, he had defined the object of study of political economy:

> Political economy is not political science; it neither occupies itself with the distribution of powers, nor with their division; it teaches us how nations acquire their means of subsistence. In other words, how these things are due to the efforts of private persons; as these persons are primarily those who also enjoy these things, political economy must not be considered as exclusively the business of statesmen; it is everybody's business.[46]

Separating economics and politics – for which he had already given Adam Smith the credits in 1803 – did not mean to Say that he was not interested in political science.

After the publication of his 'grand cours' – as he often referred to the *Cours Complet* – his writing agenda still included the project of a *politique pratique*: a textbook of political theory. A voluminous dossier of around a thousand notes, loosely classified in three books-to-be, subdivided into sixty-seven chapters, is among his papers in the Bibliothèque Nationale. The planned books were: I, *On the nature of societies*; II, *On the relations between families and the social body, or the social organization*; III, *On the relations of the social bodies between one another*.[47] It will be the task of modern political theorists to judge whether Say's manuscript notes are a coherent elementary skeleton of an original book, or just a number of side-remarks to his economics.

In this respect, the most important subject is perhaps Say's notion of spontaneous order.

Il mondo va da se, 'the world turns by itself', is a motto quoted approvingly under the envisaged chapter title: *Nations are functioning on their own, not by the steering of a government (which is just a class of society)*. Authors cited range from Aristotle and Machiavel to Jeremy Bentham and Benjamin Constant.

Just as in his economics, Say reminded himself of his positivist approach by describing his project of 'practical politics' (elsewhere also labelled by him as 'experimental politics') as 'a description of what is, with regard to the social organisation':

> *If I ever get around to completing my* Essay *of practical politics, I believe that a well readable format would be, after having made clear my position, and not letting myself get off my path, to compose the work in quite brief chapters, with titles bearing question marks. For example:*
>
> • *What is the advantage of the division of powers?*
> • *Are there circumstances in which the liberty of the press, or even of speech, may be suppressed?*
>
> *This is Machiavel's method, but what he did with a bad purpose must be done with a good one.*

Say intended to include his *Essay* on the principle of utility in his treatise of politics:

> *In political Economy one can consider utility as a fact, and the study of its principle is useless. The value of each good indicates the utility it has for man, the good he derives from its use.*
>
> *In politics, the value of public services is not subjected to free competition, but fixed according to other considerations; it is necessary to have other means for assessing their real utility. In general, in order to know whether the public is not paying too much in sacrificing for the good it derives, it is necessary to have a measure to appreciate this good.*
>
> *Two hundred thousand men are sent into a war that will cost five hundred millions. We cannot estimate the utility which the public will derive from this war, but after the grand total of this sacrifice. One must therefore be able to measure this by itself. This brings the necessity to develop what is the foundation of utility: the principle of utility. See my second course at the athénée, sessions 4 and 5.*[48]

It is clear that Say wished to extend an economic cost-benefit analysis into the domain of politics. And his example of a war is reminiscent of his biting comments on Bonaparte's human sacrifices on the battlefield.

Say's concept of statistics can be said to be part of his completed research agenda. Already in 1803, in the introduction to his *Traité*, Say had sketched the importance of statistics for economics. In 1827 he wrote an article on the subject for the *Revue Encyclopédique*, which was also published as a separate pamphlet of twenty-seven pages.[49] And he came back to it in one of the concluding chapters of the *Cours Complet*.

In modern economics, statistics is closely linked with a quantitative approach and model building. Say pronounced himself against abstract models. But he was certainly ahead of many economists of his generation to whom statistics was just a kind of descriptive economic geography, like the German cameralist approach. Or in Say's own words: 'the physical description of a country, of its mountains, of its valleys, of specific circumstances to be found there, of the rivers irrigating it, and the seas flowing along its coasts'.[50] But to him this was just *géographie physique* and not *statistique*.

Say also wished to exclude the description of institutions from statistics. He pointed to the necessity of being selective in collecting only relevant statistical data, and of collecting them in such a way as to enable comparability and causality in time. Over longer periods, Say pointed at the problem of index numbers, especially in financial data from centuries apart. Among other data, those regarding imports and exports must be considered with mistrust.

Special attention is given in his article to population statistics, as could be expected from an economist who had established the close link between economic and population growth in his analysis of the law of markets. In this respect he mentioned Necker, who for policy reasons was very interested in birth statistics. And he quoted Malthus' doubts on the reliability of British birth statistics.

Approvingly he also quoted Lagrange and Lavoisier on their statistical computations: the former for deriving French population statistics from food consumption data, and the latter for computing the number of working horses in France, derived from the number of acres necessary to produce the quantity consumed of grain. In his conclusion about the simultaneous progress of statistics, the economy and civilisation, he equally praised his Athénée colleague Dupin, and the Academy member Daru he had courted for his vote to be admitted to this body:

> However imperfect today's means of collecting statistical documents may be, they can lead to important conclusions, witness those that have been drawn by Mr. Daru and Mr. Charles Dupin, who have arrived at determining in a brilliant way the intellectual and material advancement of France.[51]

In 1828 Say reviewed the *Statistics of the Kingdom of the Netherlands*, by the statistical pioneer Quetelet, for the *Revue Encyclopédique*.[52] From the higher birth statistics for the Belgian part than for the Hollandish part, he drew the conclusion that the South was more prosperous than the North. He explicitly mentioned that Quetelet himself had his doubts about the reliability of the population figures. Say quoted the author's conclusion that a higher birth rate and a lower death rate than in France must indicate a better administration: 'Effectively all reports from this country do confirm that therein liberty is much greater, industry is better protected, and the role of the clergy is less powerful.' Say's overall conclusion was Malthusian as well as Saysian: in the first place, the growth of population must mean that people earned incomes well above their basic needs. And, second, he saw the confirmation of 'the important truth that the surest means to multiply the population of a State, is to facilitate the multiplication of agricultural and industrial output, and to ensure a wise liberty that will guarantee public confidence'.

In his *Cours Complet*, Say would insert a ninth and last 'Part' of four statistical chapters. In the *Traité* of 1803, he had labelled the simple collection of data as 'the knowledge of a lower clerk'. From his remaining papers it is clear that he was a terrific data collector himself. He did practice what he preached: when people corrected his figures, he was eager to adapt these, without caring whether it was a French student or a foreign professor pointing to his incomplete or incorrect data. However, he warned against what we would call data mining: 'calculations that can go on indefinitely and which authors can perform, if they wish, in any way they like'.[53] In the final sentences of the pamphlet of 1827, Say noticed the augmentation of average life expectancy over the past two centuries in well-governed states; and he concluded that future statistics 'will give more precise and valuable ideas on this matter to our descendants'.[54]

Producer, consumer, citizen

Towards the end of his life, but before the publication of his *Cours Complet*, Say summarised his economics in two long articles in the *Encyclopédie Progressive* (1826) and the *Revue Encyclopédique* (1828). These make it abundantly clear that the Idéologue turned economist in 1800, still was an economist with an Ideological message thirty years later. The 1826 article is perhaps the clearest example of Say's long-term optimism.

It consists of fifty-seven pages of text (forty on economics and seventeen on its history), thirteen pages glossary and a bibliography of 150 authors on political economy, from the sixteenth century onwards, in French, English, Italian, and a few in Spanish and German. Some of the authors are briefly commented upon, most with praise, but some with derision. Say's friends James Mill, Francis Place and Thomas Tooke receive positive annotations, although Mill is 'perhaps a bit too abstract'.[55] Say's most abstract opponent Ricardo is strangely absent from the list, although his *Principles* and his conversations with Say are mentioned in the historical part of the text.

The complete article was clearly written for a general public; it follows Say's familiar division of production, distribution and consumption of wealth. Say's positivist methodology of observing 'facts' is his starting point, and very soon the Physiocrats and David Ricardo are attacked on their abstract systems. The Physiocrats are equally blamed for their misappreciation of high prices as an indication of wealth; Say repeats his familiar argument of falling prices as a sign of growth and progress. At the end, a fairly long section discusses economic and colonial policy. Low taxes, no trade barriers and an end to colonies are Say's recipes.

In the historical section, a remarkably favourable conclusion is drawn regarding the *économistes* of the school of Quesnay. However, this is consonant with the treatment in the introduction of the *Traité* (1803): while Say is critical of their method, he finds that their writings obey the strictest rules of morality, and of liberty. In 1826 Say mentions that during Adam Smith's stay in France, he often visited the salons frequented by Quesnay and his followers. Dupont de

Nemours had told Say that he had often met Smith there, who had not yet made his mark but was considered 'a judicious and simple man'.[56] Say credits the Physiocrats with having made real progress regarding the notions of wealth creation and economic growth. Their recommendations, with the exception of those on taxation, 'are nearly all favourable to the public good, to sound politics, and to good morals'.[57] Approvingly Say quotes their motto 'laissez faire et laissez passer'.

Two full pages are devoted to Smith's achievements – and to his shortcomings: 'The theory of commercial production has been forgotten, just as the theory of markets which makes the nations interested in progress between one another, and which will be the surest guarantee for the future of their reciprocal friendliness.'[58] If this wording is still a tolerable and amusing, indirect example of self-promotion, a sillier proof of this comes a bit later, after Say's settling of accounts with Bonaparte.[59] On Malthus, Say comments that this author has not applied his sound (but not original) ideas on population to a broader view of economic principles. And he continues:

> About the same time, in France a book was published which embraced all of these. This work, of which I may not speak, if I could leave it out of a historical summary of this subject, has perhaps contributed to giving economic studies a more methodical and more certain direction than the one which had been followed so far; only single chapters had been treated; there was not yet a Traité d'économie politique [a footnote tells that Steuart's work is only a treatise on the balance of payments]. A methodical arrangement of subjects has allowed to grasp them as a whole, to distinguish their mutual influences, and to estimate the degree of their importance. Since then, people are carrying an enlightened judgment of the operations of public authority, and to know what are the costs of the great experiments of which they always bear the burdens.[60]

Say's historical overview concludes with his comments on Ricardo, who in spite of following the path of Adam Smith, has too often neglected his excellent method, and 'replaced it by subtle arguments leading him to results which are not confirmed by the facts'.[61] And he illustrates this by a footnote referring to his conversations with Ricardo, in which the latter asked him to accept certain points of view *for the sake of argument.* One gets the impression that after Say's visit to London in 1825, and the publication of his fifth *Traité* edition in 1826, he felt self-confident enough to openly (and sometimes shamelessly) make this kind of self-promotional statement.

In the January 1828 issue of the *Revue Encyclopédique*, Say tried to sketch 'The influence of the future progress of economics upon the fate of nations'.[62] He took the perspective of the political philosopher, more than the one of the economist. After describing the past as the successive stages of barbarism and despotism, he developed an optimistic perspective of the future:

The social organisation will become more perfect to the extent in which, in modern societies, larger populations, more developed needs, more sophistic-ated interests, and the division of labour which results from these, will require that the care of supervising the general interests will become a pro-fession by itself. Representative government will be the only answer to the needs of societies; and this also, by offering the necessary guarantees and by opening the doors to desirable improvements, is a powerful instrument of prosperity. In the end it will be adopted everywhere; and if some nation will be backward enough not to adopt it, it will stay behind all others, like the lazy or clumsy walker clinging to the middle of a marching troop, and finding himself passed by and pushed aside by everybody.[63]

According to Say, a sound education in economics is also favourable to the administration of justice, and to good institutions in general. As we have seen, he had a lifelong interest in education in general – not just economic intruction. In chapter XXVII of his last great work, the *Cours Complet*, he discussed the advantages for society of promoting a general education for everybody. This would result in higher economic growth, but it must not be forgotten that a human being is more than just a producer and consumer:

A man is not only a producer and a consumer: in ordinary life he is a husband, father, son, brother, citizen. In order to fulfill all these roles with dignity, he needs specific parts of knowledge. As a citizen, he must prima-rily be aware of the interests of society. But this is not all. Enlightenment in general softens the habits, and prepares even the most disorderly characters to listen to the voice of reason, and follow the counsels of softness.[64]

Towards the end of his life Say still proclaimed his belief in education and progress, which he had already voiced in 1800 in *Olbie*. It may sound a bit naïve, but it is also decidedly sympathetic.

10 Among masters, peers and students

'I adore Adam Smith: he is my master'

Already in the first edition of his *Traité*, Say started with a historical introduction to his discipline. He distanced himself from the Physiocrats, and paid tribute to Adam Smith.

Both Smith and Say had been influenced by French eighteenth century philosophers and economists. During his travels in France Smith had met Rousseau, Turgot and Quesnay personally. He had even contemplated dedicating the *Wealth of Nations* to the latter. Peter Groenewegen has written about the 'French Connection' in the making of economics as a science, as the third quarter of the eighteenth century saw the most prolific output of economic writings in France.[1] Philippe Steiner has produced a delightful little book on Quesnay and the French roots of the 'new science' of political economy. He includes a chapter on the economic analysis of the natural order, a concept which is also a feature of Say's economic and political thought.[2] Therefore it is a remarkable puzzle in the history of ideas that Say acknowledged so much of an influence from Adam Smith, and notably less from the French predecessors he shared with him. The same can be said of Say's reverence for Jeremy Bentham as the inspirator of his own utilitarianism, and of Malthus with regard to his ideas on population. At any rate the ideas of the Scottish and the British philosophers fell upon fertile ground with the Frenchman. Seeking for a possible explanation, one might – very hypothetically – interpret Say's lack of an extended formal education as one of the causes.

Say's manuscript notes commenting on the *Wealth of Nations* start with a critical comment on the first sentence of Smith's introduction: 'The annual labour of every nation is the fund which originally supplies it with all the necessaries and conveniences of life.'

He interprets this as a pure labour theory of value and annotates: 'I believe this is an error.'[3] A recurrent theme is his criticism of Smith's composition of his work, and of his rhetoric. Thus he complains about 'disproportionally long digressions', and even notes: 'One is always amazed that such an excellent brain as Smith's puts so much truth and so little order in his ideas.'[4] In 1803 he would keep most of his criticisms of substance to himself. Only in 1814, when he had already established for himself a reputation as the Scotsman's vulgariser, did he put his critical own ideas on value and other subjects into print. In a manuscript note for his own use, he reacted to a review in 'an English journal', which apparently accused him of being just a Smithian, as follows:

> *Those who have accused me of only having made Smith's principles more clear, have given me praise by this comment only which I do appreciate, but they have not rendered me justice. I think I have studied Smith as much as they have & I have not found explained the phenomenon of production and of consumption, which is nevertheless the foundation of all political economy. Once the principles upon which this phenomenon is founded, the development of the relations with the various professions, with the laws and habits of a society, have been well conceived, those* [principles] *only can enable us to resolve the problems we confront when we want to govern well our family or the state. And the ability to solve those problems constitutes the science.*
>
> *Although the book on the Wealth of Nations contains a large number of the elements of this science & in this respect has been enormously useful, it establishes it so little, that although it has been read and studied for thirty years by very capable men, it has not treated one question on which there is agreement, even today, which I attribute to the fact that it has not linked them to a complete system, & that he did not have this himself, whatever merit I otherwise recognise in his work.*[5]

In spite of his criticism, Say always kept referring to Smith as his master, and as a touchstone of sound reasoning and exemplary scholarship. Whether he was combating the objectivist Ricardians, or castigating his super-subjectivist brother Louis, he did not hesitate to present himself as Smith's true heir regarding method. In 1822 he thanked John Cowell, the secretary of the Political Economy Club, for admitting him, a foreigner, as an associate member. In the same letter he proposed that the Society should pronounce its veneration and gratitude for Adam Smith, 'whose writings have shown us the true way of observing matters in political economy'.[6] (This is one of the few pieces of evidence that can be interpreted as an indirect action by Say in his 'Methodenstreit' with Ricardo, in order to put himself in the front ranks of the anti-Ricardians.)

Just one day earlier he had written to his brother Louis about the latter's book *Considérations sur l'Industrie*, in which he had written that Smith had 'extraordinarily retarded' the development of political economy. Jean-Baptiste admonished him that he had made many people, including himself, very sad by his inconsiderate attacks. And when Louis had sent him his new book in 1827, he again threw upon him the example of the Glasgow professor:

> *For thirty-eight years I have studied Political economy, that means from the time when I was Clavière's secretary, before he became a minister: he owned a copy of Smith which he studied frequently; I read a few pages*

which struck me, and as soon as I could I ordered a copy which I still have. Since then, every time I have come to an opinion different from one of the authors of great judgement, I have trembled to be mistaken; I have made new efforts on the topic, and almost always I have found I was wrong. I believe you have read too superficially, for it is reading superficially only in order to find, not the intimate meaning of the author and his motives, but to read only in order to criticise him where he distances himself from our idée fixe.[7]

Regarding method, Smith was (almost) Say's ideal scholar. But in their views on the individual as economic agent, the two economists held different opinions. For the eighteenth century philosopher Smith, the model economic agent *and* citizen was still a 'virtuous' individual, with a martial spirit as one of his characteristics. The nineteenth century economist Say, like his contemporary David Ricardo, must be classified among the peace-loving economists. On several occasions he pronounced his disgust of Bonaparte's waste of human lives on the battlefield. His economic agent is a utility-maximising individual, whose tastes and values are his own business. Still his model citizen is a *virtuous* republican, and a member of the *classe mitoyenne*. The economist Say, while granting the economic agent his own utility function, had not entirely thrown away his eighteenth century baggage; he had his own ideas on what was *really* useful. Writing an *Essai sur le principe d'utilité* towards the end of his life, he did not hesitate to pronounce his own value judgements on this subject. He still denounced waste and luxury just as much as he had done twenty-five years before in his *Olbie*. This ambivalence is reflected in the subtitle chosen by Evelyn Forget for her book on Say's economics: 'markets and virtue'.

Smith is one of the three economists mentioned in an undated note Say wrote about the steps forward in economics which, in his opinion, were due to him:

> *Advances in Political Economy to my credit*
> *The theory of production costs, the reduction of which means an increase of riches for a nation ...*
> *The theory of commercial production, almost captured by Verri, has been brought to full understanding by J.B.Say.*
> *This theory is no less important than the one of the débouchés, the only one for which Ricardo gives me credit.*
> *I dare flatter myself that there is no important idea in Smith which I have not discussed in new light, or questioned if that seemed worthwhile to me.*[8]

The first three of three notions might be rephrased and (benevolently) supplemented as follows.

- Say has improved the analysis of the microfoundations of economic growth: the combined effects of the division of labour and of technical change will lead to lower cost prices, to lower market prices, and thereby to greater welfare.

- Say has defined 'immaterial production' better than his predecessors, and in particular the value added in commerce.
- Say's Law, as defined from 1814, i.e. the long-term equilibrium between supply and demand, is indeed Say's own law.

Regarding the fourth it is clear that from the beginning till the end, for Say the ideas of Adam Smith were an important touchstone in economics.

Jeremy Bentham (1750–1832) was another of the few thinkers recognised by Say as superior minds. He was Say's senior by seventeen years. From their correspondence it is quite clear that Bentham took Say seriously. Friendship is not a notion one would particularly associate with the philosopher of Queen's Square Place. But perhaps their relationship might be qualified as a respectful mutual understanding.

Their first meeting in 1814 has already been described. Just before he sailed for England, he had thanked Etienne Dumont, Bentham's French codifier in Geneva, for a copy of the *Théorie des Peines et des Récompenses*: 'Correct ideas, new and useful, a style remarkable by its clarity, precision, and force. What more can one wish?'[9] Already as *Décade* editor, or perhaps even as a staff member of the *Courrier de Provence*, Say must have been familiar with Bentham's ideas and publications which were reviewed in these journals.[10] And just before his departure to England – also before meeting Bentham personally – he had stepped forward as a convert to his philosophy in his review of the *Peines et Récompenses* in the *Mercure de France*.[11] After praising Dumont for his editorial work, he defended Bentham against the objection of being too theoretical:

> I do not believe it is possible to entirely subordinate practice to the rules derived from the law and the nature of things, but these rules are a model which one forever strives approaching, even without ever attaining it; and otherwise, who knows what the future will make possible? It is always good to have a standard, a shining beacon, whether or not it can be reached.

And after having met the philosopher himself, he asked Dumont in 1816 to be mentioned in one of his letters to him as 'one of his faithful disciples'.[12] In 1817 he wrote to Dumont again: 'In my small sphere I have made efforts that some justice be rendered to our great Bentham and his worthy interpreter.' This referred to his article in the *Censeur Européen* on Bentham's *Plan of parliamentary Reform* (also published separately as a pamphlet) and his review of *Tactique des Assemblées Législatives* in the same journal.

Say's efforts to procure a better reading lens for Bentham, and his request to him for helping the Comtes, demonstrate that not only political and utilitarian matters, but practical problems as well were discussed between them. However for Bentham substance always went before household affairs, as he wrote:

> *For mere letters of kindness we have neither of us any time. For letters about politics from me to you, there is no use. Why? Because here there is*

everything being published in a sense freely, there is no dessous des cartes,
*or at least none which you would care about. The opportunity being first
rate secure, I would have been very grateful for a short view of the state of
public opinion in Paris. You gave me nothing at all; and Swediaur nothing
about that.*[13]

In 1818 he wrote to Say that he was making converts in the House of Commons:
'The Whigs are falling off from one another, and sinking lower and lower every
day.' But this was not what Say observed in 1825, when he visited the House of
Commons with Francis Place and noticed the hostility towards the latter. There
is no reference to a meeting between Bentham and Say during this visit.

In October 1823 Bentham had given his opinion of Ricardo in the letter in
which he thanked Say for his obituary of the latter:

> *Coulson in the Globe-and-Traveller said that on morals and politics he
> had taken his principles from me: which through the medium of Mill
> was exactly true. Till he knew Mill he was not distinguishable from other
> Stockjobbers. Mill egged him on till he made him get into Parliament:
> purchase money £ 4000 of the Earl of Portarlington the borough for which
> he sat.*
>
> *A propos of a certain work, not a syllable is there in it which I did not
> think. I never on any occasion in my life said any thing I did not think: and
> scarce any thing out of print. But assuredly on that occasion I did not say
> all I thought. What use would there be in it.*[14]

This judgement surely must have strengthened Say in his efforts to belittle Ricardo's merits. It is also clear that he saw himself as a Benthamite of some kind.
We have seen that he surely was a utility economist. Was he a utilitarian economist as well? The older Say still could not completely restrict himself to the
viewpoint of the political economist, who only observed the subjective utility
judgements of the individual agents and their subsequent economic behaviour.
As a moral and political scholar (and still an Idéologue as well), he wished to
pronounce a judgement on what could be considered as really useful. The Say
papers show that already in his Athénée course of 1819 he made the same distinction.[15] In another, undated manuscript note he reminded himself to write an
essay *Du principe d'utilité*:

> *In political economy I regard utility as a given fact, the foundation of which
> I do not examine. In this work I examine the use and the real advantage we
> draw from the goods we use.*
>
> *In pol. econ. I examine the price we fix for a good. Here I examine
> whether we have a reason to fix a price for it. Yes for a healthy nourish-
> ment. No for the satisfaction of a harmful luxury snack. Yes for what pro-
> duces a real and durable good; no for what brings harm directly or after a
> while.*[16]

Some would call this paternalism; others might interpret it as utilitarianism. When Say finally got around to writing his essay on utility, Bentham was credited in the first explanatory footnote: 'The *Principle of Utility*, clearly defined by Jeremy Bentham in his *Traités de Législation* has, by lack of clear understanding, given occasion to exaggerated statements and disagreeable accusations.'

This *Essai sur le Principe de l'Utilité*, written after the completion of his *Cours Complet* in 1829, and posthumously published in the *Mélanges et Correspondance* (ed. Charles Comte and Horace Say) is divided in three sections of rather unbalanced length.[17] The themes and examples dispersed in the essay illustrate that the mature Say still held the ideas of the young revolutionary defending the freedom of the press. It is highly probable that Say composed the essay after trying in vain to have Dumont write a chapter on the subject in the sixth and last volume of his *Cours Complet* which, according to Say 'is just a long application of the principle of utility'.[18] At first Dumont wholeheartedly agreed to this proposal, to Say's great enjoyment:

> Utility is the purpose of human action, and after having considered it in the whole of my book as a given quantity, it would be a good idea to make people acquainted with its nature and principle. And in this analysis I could not find any guides more certain than Bentham and You.[19]

But in July 1829 Dumont wrote that to his great regret, he would need a much longer time to write the chapter and therefore abandoned the project. Two months later he died on a trip to Italy. The sixth volume of the *Cours* was published on 31 December. Thereafter Say tried to write the planned chapter himself, and he intended to integrate it into his unfinished political science manuscript.

Section I of his essay explains that economics is a social science, so he is not interested in Robinson Crusoe economics. In economic matters, every man is the best judge of his own preferences, but Say invents a seemingly ingenious step to bridge the gap between economic and moral reasoning:

> But man as a social being, who measures his estimation of goods by the greater or lesser amount of utility they have to man, i.e. his measure of the greatest good for the greatest number, is eminently virtuous; and I will add that if he only employs to that purpose the means which are compatible with the nature of the people who surround him and of the society to which he belongs, his principles not only display a respectable sentiment, but do conduct towards the truest and most durable good for mankind, or for his country, or for himself.

He does not suggest a measure for the proposed 'compatibility with the nature of the people and of society', but restricts himself to giving a number of examples, and concludes that a house is a more useful object than an ornament like a ring – he wisely avoids listing the market price of both. But if another person prefers the ring to the house, that is all right with Say. So he fails to provide an *ex ante* yardstick for measuring his *true* utility.

He continues with a discussion of Bentham and his pleasure/pain and utility analysis. But instead of providing us with an instrument for making choices between conflicting interests, he refers to Bentham's catalogue of pleasures and pains in the *Traités de Législation*. Say also follows him in the equal repudiation of ascetism and of arbitrariness. Religious ascetism is condemned: 'Regarding the ascetism of the cloisters, those who practice it in good faith seem tormented by idle ordeals; they are fleeing from an imaginary evil pursuing them.' And if each arbitrary opinion would be worth the same, 'there would not be any rule for the decency of behaviour'.

In section II Say defends utilitarianism against the charge of being no more than epicurism. Surprisingly, he also attacks Mme de Staël, otherwise a partner in the liberal camp, on her 'praise of the useless' in the novel *Corinne*.

In section III the question is asked if error can be of any use. Say begins by stating the importance of a free press, by which all good and bad consequences of possible measures can be discussed. Mme de Staël receives another reproach for her 'tenderness towards the useless'. Then follows a lengthy quotation from Sismondi's *History of the Republics of Italy*, as an introduction to Say's condemning of the role of the church in Italy, and more generally of the role of institutions favouring a minority at the expense of the many. Say might disagree with Sismondi on the law of markets, on religion and on bad institutions they shared the same opinions. Say linked these to the principle of utility:

> Pain and injustice (which is another pain) are directly opposed to the objective one wishes to realise by following the principle of utility.
>
> When the good produced by an institution (like wealth and power) is only enjoyed by a class of small number in society, and when the pain produced by the same institution (like expenses, idleness, wrong judgment, and deterioration of morals) falls upon the largest class, the result will be misery, depopulation, degradation of national character, etc.

In this paragraph, Say is not only speaking as an economist, but equally as the would-be political theorist who planned to write a political treatise. As an economist, he had not got any further than his comment in a letter to Malthus of July 1827, when he gave the example of the 'useless' production of trash and superfluities: 'As moralists, you and I may condemn this production and consumption; but as economist we must consider these as real.'[20]

Say was a Benthamite indeed; he was active in spreading the utilitarian gospel, but he added little to the ideas of the master. Yet his essay on utility reveals that he had remained true to the fundamental beliefs he embraced at the beginning of his career: freedom of the press, the rule of law, solid manners and institutions, and no role for the church in public life.

'It is absolutuely necessary to combat the Ricardian School'

Among Say's contacts with his contemporaries the names of Ricardo, Malthus and Sismondi stand out as the most prominent. With all of them he disagreed on one or more theoretical issues. Nevertheless he always entertained a friendly relationship with them, and on the whole he always mentioned their names respectfully. For the category of lesser known economists and other people of his generation or younger, he did not always have the same patience and consideration. For example, he expressed himself contemptuously about his first English translator Prinsep.

Regarding schools in economic thought, he considered himself as 'no longer belonging to any school' as he wrote in the first *Letter to Malthus*.[21] Still he saw himself as a worthy follower of Adam Smith, continuing on the positivist, inductive research programme of the Scotsman. The deductive, hypothetical reasoning which he also recognised in the *Wealth of Nations*, was for Say an example of 'system building', a practice he condemned equally in the Physiocrats and in Ricardo and his followers. Some of his contemporaries, like John Cazenove who wrote to him about the necessity of 'combating the Ricardian School', may have seen Say as the figurehead of the anti-Ricardians. For Say himself it was certainly flattering to be approached in this way, but it did not change his attitude.

He remained the patient teacher of economic liberty, with a keen eye for institutions and the role of the entrepreneur. He must have been confirmed in the correctness of his approach by the large number of translations of his *Traité*, all of which had come about without his active commitment. He did not overtly pose as the head of a School. However, in his *Cours Complet*, commenting on Ricardo's theory of the profit rate, he disqualified it as being 'metaphysical political economy', and irrelevant in practice. And he distanced himself again firmly from the Ricardian school: 'This school is wrong in considering each principle far too absolutely; and after having pronounced it in the form of a theorem, also in drawing rigorous consequences from it, which are very often at odds with the facts.'[22]

As we have seen in the treatment of value and price, Ricardo was Say's tormentor. It is clear that in their discussions the Englishman was on the offensive, and the Frenchman on the defensive side. The latter was neither fluent enough in English (or rapid enough in conversation), nor assertive enough to translate their fundamental differences into simple statements like: 'You're an objectivist, and I'm a subjectivist in matters of value.' Or, regarding questions of distribution: 'You are with the capitalists, I am with the entrepreneurs.' But of course it is in the nature of paradigms that they are never discussed by their believers, and therefore we must try to better understand their authors or followers by ways of rational reconstruction. Here is my modest suggestion for such an exercise.

Between Ricardo and Say, the diverging *paradigms* regarding value were:

- Value is supply determined (Ricardo) vs. Value is demand and supply determined (Say).

The *problems* to be explained were:

- Variations in labour value and price (Ricardo) vs. Relationship between produced utility and market price (Say).

The different *approaches* from which they started were:

- Long-term cost price explains objective value (Ricardo) vs. Utility explains subjective value (Say).

And their *solutions* were:

- A complete real terms labour model (Ricardo) vs. An incomplete supply and demand model of (general) market equilibrium (Say).

If we grant to Say the merit of being closer to a neoclassical solution, we must equally criticise him for his omissions and mistakes. He excluded natural utility from his analysis. He always started from the concept of individual utility, translated it into an undetermined average utility in the market, but never arrived at the idea of marginal utility. And from the fourth edition of his *Traité* (1817) he got mixed up in wrongly adding the property dimension to the problem of value. So we can agree with Schumpeter (1954) that 'he invariably mismanaged his case in controversy by replying to criticism in a desultory manner'.[23]

Of his contacts with other prominent economists, those with Malthus were the most reserved ones. They corresponded, but nothing personal was ever exchanged between the reverend Malthus and the agnostic Say. In 1814 Ricardo wrote to Malthus that Say planned to see him before his departure for France, but no such meeting has been recorded. In 1820 the *Letters to Malthus* were published – not a private correspondence but a catchy book title. In the summer of that year they met in Paris, as Say reported to Sismondi.

In 1827 the two economists entertained a correspondence, published posthumously in Say's *Mélanges et Correspondance*. Malthus sent Say a copy of his *Definitions in Political Economy*, and Say reacted in a friendly tone, praising Malthus for his clarity in general and his attacks on McCulloch and Ricardo in particular. But he objected to Malthus' reproach of having 'strangely identified utility and value'.[24] The most important point in this letter is Say's conceding that his theory of *débouchés*, questioned by Malthus, is 'in fact subjected to some limitations'. This, he writes, has been elaborated in the fifth edition of his *Traité* (1826), even while Ricardo, Mill and McCulloch had already embraced the doctrine, and the British government has made it the cornerstone of its new trading policy.[25] Another of Say's theoretical innovations 'which I have firstly brought forward, and which has been adopted in Russia, Germany, and Italy, but to my knowledge hardly by English economists' is the distinction between interest, rent and wages. To his great regret, Say had no copy left of his fifth edition which he might otherwise have sent to his opponent. But he included an offprint of his article 'Economie Politique' in the *Revue Encyclopédique*.

In a long reply, Malthus politely wrote back that he had purchased a copy of Say's fifth edition.[26] After pointing at Say's inconsistencies in his use of the notion of utility, he welcomes his restrictions on the functioning of the law of markets. In doing so he admonishes Say by lecturing to him in Say's own positivist methodology: 'To be certain of our progress in political economy, I have always held the opinion that we must frequently refer to experience, and to verify if our theories are in accordance with the facts we observe.'

Say's theory of immaterial production is questioned by Malthus because of the difficulty of measuring it. To that purpose he quotes the Russian economist Storch, and the anonymous reviewer of Say's fifth edition in the *Revue Encyclopédique*, who are both stressing the subjective evaluations by economic agents.

In Say's last reply, he once more defends his 'extension' of the definition of (economic) value as 'anything which can serve to satisfy human needs'. To the moralist, there are justified and unjustified needs. But the economist 'has only to identify and name the *common qualities* of all things capable to satisfy needs *whatever these are*, which constitute the demand from which value originates' [Say's italics].[27] As to Storch and the anonymous reviewer of the *Traité*: these authors 'have no understanding whatever of this part of political economy'.

Altogether it seems that, while Malthus and Say were the figureheads of one of the Great Debates in classical political economy, their personal contacts were only conducted in writing, in a fairly polite and distanced manner.

With Sismondi, his Genevan fellow citizen, Say had a friendly personal relationship.

In 1803 he wrote a letter to him accompanying a complimentary copy of the *Traité*'s first edition:

> You will see that I have followed Smith on all principal points. But if I am not mistaken, I have clarified other important points which he had neglected. Had he really uncovered the great phenomenon of Production and Consumption? Had he shown how commerce is really productive? Had he distentangled the ideas on real and relative dearth?[28]

Here Say summarises in brief his admiration for Smith, and his points of criticism on him. He argues that immaterial production is an equally important creation of value as physical output. And the importance is clear of the idea that rising or falling prices always must be related to the general price level. (In later editions this would be more precisely developed in the long-term relationship between lower prices and economic progress.)

In this summary of his own contributions, the law of markets is notably absent. This corresponds with the fact that he considered this an important new element in his second edition of 1814. (And it is there in his undated manuscript note of 'advances to my credit', quoted above in relation to Smith.)

We have seen that Say's *Letters to Malthus* were also partly addressed to Sismondi. In 1824 the two Genevan citizens fought a battle on the law of markets in the *Revue Encyclopédique*. But neither of the two convinced the other, so the discussion continued in 1826 in the same periodical, in a sharpened way. Say's article 'De la crise commerciale de l'Angleterre', of just five and a half pages, was not primarily an analysis of British economic problems, but rather a firm attack on Sismondi who in the September issue had accused him of worsening the crisis by his recommendation of wrong remedies:

> Monsieur de Sismondi has just returned from England. The commercial dis-
> tress of this country has struck him. Its workers *succumb from famine*; the
> Irish feed themselves with *potatoes only*; they are dressed in *just rags*, and
> according to Mr. de Sismondi that system is guilty which extols production.
> …
> Too much is produced in England, says Mr. de Sismondi …; and it have
> been *your* [Say's] *theories which have encouraged the producers to cause
> this overstocking which brings the distress of the civilised world* (page 614).
> Mr. de Sismondi is paying us too much honour. There is not a single
> speculator in England who has worried about our books when he founded a
> company, or expanded his commerce.[29]

After explaining that there can never be too much production of goods that can be sold at a profit, Say accuses Sismondi of wishful thinking about society, and of neglecting facts that do not fit his analysis. In this respect, he is in the company of David Ricardo, whose theory of money is 'perhaps the only part of the science where he has taught us new and important truths'. But in his theory of taxation, 'he is founding his conclusions upon abstractions, and abandons the experimental method'.

Say does agree that England – such a rich country where yet so many are suf-fering – is in crisis, but he blames the monetary overexpansion, followed by overcontraction, for this:

> Starting enterprises have been halted; merchandise is sold well below its cost
> price, and even those manufacturers who had worked with the utmost pru-
> dence have been unable to continue production; that causes the working
> population to cry famine; that causes the government to lower the import
> duties on corn; that causes the cries of the big landowners who cannot sustain
> the competition with foreign corn because of the taxes burdening them.

The English institutions of substitution and primogeniture are deplorable, and are partly responsible for the sorry state of the economy. Finally, Say completely disagrees with Sismondi and his mixing up of capital and revenue for which the latter blames him.

This *Revue* article seems intended as a final settlement of accounts by Say with Sismondi and Ricardo at the same time. In the same issue of the journal, he took on Count Florez Estrada who had written a pamphlet on the English economic crisis, blaming a shortage of gold for it.[30] Say corrected him in writing that on the contrary, a monetary oversupply was the cause.

In 1828, in one of Say's last letters to Sismondi, he felt confident enough to write that *the abstractions of Ricardo and McCulloch have altogether fallen down in England.*[31] If he did not openly aspire to be Head of a School, implicitly he went a long way in that direction.

When widening our scope from individuals to groups of contemporaries, it is striking that a limited number of often overlapping networks played a significant role in Say's life and in his work. The Protestant Genevan connection was important in his family life and his business ventures: his aunt Duvoisin was one of the financiers of the Auchy spinning mill, and his cousin Michel Delaroche was an important sounding board and advisor for his private investments. With Genevan intellectuals and scholars like Sismondi and Dumont he entertained a correspondence and a personal friendly relationship, even if he might disagree with them on certain issues.

The Genevan pastor, and the French editor of Bentham, Etienne Dumont (1759–1829) had been on the staff of the *Courrier de Provence* where the young Jean-Baptiste Say was employed. From 1785 till 1789 he had lived in London, where he formed a close relationship with Sir Samuel Romilly; with the latter he visited Paris in 1788. His correspondence with Say has already been quoted above.[32]

With the name of Dumont begins the overlap with the utilitarian – and mostly English – circuit. It has already been remarked that Bentham's ideas fell upon fertile ground with Say as he had been impregnated already with French eighteenth century ideas, like those of Helvétius and Chastellux.[33] Even more than Say's utilitarianism, his liberalism was French and home-grown. By 1800, when he published his *Olbie*, the influence of the Enlightenment salons, combined with his first-hand witnessing of the Terror and other totalitarian developments of the French Revolution, had resulted in a liberal attitude, although perhaps the amount of social control he proposed for the state of Olbia was a bit oppressive for the individual citizen. His individualism was soon strengthened by his personal confrontations with the First Consul, when he found himself in the company of other dissenting liberals in the Tribunat like Benjamin Constant. Both in his economic thinking as an elementary methodological individualist, and in his political standpoints he further developed his individualism in the later editions of the *Traité* and in the *Cours Complet.*

'You have signalled the great and happy effects of machinery'

Even to his students, Say's ambiguous relationship with his master Adam Smith was clear. In 1823 one of them wrote: 'Would Mr. Say, who so openly confesses his well-meant admiration for Adam Smith, perhaps not have treated him too critically in his last lecture?' A number of around twenty students' letters, plus seven others classified as *difficultés* in the Say papers, testify to his willingness to communicate with his pupils.[34] Already in his first lecture he had suggested to his audience to write down their questions for him – another sign that he preferred not to improvise upon oral questions. The letters are not just interesting for their subject matter, but also for the insight they give in the varied composition of his audience: French students, professional people and foreign listeners. The majority of the letters are dated from the years 1822–1823 and 1829–1831, so it is plausible that he must have received dozens more in the years 1823–1829. All but one are serious letters; one anonymous author reproached Say for his 'incoherent phrases and absurdities'.[35]

Two requests were of a practical nature. On behalf of a number of Sorbonne students, a Monsieur Baltahasard asked Say if he could please start his lectures a little later, so as to make it possible for them to attend these. Three weeks later the request was repeated by someone signing Balland, but obviously in the same handwriting. On the other hand some inhabitants of Versailles asked the professor to start a little earlier, in order to enable them to take the last coach home.[36]

Four Englishmen, one American and a Cuban professor of economics by the name of Velez were the foreign letter-writers. The English primarily wrote about topics of exchange rates and international trade. The American, Charles Johnson, found it necessary to point out to the former spinning mill owner the existence of Eli Whitney's 'cotton gin':

> *You have signaled the great and happy effects of machinery, and you have pointed out the advantages of cotton spinning machines. But Monsieur, there is another machine, invented in America about thirty years ago, the effects of which, I believe, are even more remarkable then those of the spinning machines. This is the 'Cotton Gin' invented by Mr. Whitney, and intended to separate the kernels from the cotton proper.*

In his opinion, its existence was hardly known even in England, and therefore he found it appropriate to signal it to Say.[37] The Cuban Velez clearly had not completely understood Say's subjectivist approach in economics, as he complained that 'this science, having as its object of study exclusively the accumulation of riches and values, wishes to stamp out in each individual love and the most sacred friendship, as if they were pieces of cloth'.[38]

Among those who identified their professions, there were a student of law, a young lawyer, an industrial entrepreneur and a sculptor. One of Say's answers he wrote down relates to his reasoning that the lowering of prices is a good thing, and a sign of progress:

> [An auditor] *says that far from regarding low prices as a good thing, it must be regarded as a bad one. But a low price is only bad if caused by the dearness of other products. When a shoemaker, in the same time in which his day wage has fallen by fifty percent, has seen all his consumption goods (bread, meat, amusement etc.) fall by fifty percent as well, the lowering of his day wage would not affect him. And if the lowering of all prices would be the result of a more efficient way of producing (like the use of machines, the cultivation of fallow ground, the use of transportation canals etc.)*

nobody would suffer although all prices would fall. But in the continuation of this lecture we will see which are the occasions in which it is impossible that prices will fall enough to enable the goods to get within reach of the indigent class.[39]

Another student, Bidaux, had already completed the Ecole Polytechnique and wrote to Say four times with corrections of his calculations of the bullion to grain relationship since classical antiquity. On one of these Say wrote: 'Verified as being right, and corrected accordingly.'[40]

How Say interspersed his answers to these letters in his lectures, cannot always be precisely reconstructed. In the tenth lecture of his first Conservatoire year, on 10 February 1821, he did so for the first time. He answered three questions, one of which ran as follows: 'One of your assiduous students has not completely understood what you said, last Saturday the third, on the evil effects for society of the extravagance of individuals.'[41] Say noted that he had answered this question at the beginning of his lecture. The negative effects upon the economy of prodigal ('improductive') consumption were a central element in Say's thought, as being detrimental to growth, and socially harmful as well. In his answer he might well have praised the modesty, and the propensity to save and invest of the *classe mitoyenne*.

In his lecture notes of later years, he was less precise about the answering of students' questions. But he has written down a general observation on his views regarding the coherence of his theoretical concepts and his pedagogical objectives. He might well have written this around 1815, when he started his Athénée teaching, as it has the flavour of thinking aloud to himself, and only refers to his *Traité* and not to the *Cours Complet*:

> *Questions to be resolved. All questions must be solved in my Traité otherwise it would not be complete. What can one ask in an examination for an answer to a question? The explanations which clear it up completely. The explanations which let one completely understand a principle, which demonstrate its relation with other principles, and the examples which make visible that this principle is but a general expression of particular facts. This is what my lectures should be. Each of them must be founded upon one or several principles, of which they are just the explanation. These principles constitute the analytical table of the lecture & can be dictated to the students in order to let them understand the analysis.*

In the margin, Say repeated this last sentence:

> *By beginning the lecture with dictating the analytical table, the explanations will be better stamped on their memory.*[42]

This clearly illustrates that from the beginning of his teaching career till the end of his life, Say remained the citizen of 'Olbia' who felt destined to teach the principles of political economy to his fellow citizens.

11 Alive after 200 years

Three revolutions

Jean-Baptiste Say died 180 years ago. Surely his life had a background of 'troubled times', as the subtitle of Palmer's book indicates. It began under the *Ancien Régime*, embraced the entire French revolutionary period and ended during the reign of Louis Philippe. Say actively took part in three revolutions: the French Revolution, the Industrial Revolution and the academic introduction of a new discipline.

Interest in his scientific heritage has revived in the past decades: first by the reconsideration of French eighteenth century economics, as one of the by-products of the bicentenary of the French Revolution in 1989; second by the taking-up of the *Oeuvres Complètes* project coordinated by André Tiran at the Université Lyon 2 *Lumière*; and third by the interest of established scholars of reputation such as Robert Palmer and Samuel Hollander, leading to a number of important monographs and articles on Say. I humbly hope to have added some relevant historical and biographical background information in this volume.

At any rate, the revival of J.-B. Say studies has not been limited to the domain of economics. The studies by Palmer, Steiner and Whatmore have shed light upon the historical, sociological and political theory dimensions of Say's life-time and his works.

Evelyn Forget has written a scholarly study on Say's economics, and produced a very useful English translation of Say's *Olbie*.

Other modern approaches present a clearly partisan view on Say's economics: Hollander has recruited him into the purely Ricardian-classical camp; Kurz and Gehrke have proclaimed Ricardo's victory over him; and Rothbard has identified him as a proto-Austrian economist par excellence. Steven Kates has surfaced as a true believer in the validity of Say's Law for modern economics. With the exceptions of Rothbard and Kates, all of them have already been quoted above – approvingly and disapprovingly. In this epilogue I summarise and comment upon their essential contributions. Some earlier assessments, like the one of Schumpeter (1954), can still be warmly recommended.

Sowell (1972) on Say's Law is still a perfect starting point for a broad analysis of the subject.[1] However, it must be noticed that he too has added to the confusion by wrongly translating Say's defence against Malthus' reaction to his fifth edition of the *Traité* (1825) with regard to the definition of a product as something that can be sold for (at least) cost price – the definition which also earned him Schumpeter's ridicule. Say concludes: *Ma théorie des debouches demeure entière* (My law of markets remains complete). Sowell translates: My theory of markets *becomes* complete.[2] Elsewhere Sowell rightly draws attention to Say's 'real conversion' regarding the limits of production, as treated in his fifth edition.[3] This was discussed in the preceding chapter in relation to his discussions with Malthus and Sismondi.

Some others are wide off the mark, like the Marxist Anikin (1975) who wants us to believe that Say, after falling out with Bonaparte, 'bought shares in a textile factory' and 'became rich'. He even thinks that Say 'moved to Paris as a wealthy rentier' and 'became a loyal servant of the Bourbons'.[4] We can smile at his conclusion that Say was only 'the founder of 19th-century vulgar political economy', and 'the father of the bourgeois apologetic theory of distribution'.[5]

Say and the historians

Robert Palmer and Richard Whatmore were the first authors to fully render justice to Say as a historical character in the period of the French Revolution. Both have strictly limited themselves to the printed texts of the period, and nevertheless they have opened truly new perspectives. Palmer's book is modestly subtitled as 'writings selected and translated' but effectively it is a concise history of Say's most important ideas in just over 150 pages.[6] His chapter titles qualify the young Say as a 'mild revolutionary', the author of *Olbie* as a 'sober utopian' and the scholar isolated by Bonaparte as 'the frustrated economist'. These are followed by 'the innovative economist', 'the commentator on England' and 'the professor of political economy'. Palmer deserves praise for his balanced choice of Say texts, and for their translation as well. Without consulting the Say papers (and perhaps unaware of their existence), he has sketched a picture of Say that is largely identical to mine. Say's position in the turbulent times of his life is labelled as follows: 'Never active in the Revolution, he also never opposed it, even during the Terror, and his later writings are free of the retrospective lamentations in which even liberals indulged.'[7] If I were to rewrite this sentence, I would commence with describing Say as 'active on the sidelines' during the Revolution, and only add 'other' to liberals at the end. Altogether, Palmer's book can be recommended just as much as Forget's as a valuable introduction to Say's life and work.

Richard Whatmore only names Say in the subtitle of his *Republicanism and the French Revolution*.[8] The first half of the book describes the relationship between political economy and republicanism, the political economy of French decline and the political economy of the Terror after the Revolution. In the second half, Say's ideas are measured against the yardstick of the concepts of (primarily French) *philosophes* and revolutionaries on republicanism, secularism and the organisation of commercial and industrial society. Whatmore has constructed a fascinating picture of Say's ideas as part of the development in the French history of ideas, not so much in economics but primarily in political science. His concluding sentences are:

> [Say's] view of enlightenment philosophy leads to the conclusion that seeking a purportedly radical public sphere in late eighteenth-century French thought is ultimately a white elephant. Such a project cannot capture the real divisions between *philosophes*, revolutionaries, and their antagonists, concerning small and large states, forms of government, ancient and modern republicanism, the nature of civilization, the merits of commerce and industry, the kinds of ranks which characterize a modern social order, the civil value of different religions, and the merits of the political and social cultures offered by other nations, particularly Britain, Switzerland, China, and North America. Say believed in a Revolution, the product of a critique of *philosophe* projects for restoring French glory, which was among the most radical intellectual experiments in modern history: the creation of a republic without social hierarchy in conditions of advanced civilization.[9]

Is this the same Jean-Baptiste Say whose life and ideas have been sketched above? Yes and no: the young Say was a republican revolutionary and a secular, moderate egalitarian. He kept true to these ideals, but in later life his ideas were more concerned with the conditions for economic growth and peace than with restoring French glory, and he saw his own role not as the author of a political blueprint for society, but as the writer of a treatise on the correct economic ideas underlaying its institutional design. So my accent is slightly different from Whatmore's, but his book is a magnificent exercise in intellectual history.

The Ricardian partisans

Samuel Hollander has written a book on the economics – explicitly economics only – of Say.[10] He presents him as the classical of classicals, i.e. Samuelson-canonical. (His book is dedicated to Paul Samuelson.) By the way, classical is also equivalent to Ricardian in the Hollanderian interpretation, meaning supply-and-demand, cost-price-cum-utility economics. After a methodological chapter on Say and the classical canon, Hollander concludes by presenting Say as a Ricardian: 'If all this is not pure Ricardo it is nothing.' Hollander has thoroughly done his homework. Unlike many English and American authors, he has studied all of Say's original writings, from the first edition of the *Traité* (1803) till the last posthumous editions of the *Oeuvres Diverses* (1848) and Steiner's edition (1996a) of Say's 1819 lectures at the Parisian Athénée.

As usual, Hollander does not underestimate his readers, who need a strong stomach and a fair knowledge of French to follow the many quotations from the various editions of Say's work. The manifold references in the text demonstrate scholarship but do not make for easy reading. Take for instance the following paragraph:

[Mill's] *Principles* cites warmly Say's contribution to the excess-demand issue with special reference to the case against the 'systems' of Malthus, Sismondi and Chalmers (Mill 1963–91 [1848], 3: 575–6). There is the commendation of Say along with Ricardo for the proposition 'demand for commodities is not demand for labour' relating to the accumulation process (Mill 1963–91 [1848], 2: 78; see above, p. 176). And in value theory, Mill was impressed by Say's solution to the 'paradox, of two things, each depending upon the other' that demand varies inversely with price but price rises as demand increases – involving the *equation* of demand and supply.
(Mill 1963–91 [1848], 3: 466; see above, p. 101)[11]

Two lengthy chapters on value, distribution and growth discuss the Say–Ricardo debate on value and price. The first took place before Ricardo's death in 1823, and the second after (this has also been my approach in time – but not in content). Following the subsequent editions of the *Traité*, Hollander concludes that 'Say and Ricardo were operating on the same wavelength', or that 'All this [written by Say] is in line with the classical canon'. The latter conclusion is drawn from a quotation from the *Cours Complet* where Hollander translates *prix* as 'cost price' and *à bon marché* as 'at lower cost'. I must confess that I can only read *prix* as 'market price', and *à bon marché* as 'at lower market price'.[12] Who is bending what here?

The following quotation is read by Hollander as 'wholly orthodox observations regarding the outcome of entrepreneurial innovation ... where again long-run calculable costs are conspicuous'. On the contrary, I am inclined to credit Say here for his original insight in the innovation process on the shop floor, if perhaps he is overestimating the velocity of its diffusion and of bringing about lower prices; and instead of 'conspicuous calculable costs' in the long run, I would suggest to read here a non-calculable yet predictable lowering of costs (and prices) by product and/or process innovation:

> Scientific insights alone are insufficient for the advancement of the arts [technologies]: also necessary are more or less risky experiments, the success of which does not always compensate their costs; while when they succeed, the competition mechanism rapidly erodes the profits of the entrepreneur; but society as a whole remains in possession of a new product, or – which amounts to the same – of a permanent lowering of the price of an already existing product.[13]

In the chapter on Riches, it is increasingly hammered out to the reader how Ricardian Say really was. In less than a full page (187–188), we are treated to 'a wholly Ricardian formulation' and to a 'wholly Ricardian statement' as well as 'these wholly Ricardian statements'.[14] The reader may judge for himself.

In the chapter on the law of markets, Hollander makes it plausible – contra Baumol (1977) – that in spite of the essentially microeconomic formulation of Say's Law in the first edition of the *Traité* (1803), this already contains the essence of the rapid and powerful equilibrating mechanism which Baumol first encounters in the second (1814) edition. Hollander is right that the germs were there in 1803, but we have seen that Say himself, in his correspondence with Michel Delaroche, was convinced that his 1814 chapter was new and superior.

In the concluding chapter, Hollander sets himself the task of explaining why 'an unwillingness to be in the least generous manifests itself in his [Say's] depriving Ricardo of almost any credit for a serious contribution'. He concludes that Say 'engaged in a systematic campaign, especially after 1823, to distance himself in the public estimate from Ricardo and the Ricardians rather than to emphasise common ground'. To this we can agree. But what is Hollander's explanation? 'I suspect we must have recourse to psychological matters.'[15]

This is Hollander the economist who lets the written texts speak for themselves. He has not convinced me, for I continue to believe that Ricardo and Say were starting from incompatible paradigms regarding value and price. My own psychological interpretation is that Ricardo understood Say better than his opponent understood him. Therefore Say's reaction was more bitter. And in Say's own time, many of his correspondents praised him as a worthy opponent of the English model-builder, perhaps even as the head of the anti-Ricardians. Certainly after Ricardo's death in 1823 this support may have strengthened his own anti-Ricardianism regarding methodology in general, and value theory in particular.

Even more pro-Ricardian than Hollander are Kurz and Gehrke in their contribution on Say and Ricardo, in the first of two recent Say conference volumes.[16] From the outset, they are clear about the position from which they examine their subject:

> Regarding the fact that during the period from their first meeting until the premature death of Ricardo in 1823, Say has repeated several times that he wished to take the British theorist as his point of reference and to assimilate his system of analysis, it will be our interest to determine whether he made any progress in this field. With the exception perhaps of the law of markets, it cannot be confirmed that Say has exerted any influence on Ricardo, while according to Say himself things were quite different in the opposite direction. Therefore the question is to determine the extent of this influence. As a consequence, Ricardo's analysis will provide us with a standard to examine the degree of excellence of Say's analyses regarding the theory of value and distribution.[17]

Furthermore they promise to let the two authors speak for themselves, and to 'reduce our comments and interpretations to a minimum'. In their chapter of eight sections, seven are concerned with value and distribution, and the eighth with the law of markets. Despite their stated objectivity, they had already disclosed their conclusion one page earlier:

> While Ricardo did appreciate certain points of Say's analysis, from the start he pronounced a critical judgment on other points, precisely on the theory of

value and distribution. It did not take him long to put his finger on the problems, incoherences, and contradictions present in Say's analysis, all of
which, according to Ricardo, could absolutely not be resolved within the
frame of the successive editions of the *Traité*.[18]

After describing the first meeting and the first exchange of ideas between Say
and Ricardo, Kurz and Gehrke continue on their methodological differences –
Say's inductive vs. Ricardo's deductive method – and their different views on
the possibility of applying mathematical methods in economics – Ricardo's car-
dinal vs. Say's ordinal viewpoint. Also, Say held a fundamentally harmonious
view of economic life as a potentially positive sum game for all classes of
society, whereas Ricardo saw a conflict of interest between the landed aristocracy on one side, and the other classes on the other.[19]

Kurz and Gehrke then concentrate on three fundamental disagreements
between Say and Ricardo: 1. the distinction between value and riches; 2. the
measure of value and the definition of revenue; 3. the theory of distribution.
Their comparison of the printed sources is broad and thorough, except that they
only quote the Prinsep (1821) translation of the *Traité* (from the fourth (1819)
edition). Thus they miss some examples of Say's very clear wrestling with and
rearranging of the subject as a consequence of his debates with Ricardo.[20] The
changes he made in the third and fourth edition are only represented by Ricardo's reactions and not by Say's own wording.

Also Kurz and Gehrke are confused about Say's distinction between 'natural'
and 'social' riches. Indeed it was one of Say's unfortunate ideas to exclude free
or natural riches from the domain of economics, and to concentrate solely upon
utility produced by humans in his explanation of value and price. But Kurz and
Gehrke are misled in writing that Say's thought 'seems to be rooted in physioc-
racy';[21] Say always pronounced himself against the 'Economistes'.

Kurz and Gehrke are clearly malevolent in their interpretation of Say's
hypothesis that it is possible 'by causes, the discussion of which is outside the
subject of our present speculation' that corn prices will remain constant in spite
of a higher production level. They blame him for 'not giving any explanation'
for this phenomenon. No indeed, Say is not pretending to do so, as he clearly
specifies his *ceteris **non** paribus* clause.

The two supporters of Ricardo become ever more partisan and noisy in their
comments on Say's sloppy reasoning, and his getting mixed up in trying to
combine his microeconomic analysis of value and price with his macro hobby-
horse of continuing growth, accompanied by a general lowering of prices. This
is their appreciation of Ricardo's letter to Say of 5 March 1822, confronting the
latter with the inconsistency of his vocabulary: 'Hit, down! This demonstration
was the final blow in explaining to Say that his concepts of value and riches
were leading to the highest possible confusion.'[22]

Regarding the subject of Say's Law, which was embraced by Ricardo, Kurz
and Gehrke start from the question – since long irrelevant – whether Say deserved
any credit of priority for stating the law of markets, or whether – following Marx

– he might almost be accused of plagiarism. They conclude that while the two economists held a generally similar opinion on the subject, Ricardo's defence was superior to Say's. To that purpose they quote Ricardo's letter to Malthus from September 1820, where he accuses Say of making the same error as Torrens by blaming the entrepreneurs for not producing enough merchandise in a slump to counterbalance the unsold production. Ricardo seeks the cause in 'the bad adaptation of the commodities produced to the wants of mankind which is the specific evil, and not the abundance of commodities'.[23] But this is not really very different from Say's analysis.

The chapter concludes: 'We know that, for better or for worse, not all readers, including Say, were ready to follow the guidance of Ricardo.' Thank you very much Kurz and Gehrke! Although they have put a lot of effort into representing the Say–Ricardo discussion in great detail, it is disappointing that they have not risen to a more distanced and historically relativist position, examining those elements that are still valuable in the analysis of the Frenchman and of the Englishman. It may be true that Ricardo had a complete and closed model of price determination, whereas Say only had an incomplete and open analysis. However, the latter deserves at least some recognition for his subjectivist approach.

Three balanced assessments

More objective in this respect are the writings of Philippe Steiner on the same topic. His contributions to the corpus of J.-B. Say scholarship can be seen as a highly readable book-in-instalments on the essential elements of Say's economic thought: his methodology, his relation to Adam Smith, his theory of the entrepreneur and his debate with Ricardo. As an editor of Say, he has written valuable introductions to Say's Athénée lectures and to the variorum edition of the *Traité*. His comments have been amply and approvingly quoted above.

In the first of two recent conference volumes on J.-B. Say, Steiner has reconstructed the Say–Ricardo debate viewed not from the angle of value and price, but starting from Say's conception of production.[24] At the end of his article he presents a very useful and objective chronology of Say's contacts with and comments upon Ricardo.[25] It is Steiner's conclusion that Say's theory of value and price was closely linked with his ideas on technical progress, enabling man to more efficiently use the 'free' forces of nature:

> Although Say did not formulate a law of demand or a law of the market, he must be credited with original and substantial considerations, even if these underwent changing formulations and were incomplete with regard to later developments, in not answering the questions raised by Ricardo.[26]

In other contributions, Steiner has analysed Say's achievement in his theory of the entrepreneur, in his view of economics as the science of modernity and in his ideas on the future of colonies.[27]

Steiner is one of my two favourite modern authors on Say. The other is Evelyn Forget, who – in my opinion – has produced the most valuable single book assessment of Say's economics, in which she has also provided the first English translation of Say's *Olbie*.[28] She examines Say's economic and political analysis from a broad perspective of the history of ideas, in which his starting point in the philosophy of the Idéologie is an essential element. She leads her readers from the psychology and physiology in this movement to its social theory, in which the concept of spontaneous order is an important element.

Before presenting her translation of *Olbie*, Forget examines Say's theory of value, his analysis of income distribution and the law of markets in all of his published works. To most of her argument I wholeheartedly agree, as has been made clear already in Chapter 3 above. Particularly valuable is her summary of Say's methodology, as presented in the first edition of the *Traité* (1803). In his preliminary discourse, Say draws a parallel between the recent steps forward made in physics, and the recent developments in political economy. By analogy, the laws of economics are not man-made, but to be discovered as laws of nature. To Forget, his attack on 'system' is another example of his permanent reasoning as an Idéologue.[29]

Her conclusion with regard to the law of markets leaves room for nuance in Say's own interpretation of it:

> From his earliest writings in economics, then, Say was quite prepared to allow for misallocation of capital in the form of a glut of particular commodities accompanied by an underproduction of others. Moreover, he did recognise the possibility of general cyclical overproduction, and attributed this to state of affairs to extraordinary circumstances brought about, usually, by inept public administrations that disrupt normal markets and trade channels and are reflected in unsustainable price expectations and speculation.[30]

Altogether Forget's book is a fine introduction to Say's economics. Strangely enough the name of Bentham is entirely absent in it, but utility and utilitarianism are decently treated. In the second Kates volume discussed below, she elaborates upon the relationship between Say's theory of the entrepreneur and the law of markets.

André Tiran is an exception among J.-B. Say scholars in concentrating heavily on his monetary thought. In his dissertation (1994) and in other publications he has discovered new perspectives on this subject, both as a single topic and as a complement to the functioning of Say's Law.[31] Tiran notes that Say, although primarily concentrating on real world economics, was by no means naïve in monetary matters, even when his theories were sometimes falsified by the facts. We have seen that in 1814, when preparing his English journey, he ordered the latest monetary pamphlets by Hamilton, Huskisson and Bosanquet, together with the *Report of the Bullion Committee*. In discussing Say's version of a quantity theory of money, Tiran lists nine authors, from Locke to Smith, who had been studied by Say regarding this subject.[32] All credit facilities are taken into account in Say's analysis, as far as they influence the velocity of circulation, and economise upon the use of 'real' money, i.e. precious metal currency. This is also an important dimension for judging Say's sophisticatedness in his own versions of the law of markets, where the monetary accommodation of rising or shrinking effective demand comes into the picture. Another French economist who has appreciated Say's original contribution in this respect is Alain Béraud.[33] In his interpretation, 'if a growing production entails a greater demand for means of exchange and a tendency towards a lower price level, it is always possible to avoid lower prices by activating balances which Say considered as money signs'.

Tiran summarises Say's ideas on the quantity of money, its velocity of circulation and their effects on prices in four points.[34]

1   The quantity of money is not the decisive influence on the price level. An augmentation of the supply of one commodity influences the prices of all other goods.
2   There is one general velocity of circulation for money and for commodities. There is no single good that has a paramount influence on this velocity. The level of economic activity determines the velocity of circulation of all commodities, including money.
3   In periods of crisis the velocity of circulation is notably lowered, certainly for goods that depreciate slowly and can be used as a store of value. But it is accelerated for other, depreciating goods.
4   The quantity of metal coin is given in the short run, by its difficulty of production. Changes in the supply and demand of money only slowly influence prices and circulation.

Altogether these concepts were not sophisticated enough to explain all monetary phenomena observed by Say. Tiran quotes a number of paragraphs from the *Cours Complet* where Say is inventing complex arguments to explain events contradicting his theory of neutral money, like the crisis in commercial credit in England, or the possible duration of adaptation to higher prices (or even the anticipation of higher prices). In the preceding chapter it was made clear that Say, in replying to Sismondi's analysis of British economic problems, and in discussing Florez Estrada's opinion on the British shortage of credit – both in the *Revue Encyclopédique* – started from an exogenous oversupply of money (followed by overcontraction) which does not fit his general analysis of a quantity of money adapting to the growth of an economy.

Tiran's first quotation from the *Cours Complet* reads:

> In spite of the principles teaching us that money only plays a simple intermediating role, and that fundamentally products are paid for with products, a greater money supply is always favourable for larger sales and for the reproduction of new values.

In the second Say puts forward a hypothetical, psychological explanation:

> Perhaps the confused feelings people have about the gradual depreciation of the value of money, may cause that that the consumers are always prepared to get rid of their money for other products, the value of which is not prone to an equal loss of value.[35]

Tiran has done an excellent job by carefully looking at the development of Say's monetary thought. Unlike Hollander, and unlike Kurz and Gehrke, he has not fallen into the trap of either interpreting Say too benevolently or too strictly. The result is a positive appreciation of Say's well-considered reasoning on certain monetary topics, while he also points at a number of clear analytical deficiencies.

Two true believers

Murray Rothbard has hailed J.-B. Say as the forerunner par excellence of Austrian economics.[36] According to Rothbard, he was a 'splendid writer' and a better methodologist than Adam Smith. Say's utility-based value theory was superior to Ricardo's, as was his theory of income distribution. He brought the entrepreneur back into economic thought, from which Adam Smith had purged him. He has given the best explanation of the law of markets, and the best theory of taxation:

> In short, J.B. Say, unique among economists, offered us a theory of total government spending as well as a theory of overall taxation. And that theory was a lucid and remarkable one, amounting to: that government is best (or 'least bad') that spends and taxes least. But the implications of such a theory are stunning, whether or not Say understood them or followed them through.[37]

Steven Kates has written a provocative 250-page pamphlet on the history of Say's Law and its misinterpretation in *The General Theory*.[38] He argues that Keynes is responsible for a fundamental misunderstanding of classical – and in fact all pre-Keynesian – economics which has disfigured mainstream macroeconomics since 1936. This is no small reproach, but Kates makes his point in a well-documented and convincing way. His book not only summarises the entire literature on Say's Law but also offers a new perspective on the place of this theorem in the Anglo-American literature (as well as in Röpke and Haberler) between James Mill and Maynard Keynes.

Then what is the Katesian Revolution? In Kates' own words:

> Keynes used Say's Law to distinguish his own economic theory from those of others ... What Keynes argued was that involuntary unemployment was a formal impossibility in the economic theories of his 'classical' contemporaries,

precisely because they had tacitly accepted Say's Law as valid. This represented a quite extraordinary attack on the economics profession.... If this accusation were true, there could be no more devastating criticism made against economists and economics as a science. A discipline which purported to deal with economic matters, but which did not accept the reality of economic fluctuations, or acknowledge and explain the existence of unvoluntary unemployment, would undoubtedly have been of little use. No criticism of it would have been too harsh.[39]

It is Kates' claim that not only did the classical economists, contrary to Keynes' distortion of their views, fully accept the possibility of recessions and involuntary unemployment, but they even founded the classical theory of the business cycle on the law of markets: 'This was done by explaining recessions as resulting from misdirected production or other factors which drove demand and supply out of alignment.'[40]

After introducing the place of Say's Law in *The General Theory*, Kates has four chapters on classical economists and the Law in English classical theory. He writes two chapters on Keynes' discovery of the Law – mainly through reading Malthus – and on possible influences that may have set him on the path of the term itself and the central importance of effective demand. In the former of these two chapters he documents the date of the Malthusian influence on Keynes' ideas from recently published students' notes taken in the Michaelmas term of 1932. In the latter he plausibly suggests how Keynes may have found the not yet familar term Say's Law in American textbooks. In three concluding chapters the post-1936 discussion of the various concepts of the Law is well summarised and critically assessed.

Kates begins his argument with firm statements. He concludes with a trumpet-call:

Keynes described Say's Law as fallacious. The law of markets was devised to demonstrate that theories based on failure of effective demand were themselves fallacious. Between the polemical skills of Keynes, the obfuscations of Lange and the penetrating summary statement by Becker and Baumol, the actual meaning and significance of the law of markets disappeared from economic theory. The Keynesian Revolution was a revolution indeed, but the full significance and nature of that revolution have not yet been understood.

Kates has written a thorough overview, however without discussing the subsequent editions of Say's *Traité* and *Cours Complet*. Say's *Letters to Malthus* are referred to, but very scantily. This is one of the small number of J.-B. Say titles in the Keynes library (which to me illustrates the fact that Keynes read a lot more of Malthus than he did of Say). An account of the Say–Sismondi discussion on the subject, which is essential for a complete understanding of Say's own development, is almost entirely absent. And for the early versions of the

Law that can be distinguished in the *Wealth of Nations*, one should go back to Sowell's *Say's Law* (1972).

On the occasion of the bicentenary of Say's *Traité* (1803), Kates has edited a volume of essays pro and contra the relevance of Say's Law.[41] In view of his own parti-pris pro, Kates must be praised for presenting a balanced assessment. On the one hand, Mark Skousen tells us: 'The road to recovery, like the road to long-term economic growth, belongs on the supply side. This is Say's legacy.'[42] On the other, Steve Keen writes: 'Say's Law is irrelevant to the world in which we live. Rather than discussing Say's Law any further, we should consign it to the dustbin of the history of economic thought.'[43]

The contributors William Baumol and Evelyn Forget have a long-standing reputation as J.-B. Say scholars. The former's *Economica* article 'Say's – at least – Eight Laws' (1977)' only discusses seven versions of the law, as the author concedes. His contributions are a reprint of his *Journal of Economic Perspectives* (1999) article and a brief and brilliantly clear-written introduction which not only summarises the most relevant points of discussion but in itself is a model plea for doing history of thought as part of an economist's education. Baumol states that even Say himself did not claim credits for being its first enunciator. Yet in his manuscripts there are some notes suggesting that he claimed the authorship of its clearest statement, and in his correspondence with Michel Delaroche he claimed the novelty of his exposition in the second edition (1814) of the *Traité*. This is also reflected in the wording of the final sentences of the *Cours Complet* (1828–1829) which do confirm his belief in long-term industrial growth and in the validity of his law – precisely the version Baumol credits him for.

Forget focuses upon Say's own Law in the broader context of his views on entrepreneurship and decision-making. She knows there are more references to the law in Say's works than just in the *Débouchés* chapter. Yet in examining the Law in the context of Say's other economic ideas, she concludes that there is an inconsistency with his analysis of the entrepreneur's role. The Law supposes a rapid equilibrating mechanism in case of a misjudged composition of total supply by the entrepreneurs, but in Say's *Cours Complet* the entrepreneurs, for various reasons, cannot always be trusted to perform that role. In Forget's summary:

> If a country lacks an industrial climate and does not foster the development of entrepreneurs, that nation will lag behind its neighbours in industrial development, and sometimes languish with economic opportunities not seized. Suddenly, the law of markets seems a lot more contingent and a little less spontaneous.

Kates himself discusses the policy consequences of what he calls the disappearance of Say's Law: 'The law of markets had been one of the pillars of economic thought before the publication of the *General Theory*. Its disappearance has damaged economic theory and policy beyond recognition.'

In his chapter 'Austrian Appreciation of the Law of Markets', Steven Horwitz notes the lack of interest in it in classic Austrian theory, but he does not mention the praise bestowed by Murray Rothbard on Say as the proto-Austrian par excellence. While others have pointed at a lacking or underdeveloped treatment of money in discussions of the law, Horwitz puts the examination of the money supply and the adjustment of the price level at the core of his defence of it and concludes: 'Say's Law is an explanatory principle of the spontaneous order of the market.'[44]

Bruce Keen revives the Marxian critique of Say's Law by reasoning that it is only applicable to 'a market economy without capitalists and the accumulation of wealth'. His interpretation of the law is incompatible with the existence of a surplus and of accumulation. As Marx himself disliked 'the dull Say' it is not surprising that till the present day, the two conflicting paradigms of capitalist development do not meet.

This Kates volume has addressed an important issue in the history of economics not as an antiquarian problem but as a question of present-day relevance. Yet I was left with the question whether Kates and some of his associates might not be victims of the same syndrome they pretend to attack. They combat the standard-Keynesian orthodoxy which represents 'Say's Law' as a theorem embracing everything that is wrong with classical economics. But aren't they fighting a comparable straw man in suggesting that Keynesian orthodoxy is part and parcel of twenty-first century mainstream economics? And if a principle is embraced by neo-Austrians and New Classicals alike, does this not signify that it must be a very broad notion indeed, badly needing further specification?

Alive and controversial

Jean-Baptiste Say was the most famous French classical economist. Even under the (wrong) label of being just the popular vulgariser of Adam Smith, he was tremendously successful in Europe and the US as a textbook author during the larger part of the nineteenth century. In the twentieth his reputation faded, only to become a byword for outdated classical misconceptions, ridiculed by Keynes as Say's Law. In the twenty-first century we seem to be witnessing a true Say revival, not only by reappraisals of his ideas on entrepreneurship and his Law, but also by new interpretations of his achievement as an institutional economist, primarily by Richard Whatmore and Evelyn Forget. The edition of his manuscript of *Politique pratique* will lead to deeper insights in this respect.

The divergent opinions on Say's economics summarised above clearly demonstrate that there still exists a sometimes fundamental disagreement on Say's contribution to classical economics and on 'what he really meant' – to use Baumol's wording. Sometimes he was his own worst enemy, who could not choose between the roles of scholar and of teacher. Regarding Say's work, Schumpeter has already noted that we must distinguish between superficiality of thought and superficiality of exposition. Some of the participants in modern discussions of

Say's economics have even demonstrated a truly partisan attitude, like Kates (pro) and Kurz and Gehrke (against). A number of their opinions might be condensed as headlines of sports match results in the following way.

On value

- Ricardo beats Say by knock-out (according to Kurz and Gehrke).
- Ricardo beats Say on points – in the misinterpretation of referee Hollander (according to this author).
- Say beats all other classicals as a proto-Austrian economist (according to Rothbard).

On 'markets'

- Malthus' paradigm beats Say's (Keynes).
- Ricardo's explanation is superior to Say's (Kurz and Gehrke).
- Say (1814) beats Mill and other classicals in priority (Baumol).
- Say's analysis beats Keynes and the Keynesians (Kates).

Someone whose legacy can still inspire such totally diverging interpretations after two centuries, may rightfully be called 'still alive'. Jean-Baptiste Say, in the last sentence of his *Cours Complet*, used a long-term perspective:

> The theory of débouchés, by showing that the interests of men and nations are not opposed one to another, will necessarily spread the seeds of concord and peace, which will germinate over time, and which will not be the smallest benefactions of the more precise opinion that people will have learned about the economy of society.

In the spirit of Say's optimistic perspective, this book is dedicated to my granddaughters. May they grow up as worthy members of a 'classe mitoyenne', and enjoy the 'free communication of friendship, the taste of reading and of travelling' (Say 1803).

Notes

1 Youthful revolutionary

1 Say papers, *Journal Anglais*, 1814.
2 Mme Duvoisin to le Sage, 1786; Bibliothéque Publique et Universitaire, Geneva. Published by Hitoshi Kitami.
3 Flandrin (1976) p. 191.
4 Comte (1834).
5 Quoted in Valynseele (1971) p. 27 n 31.
6 Blanc (2003).
7 Ibid.
8 *Cours Complet*, part 8 vol. VI: On taxes that contribute nothing to the treasury.
9 La Société des Amis des Noirs (1788–1793) and its successor, la Société des Amis des Noirs et des colonies (1796–1799) were the first anti-slavery organisations in France. Condorcet chaired a number of sessions of the first society. J.-B. Say and his wife were members of the second. Its minutes have been published in Dorigny and Gainot (1998).
10 Whatmore (2000) p. 78.
11 *De la Liberté de la Presse* pp. 15–16.
12 '*Pièce trouvée par mon père à la prise de la Bastille*' in Say family papers.
13 The French economist and statesman Jacques Necker (1732–1804) was born in Geneva; in 1789 he was director general of finance – effectively the French prime minister. He was the father of Mme de Staël.
14 Whatmore (2000) p. 85.
15 Tiran (1995) pp. 17–18.
16 Ibid. pp. 18–19.
17 *La Décade*, 10 prairial an II (29 May 1795) p. 412. In the Say family papers there is a testimony of Say's membership of the Arts Company.
18 Say papers, F 376–15.
19 The precise further family relations of the Duvoisins (other than Say's aunt, his father's sister) are not documented. They do not figure in Valynseele's genealogical work (1971). In 1798 Say made a note that 'my relatives Duvoisin' settled near Geneva, and in 1807 he recorded the death of his uncle Duvoisin.
20 The *écu* disappeared during the French Revolution, but the 5 franc silver coins minted throughout the nineteenth century were often still called *écu* by the French. By the middle of the 1790s, the assignats had undergone an enormous depreciation. Say's letter was written one year before the currency reform of 1795, which reintroduced the franc (at a slight discount from the livre). So his annual fixed income was 5000 francs.
21 The *Décade* office and Say's apartment were on the Rue Thérèse in the Parisian second arrondissement.

22 Kitchin (1966) is an excellent book on the subject. More recent is the very thorough PhD thesis of Regaldo (1976). Say's complete set of volumes, with his own copy of the founders' contract, is in the library of A. Heertje.

23 Kitchin (1966) p. 18; Letter of 22 vendémiaire, an III (13 October 1794), Duval papers.

24 *La Science du Bonhomme Richard*, par Benjamin Franklin, précédée par un Abrégé de la Vie de Franklin, par J.-B. Say; Paris 1794.

25 The law of Germinal, year III (March 1795) replaced the livre of 20 sous (each counting 12 deniers) by the decimal system of the franc (of 100 centimes). The conversion rate was 0.98765 F to the livre.

26 Letters of 5 and 22 vendémiaire, an III (September and October 1794), Duval papers, with sums of 600 and 400 F respectively. The Thermidorian Reaction had set off a new economic and monetary crisis. Committed to free-trade principles, the Thermidorians dismantled the economic regulation and price controls of year II. The depreciation of the assignats, which the Terror had halted, quickly resumed. By 1795 the cities were desperately short of grain and flour, while meat, fuel, dairy products and soap were entirely beyond the reach of ordinary consumers. By the spring of 1795 scarcity was turning into famine for working people of the capital and other cities. Surviving cadres of sansculottes in the Paris sections mobilised to halt the reaction and the economic catastrophe it had unleashed.

27 Whatmore (2000) p. 112.

28 Ibid.

29 The four classes of 1803 were: 1. Mathematical and physical sciences; 2. French language and literature; 3. History and ancient literature; 4. Fine arts. The second class of the Institut was responsible for the French language, and corresponded to the former Académie française. When King Louis XVIII came to the throne in 1816, each class regained the title of 'Académie'; accordingly, the second class of the Institut became the Académie française. Since 1816, the existence of the Académie française has been uninterrupted.

30 Kitchin (1966) pp. 3–5.

31 Say to Paschoud, 1 March 1797; Bibliothèque Publique et Universitaire, Geneva. Copy in Hashimoto photocopies collection.

32 *Mémoires de Gibbon; Suivis de quelques ouvrages posthumes et de quelques lettres du même auteur*. Recueillis et publiés par Lord Sheffield; traduits de l'anglais. Published 1797 'Chez le Directeur de la Décade philosophique in Paris'.

33 Lécuyer and Oberschall (1968) p. 40.

34 Ibid.

35 Picavet (n.d.) p. 538.

36 Kitchin (1966) pp. 118–119, 121.

37 Tiran (1995) p. 66.

38 Forget (1999) quotes Staum (1996) on the following attributes for important medical or philosophical authors belonging to the Idéologie: 1. attendance at the salons of Mme Helvétius, Destutt de Tracy or Condorcet in the period 1794–1807; 2. being on the staff of, or a contributor to *La Décade*; 3. moderate republican after 1794, and in opposition to Bonaparte after 1801.

2 At the crossroads of literature, politics and economics

1 Say's first son Horace was born in 1894, and his first daughter Andrienne in 1896.

2 In 1796 Vernes published his novel *Adélaïde de Clarencé, ou Les Malheurs et les Délices du sentiment*, which was for sale at the office of the *Décade* in the Rue Thérèse. This was a novel with a Rousseau-like theme: Vernes' father, a Genevan pastor, had been a friend of Rousseau. In the letter of 1797 Say told him about his dealings with other Parisian booksellers in promoting the sales of this novel.

3 François-René Molé [Molet] (1734–1802), French actor.

4 Mahérault was theatre commissioner from 1799 till 1806; Say's mentioning Olbie dates this letter to 1801 or a little later.

5 Forget (1999) p. 216.

6 Say to Duval, undated letter (possibly 1799), Duval papers nr. 87. In 1812 he thanked Michel Delaroche for lending Lactretelle's *History of France during the eighteenth century* to his son Horace, *as the history of the preceding century is a first necessity for any person wishing to be concisely informed* (Say to Delaroche, Copies de lettres, 25 February 1812).

7 Note for Prairial, an IV; Say papers, F 376–15. Before his 'Acta', started in 1806, Say only made a very summary list of events in his life.

8 Kitchin (1966) p. 193; *La Décade*, 20 prairial, an XII (June 1803).

9 Tiran (1995) pp. 78–79.

10 Ibid. p. 81.

11 Bonaparte's failure to win Acre (Akko in modern Israel) from the Ottomans, assisted by a British fleet, was the turning point of his Egyptian campaign. The Dutch historian J. Presser, quoting Albert Sorel, describes the French return to Egypt as 'Russia in the heat': wounded officers who had paid for their transport, were thrown from their stretchers without mercy (Presser (1960) p. 69). Horace's obituary was published in the *Décade* issue of Frimaire, year VIII. Valynseele (1971) summarises his career on pp. 32–33.

12 Kitchin (1966) pp. 120–121.

13 Tiran (1995) p. 74 n 3.

14 Engraving reproduced in Forget (1999) p. 24.

15 Miss Williams had been imprisoned as a Girondin sympathiser during the Jacobin Terror. After her release she travelled to Switzerland with the publisher John Hurford Stone, with whom Say would consider a business association in 1812.

16 B. Gainot in Dorigny and Gainot (1998) p. 365.

17 Quoted by Dorigny and Gainot (1998) p. 381.

18 Ibid. p. 382.

19 *La Décade*, 10 germinal, an IV (30 March 1796).

20 '…ouvrir toute l'influence aux Lumières.' Quoted by Tiran (1995) p. 58.

21 In a personal communication of December 2011, Prof. Israel wrote:

> You are absolutely right, though I would say in mitigation that the volume was not meant to go beyond the start of the French revolution. The reason I did not mention the Décade at all in DE is that I didnt then know about it. I do now and have been reading it extensively. You will be pleased to hear that it figures extensively in the smaller book I have written on ideology in the French Revolution that will be going to the press soon.

22 Quoted by Tiran (1995) p. 69 n3.

3 A dissident under the Consulate

1 Say papers, F 376, 15–16: *I am nominated into the Tribunat, and renounce the editorship of the Décade philosophique.*

2 Presser (1960) p. 160.

3 Ibid. (The imprint of *Olbie* was 1800, but apparently the book came out late in 1799.)

4 The revolutionary author, Sieyès' associate Charles Théremin, was a fellow member of Say in the Society of the Friends of the Blacks.

5 Whatmore (2000) chs 5 and 6 in particular.

6 Pierre-Louis Roederer (1754–1835) was a member for the Third Estate in the Estates-General of 1789. Changing sides several times in subsequent years, he became prominent during the Thermidorian Reaction. In 1796, he was made a member of the

Académie Française, was appointed to a professorship of political economy, and founded the *Journal d'économie publique, de morale et de legislation*. He was an active supporter of Bonaparte's coup in 1799.

7 Translations by Forget (1999) p. 200.
8 The neoclassical Panthéon in the university quarter of Paris was built between 1758 and 1790 as an abbey church dedicated to St Geneviè, and after many changes now functions as a secular mausoleum containing the remains of distinguished French citizens.
9 Forget (1999) p. 220.
10 *Cours Complet* (1828) I p. 166.
11 *Olbie* footnote, in Forget (1999) p. 204.
12 *Olbie* (End) Note V, in Forget (1999) p. 237.
13 Pierre-Laurent Bérenger (1749–1822) was a French poet and moralist. Emmanuel Joseph Sieyès (1748–1836), best known as Abbé Sieyès, was one of the chief theorists of the French Revolution; his most famous pamphlet was *What is the Third Estate?* (1789).
14 Shovlin (2006) p. 178.
15 In Forget (1999) p. 206.
16 Cesare Beccaria (1738–1794) was an Italian philosopher and penal law jurist.
17 Forget (1999) p. 210.
18 Shovlin (2006) p. 217. In 1802, Roederer also advocated the creation of the Légion d'Honneur by referring in the Legislative Body to the specifically French sense of honour.
19 In Forget (1999) pp. 229–230.
20 Ibid. p. 221, 223.
21 *Publications diverses* (of J.-B. Say), Say's annotated copy, privately bound and including a number of his pamphlets and offprints, in A. Heertje's library. Probably annotated after 1826; translation from Forget (1999) p. 242.
22 Whatmore (2000): Conclusion, pp. 217–219.
23 Steiner, in Say (2006 var. I*) p. XIX.
24 Whatmore (2000) p. 145.
25 Steiner, in Say (2006 var. I*) p XXIII n33.
26 Translation by Whatmore (2000) p. 149.
27 Translation by Palmer (1997) p. 53.
28 *Traité* (2006) I pp. 29–30.
29 Ibid. p. 58.
30 Forget (1999) p. 154.
31 The Prinsep translation was made from the fourth edition (1819).
32 [*Traité* 1803] Translation in Palmer (1997) pp. 71–73.
33 Quoted by Forget (1999) p. 33.
34 After 1790 Jacques Necker, Louis XVI's former finance minister, had exiled to Switzerland. The so-called 'Groupe de Coppet' around Mme de Staël and Benjamin Constant was still in its infancy at the time of Say's visit.
35 Say papers, F 376–60. Ch. A. de Calonne was the French controller general of finances between 1773 and 1787. He opposed Necker's measures during the latter's first ministry (1776–1781).
36 *La Décade*, 20 pluviôse, an IX (9 March 1801).
37 Tableau Chronologique, in Potier and Tiran (2003) p. 745.
38 Quoted by Forget (1999) p. 262 n 5.

4 Reluctant entrepreneur

1 The letters to Duval are in the Amaury Duval papers, *Musée Rolin*, Autun.
2 Landes (1966) p. 317.

3 Bergeron (1972) pp. 67–80.
4 Teilhac (1927) p. 25.
5 *Copies de mes lettres*, 3 December 1811.
6 Teilhac (1927) p. 26.
7 Officially the franc had replaced the livre in 1795. But even today the French still use the franc as an accounting unit parallel to the euro.
8 Holtman (1967) p. 612.
9 All letters by Say quoted in this and the following chapter are from Say's *Copies de lettres* in the Say papers.

10 *Les frais de commerce qui comprennent outre les appointements, les impositions, le chauffage et l'éclairage des bureaux et ateliers, l'entretien des machines en huiles, graisses, garnitures de cardes, peaux, draps, fil, soie, papier à ployer, à écrire, cordes et ficelles, nourriture de chevaux, toiles à tabliers, à paillasses, à bâches, couvertures d'ouvriers, partie des matériaux de menuiserie, serrurerie, fonderie, métaux, creusets, charbon se sont montés à 59278.74.*

Most probably, Say's 'interest' means capital cost including calculated interest on stocks. A net interest of 62,000 F would indicate a value of roughly one million for the company. At its dissolution in 1812 it was calculated at around 600,000 F.
11 'Industry' in Say's vocabulary always means 'human productive activity'.
12 Economic soup, also known as Rumford's soup, was boiled from potatoes, beans and old beer. The recipe had been invented by Count Rumford for prisoners and the poor in Bavaria. Rumford's experiments with 'houses of industry', savings banks and soup kitchens were mentioned favourably in the *Décade* in 1799.
13 A very hypothetical calculation might be that Say imagined himself to be one-quarter entitled to assets worth over 600,000 F. By depreciations and bankrupt debtors this sum had effectively shrunk to 400,000 F.
14 The sale of the meadows owned in Normandy was not successful; at the end of 1819 Say was still corresponding with a local cashier on the transfer of rents, and finally in 1822 the sale took place.
15 Say to Duval, 1808; Duval papers, Autun.

5 A rentier in a depressed economy

1 Six children were born to Say and his wife, four of whom grew up to adult age: Horace Émile (1794–1860), Adrienne, later called Andrienne (1796–1857), Hippolyte (1799–1805), Amanda (1802–1814), Octavie, called Fanny (1804–1865), Alfred (1807–1864). Valynseele (1971) mentions five children, omitting Hippolyte.
2 Quoted by Steiner, in Say (2006 var. I*) p. XIII (original emphasis).
3 John Hurford Stone (1763–1818) was a British radical political reformer and publisher who spent much of his life in France. His printing business published works by Thomas Paine, Thomas Jefferson and Constantin Volney, among other. He was bankrupted in 1812 by the high cost of printing the thirty-volume *Voyage de Humboldt et de Bonpland*.
4 Henri Casimir de Rham had emigrated from Switzerland to New York in 1805, and became a successful banker there. In July 1814 Say wrote him a detailed letter accompanying a procuration for cashing the interest on American loans he owned; this was a complicated affair as the US Consulate in Paris had been temporarily suspended, and de Rham would have to obtain official permission from the French Consulate in New York.
5 Teilhac (1927) p. 17.
6 Sismondi (1807) and Frossard (1807) to Say; quoted by Steiner, in Say (2006 var. I*) pp. XXV–XXVII.
7 Say to Paschoud, 19 May 1814, in *Copies de lettres.*

8 Not all booksellers paid the same price. Gravier paid 7.50, and Bossange 8.50.

9 Frédéric César de La Harpe (1754–1838), Swiss political leader and Vaudois patriot, tutor and confidant to Tsar Alexander I of Russia and a central figure in the creation of the Helvetic Republic (1798). He may have played a role in Say's dedicating his *Traité* to Alexander I in 1814.

10 The French bookseller Joseph DeBoffe had his shop in Gerrard Street from 1792 till 1807, so the information of Say was no longer up to date. An English translation of the *Traité* would only be produced in 1821, from the fourth edition of 1819.

11 Say papers, undated (1814?) and unnumbered note.

12 Say papers, F 375–2.

13 The parallel of lower prices and progress is a distinguishing characteristic of Say's analysis. In 1803, he takes the Physiocrats to task on this subject. He quotes Dupont de Nemours, who believes that lower prices mean lower wages for poor people, and will result in a lower national income ('revenu national'). Say argues that lower prices will lead to a reallocation of labour and capital, and result in higher total output and income.

14 *Traité* (2nd edn 1814) p. XLIX n 2:

> Verri said that reproduction was nothing more than the production of value, and that wealth consisted of the value of goods. Galiani ... said that labour was the source of all value; but Smith has appropriated these ideas and linked them, as one can see, to all other phenomena, and proved them by their consequences.

The Italian mercantilist Ferdinando Galiani (1728–1787) published his *Dialogue sur le Commerce des Blés* in French in 1769. The Italian philosopher, historian and economist Pietro Verri (1728–1797) published his *Elementi del Commercio* in 1769, arguing in favour of laissez-faire in trade.

15 Ibid. I p. 4.

16 *Traité* (var.) p. 592.

17 Steiner, in Say (2006 var. I*) p. XXVIII.

18 Baumol (1977). Actually Baumol is only listing seven 'propositions' of Say, jumping from four to six in his enumeration.

19 *Traité* (2nd edn. 1814) II pp. 75–76.

20 Steiner (2003).

21 Say [1814], *Traité* (var.) I p. 37.

22 Steiner (2003) p. 331.

23 Say (1828), *Cours Complet* I p. 300; quoted by Steiner (2003) p. 337.

24 Koolman (1971).

25 Ibid. p. 286.

26 Say, 'Lettre à Monsieur le President de la troisième Classe de l'Institut', Amsterdam University Library mss. 65 Ee 5. As it is undated, this version may have been Say's private copy. Annotated on top: 'Economie politique; Répondue le 24 Juin 1814'.

27 *RAPPORT fait à la Classe d'Histoire et de Littérature Ancienne de l'Institut, par M. GINGUENÉ, l'un de ses membres, sur le* Traité d'économie politique de M. SAY; 7 pp. leaflet printed as *Extrait du Mercure de France – Juin 1814.* The *Mercure gallant* originated in the seventeenth century as a newspaper and literary magazine. The title was changed to *Mercure de France* in 1724. The gazette was briefly suppressed from 1811 to 1814 and ceased publication in 1825. The name was revived in 1890.

6 Spying in Britain

1 Say to Dupont, 5 April 1814; quoted by Steiner, in Say (2006 var. I*) pp. XIII–XIV. Palmer (1997, p. 79), writes that Say only implicitly speaks about 'laissez-faire', so this is an exceptional use of the term. Say also used it in 1826 in relation to the Physiocrats, in his article *Economie politique* (p. 267).

2 He asked for the pamphlets of Hamilton on the *Sinking Fund*, and of Huskisson on *Paper Currency*; also, 'if they are not too expensive', the *Report of the Bullion Committee* and Bosanquet's *Practical Observations on the Report of the Bullion Committee*.

3 Louis Becquey (1760–1849) was the director general of commerce in 1814. Under his directorship of 'Bridges, Roads and Mines' (1817–1830) he introduced the 'Plan Becquey' for a system of canals in France.

4 Unnumbered 4 pp. note dated July 1814, in Say papers.

5 Say papers, F 376–37.

6 Landes (1966) p. 322:

> Iron manufacture was essentially a kind of cookery – requiring a feel for the ingredients, an acute sense of proportion, an 'instinct' about the time the pot should be left on the stove. The ironmasters had no idea why some things worked and others did not; nor did they care.

7 Kirkman Finlay, MP, was chairman of the Glasgow Chamber of Commerce in 1814 and 1816. In 1840, the economist Robbert Torrens wrote *A letter to Kirkman Finlay*.

8 He would remember this visit in an 1828 review in the *Revue Encyclopédique*.

9 Say to Becquey (?), 14 October 1814; in Hashimoto (1971).

10 The correct title of this annual was *Retrospect of philosophical, mechanical, chemical, and agricultural discoveries*; it published mainly technical articles copied from English and foreign sources.

11 Ricardo (ed. P. Sraffa 1951–1973) VI p. 157 n1.

12 This is documented in their correspondence; Say papers and British Museum, Add. Manuscripts 35152.

13 Mill to Ricardo, in Ricardo (ed. P. Sraffa 1951–1973) VI pp. 156–157.

14 John Herbert Koe (1783–1860) had been Bentham's secretary, and became a County Court judge.

15 Ten letters from Bentham to Say, 1818–1824; Say papers, Bibliothèque Nationale, Paris. Six letters from Say to Bentham, 1820–1824; Bentham papers, University College, London. Nineteen letters from Say to Place, 1817–1828; British Library, London.

16 Macvey Napier (1776–1847) was a Scottish legal scholar, and an editor of the *Encyclopaedia Brittanica*. He was editor of the *Edinburgh Review* from 1829. In 1816 he asked Say for information about the Banque de France, and was provided with the data he requested. Say's reply of 13 August 1816 was printed in Say's *Oeuvres Diverses*. Dugald Stewart (1753–1828) was a Scottish philosopher and mathematician. He wrote the first account of the life of Adam Smith. As professor of moral philosophy in Edinburgh, he also taught a course of political economy.

17 *De l'Angleterre et des Anglais* (1815); we quote the page numbers of the Steiner edition: *Jean-Baptiste Say, Cours d'économie politique et autres essais* (Steiner (1996a) pp. 51–52). Incidentally, here we have the only sentence in Say's works where he seems to give a positive verdict of Bonaparte. It is possible that he intended to make it sound a little sarcastic, like many other qualifications of the little general in his letters and publications. But the pamphlet came off the press during Napoleon's 'Hundred Days' return from Elba, in April 1815. So probably the best explanation is that Say – for once – chose for an opportunistic, positive labelling of 'this prince and his enormous talents'.

18 Steiner (1996a) p. 54.

19 Ibid. p. 58.

20 Ibid.

21 Ibid. p. 59.

22 The English Quaker Morris Birkbeck (1764–1825) published his *Notes on a Journey through France* (1814) after travelling around in the recently defeated country. He later moved to the United States.

23 Ibid. More than a century later, the historian Toynbee was to draw an almost identical picture as the ultimate consequence of a Ricardian economy:

> That world of gold-seeking animals, stripped of every human affection, for ever digging, weaving, spinning, watching with keen undeceived eyes each other's movements, passing incessantly and easily from place to place in search of gain, all alert, crafty, mobile – that world less real than the island of Lilliput which has never had and never can have any existence.

Quoted by Stedman Jones (2008) p. 220.

24 Ibid. p. 61.
25 Ibid. p. 60. Say is adding a footnote on British universities, which he had visited during his trip:

> There still are very good studies in Oxford, although a bit outdated. There is a more liberal approach at the University of Glasgow. The present professors in Edinburgh are sustaining the glory of this famous University. Philosophy and patriotism are combined with a taste for letters, and they are conferring a certain importance and solidity to literature, without however leading to puerile rhetoric. The *Edinburgh Review* is perhaps the best literary journal in the world; it is read from Philadelphia to Calcutta.

26 Ibid. p. 65 (original emphasis).
27 Say mentions spinning and weaving mills of cotton and of wool; breweries and crystal factories, muslin embroidery and butter churning. 'In New-Castle and Leeds, self-propelling steam engines are drawing behind them the carts with coal.'
28 Steiner (1996a) p. 75.
29 Ibid. p. 79. In his *Cours Complet* (1828–1829), in his fourth Part (out of nine), 'On the influence of institutions upon the economy', Say was to add as ch. XXVI a Digression on the origin, development and probable ending of the English India company.
30 Ibid. p. 80.

7 A dissident under the *Restauration*

1 Translation by Palmer (1997) pp. 83–84.
2 Ibid. p. 85.
3 Ibid. p. 86; the sum mentioned by Say roughly corresponds to the amount mentioned above, from his *Journal of personal affairs*.
4 Quoted in Palmer (1997) p. 88.
5 Say to S…, 9 May 1815; *Oeuvres Diverses* pp. 403–404. It is unclear whether this letter was effectively posted, or written as a document of self-justification. In a footnote, Say writes that:

> During the Hundred days, Bonaparte had asked Sauvo and Bassano to probe me about taking up my pen and proving that the rates of government paper was higher in France than in England, and that consequently the credit of the imperial government was superior to that of the British government. I refused and made this letter to prove that what they wished me to prove was false.

6 Say papers, A 11–17; Lazare Carnot (1753–1823), the 'Organiser of Victory' of the French Revolutionary army, was an exceptional soldier and a very good mathematician. After 1789 he organised the French conscription. During the Hundred Days he served as Napoleon's Minister of the Interior. He wrote to Say as 'my dear former colleague' although they never belonged to the same political body.
7 Say papers, A 44–53; François, Comte Barbé-Marbois (1745–1837) was a prominent civil servant under the First Republic and under Napoleon. During the First Restoration, he was made Peer of France by King Louis XVIII, and confirmed in his office

as president of the Cour des Comptes. Deprived of his positions by Napoleon during the Hundred Days, he was appointed minister of justice under the Duc de Richelieu (August 1815), tried unsuccessfully to gain the confidence of the Ultra-Royalists, and withdrew in May 1816.

8 The Athénée was the successor to the eighteenth century Lycée, combining the Musée de Paris with the Musée Scientifique. The aim of this institution was to provide good-quality education to the general public. After the return of Louis XVIII to Paris, the Lycée remained active under the name Athénée Royal until 1848. In 1815 Destutt de Tracy was its president, and Say's old friend and colleague Ginguené a board member. Steiner (1996a), in his introduction to Say's Athénée lectures (p. 38), finds it plausible that Say taught in 1815–1816, 1816–1817 and 1818–1819, but not in 1817–1818 and 1819–1820.

9 In August 1815 Say received an official refusal from the ministry. See Blanc (2003).

10 In the 1980s, an international project compared the institutionalisation of political economy at European, American and Japanese universities. For France, see Levan-Lemesle and Hecht (1986). According to Kadish and Tribe (1993), the demand for political economy in Britain was lagging behind that in other European countries. In the Netherlands, by contrast, King William I saw economics as the science of modernity and promoted the institution of 'staathuishoudkunde' chairs in law departments. So there was no close parallel between the theoretical advancement of the science, and a broad academic institutionalisation in the same country.

11 Probably the bookseller-publisher Arthus Bertrand.

12 Nicolas Clément (1778–1841) was a successful chemist in his own right as well as in his cooperation with C.B. Desormes. In 1819 he became a professor at the Conservatoire des Arts et Métiers, holding one of the three chairs in higher technical education established that year. Clément had to his credit, among other things, a beet-sugar refinery, a distillery that manufactured alcohol from potatoes and an alum refinery. After marrying Desormes' daughter he called himself Clément-Desormes. Samuel Widmer (1767–1824) had been active in the Society of Arceuil, which under Napoleon promoted chemical research, and organised industrial exhibitions. Textile printing was improved by the German-born, successful industrial Christophe Oberkampf and his nephew Samuel Widmer with the introduction of roller instead of block printing. This particular industrial process integrated bleaching with the application of new dyeing methods, notably Samuel Widmer's invention of a solid green dye. Widmer's obituary was published in the *Revue Encyclopédique*, August 1824.

13 Say papers, unnumbered file *Settlement with my partner Clément*.

14 According to Say's *Copies de letters* in the Say papers, he asked Clément in 1820 to collect information for him in England on the construction of canals, and the techniques of paper mills. In 1824 Say mentioned his 'friend' Clément in the *Revue Encyclopédique* as his informer on technical progress and the lowering of cost of production.

15 Ricardo (ed. Sraffa 1951–1973) VII p. 226. The generally very precise Sraffa has it wrong that the working partner would have been Say's brother Louis.

16 Ibid. p. 166.

17 *Copie de la lettre adressée par* M.J.-B. SAY *à Messieurs les Membres du Conseil d'Administration de la Compagnie d'Assurances générales*; 31 May 1818, Say papers, F 376–41. Reproduced in Schoorl (1980) pp. 157–158.

18 This so-called memoir of Bonaparte, originally published by John Murray in London, was soon discovered to be a fake. Among the names of its possible real authors, Mme de Staël and Benjamin Constant were mentioned.

19 Reviews in *Le Censeur Européen* IV (1817) pp. 74–96 and V (1817) pp. 105–128, signed J.B.S. Anon. [J.-B.Say], *De l'influence ministérielle sur les élections en Angleterre*; De l'imprimerie de Bossange, Et se trouve au bureau de Censeur Européen, Rue Gît-le-Coeur, no. 10.

20 Say to Place (in French), 21 December 1817 (original emphasis). B M add. mss. 25153–31.
21 Say to Duval, 11 December 1819. *Duval papers.*
22 *Éloge funèbre de Sir Samuel Romilly, Baronet, prononcé le 18 Décembre 1818 devant la société des amis de la Liberté de la presse & sur son désir exprès par J.-B. Say.* Say papers, unnumbered 30 pp. file. Even in spite of an annotation to have it included in the posthumous *Mélanges et correspondence* (ed. Ch. Comte and E. Daire, 1848), this intention was not fulfilled.
23 Say to Place, 15 December 1818 and 12 August 1820; B M add. mss. 25153–54 and 35159–165. The name of Adrienne Say, once she had become Mrs Comte, was always spelled as Andrienne.
24 Say to Place, 29 September 1823; B M add. mss. 35153–220. Place to Say, 6 October 1823; B M add. mss. 35153–225.
25 Ricardo to Malthus, 18 December 1814; Ricardo (ed. P. Sfraffa 1951–1973) VI pp. 161–165.
26 Ricardo to Trower, 14 December 1822; ibid. pp. 241–247. Hutches Trower (1777–1833) was a stockbroker and a lifelong friend and correspondent of David Ricardo.
27 Ricardo to Malthus, 18 December 1814; ibid. pp. 163–164.
28 Say papers, dossier *Valeur et prix*, I 403, and an unnumbered one *Rognures sur la valeur.*
29 Say to Ricardo, 21 July 1817; Ricardo (ed. P. Sfraffa 1951–1973) VII p. 166.
30 Ricardo (1819) II p. 297n.
31 Ibid. I p. 12n, 14n, 18n.
32 *Traité*, 4th edn. II p. 4n; Latin quote: 'It is good to learn from one's enemy'. The informed reader knew who the enemy was.
33 Ibid. p. 9.
34 Ricardo to Say, 11 January 1820; Say to Ricardo, 2 March 1829; in Ricardo (ed. P. Sraffa 1951–1973) VIII pp. 149–150 and 161–162.
35 Say papers, dossier I 403:

> This was part of a refutation of the thesis that labour is an exact measure of value. I have withdrawn it as being too metaphysical. The only side where Smith's doctrine in this matter can be maintained is the following. No merchandise can for a long period be offered below its cost price, because no one will condemn himself to a constant loss when he can do otherwise.

The note continues with examples that, in time and space, the price and quality of labour can be quite variable.
36 Smith [1776] *The Wealth of Nations* (5th edn. 1789), Say's copy in Bibliothèque de l'Institut, Paris; note on ch. V p. 44. Hitoshi Hashimoto (1980, 1982) has published Say's comments and notes from this private copy.
37 Say papers, dossier I 403; notes *Nature des Richesses* and *Ricardo et Say d'accord.*
38 *Traité* (5th edn. 1826) pp. XXXIII–XXXV.
39 Quoted in Sowell (2006) p. 108.
40 *Traité* (5th edn. 1826) p. 169 (original emphasis).
41 *Mélanges et Correspondence*, pp. 86–91.
42 Ricardo (ed. Sraffa 1951–1973) VI pp. XXVI–XXVII. Sraffa consulted the Ricardo letters from the Say papers in the 1930s, and sent them back to the latter's descendants in Nantes; they were probably burnt there in a bombing fire during the war. Say annotated the wrapper of Place's translation: 'Stored herein is the English translation Place had tried to make, which is worth nothing.' See below Chapter 8 for the meeting of Say with Place in London in 1825, and their communication about the Ricardo correspondence.
43 Say to Ricardo, 19 July 1821 in *Mélanges et correspondence*. Speaking of welfare as

the balance between human needs and useful goods, Say added the following in the printed version:

> ... if, by a hypothesis impossible to be completely fulfilled, we would be able to obtain all imaginable utilities from free services, we would all be richer than David Ricardo, as there are desirable things surpassing the purchasing power of the largest fortunes.

In this letter he also inquired about the possibility of becoming a foreign member of the Political Economy Club.

44 Steiner (2010).
45 Ibid. p. 576.
46 Ibid. p. 574.
47 *Cours Complet* I p. 238n.
48 Kurz and Gehrke (2003).
49 It must be remarked that no copies of Say's letters have survived from May 1816 till June 1819. The letter of April 1815 was not formulated as a reminder of a final instalment, so the complete settlement of Grivel's debt must have been arranged between 1816 and 1819.
50 Say papers, *Copies de lettres*, June–August 1815.
51 Ibid., letters of August and November 1815. John Murray was Ricardo's publisher.
52 Ibid., Say to Treuttel & Wurtz, 11 October 1822. As no copied letters have survived from May 1816 to June 1819, it is possible that Say sent other reminders to London during this period.
53 Say to Déterville, 23 June 1819; Say papers, *Copies de lettres*.
54 Say to Déterville, 8 April 1826; ibid.
55 Say papers, *Copies de lettres*, 9 November and 13 December 1815.
56 The fame of Isigny butter goes back to the sixteenth century. In the nineteenth century, the population of Paris alone consumed 800 tonnes of butter a year.
57 Say to Dumont, 18 September 1918; published in Kitami (2003).
58 Say (1817), *Petit Volume, contenant quelques aperçus des hommes et de la société.*
59 Bentham to Say, 4 June 1818; Say papers, A 67–6.
60 Storch to Say, 22 January and 20 November 1816; Say papers, A 116–97/98.
61 King Charles XIV to Say, 18 December 1818; Say papers, A 5–11.
62 Potier (2006, 2010).
63 Say [1821].
64 Gutierrez to Say, 7 January, 23 May and 25 July 1817; Say papers, A 89–48/50.
65 Neither Potier (2006) nor Potier (2010) mentions the existence of a second Italian edition to which Chitti seems to refer here. The criticism of Gioja was still vivid ten years later, when Say wrote to an unnamed journal editor – very probably Jullien of the *Revue Encyclopédique* – about a Milanese journal in which Gioja criticised Say and Dupin. See Hashimoto (1971).
66 Morstadt to Say, 12 March and 11 April 1818, 12 October 1820 and 7 August 1821; Say papers, A 104–72/75. L.H. Jakob had been the German translator of the first edition of Say's *Traité*.
67 On 13 February 1820, Charles-Ferdinand, Duc de Berry was murdered on the steps of the Paris Opera while helping his pregnant wife into a carriage. Berry was the nephew of Louis XVI, and a possible heir to the throne. In September the Duchess gave birth to 'The Miracle Child'.
68 Rau to Say, 29 November 1820; Say papers, A 110–93.
69 Prinsep to Say, July 1821; Say papers, A 108–81.
70 Biddle to Say, 29 May 1824; Say papers, A 69–19. Say prepared a French translation of this letter.

8 Late recognition

1 Say (1818a), Paris (Déterville), 23 pp. Say (1818b), Paris (Déterville), 35 pp. Until recently, the food market of the La Villette quarter was an important link in the provisioning of Paris.

2 Say to Lafitte, 30 January 1821, in *Oeuvres Diverses* (1848) pp. 564–570.

3 Guillaume Louis Ternaux, called 'Ternaux l'Aîné' (1763–1833), was a rich entrepreneur and French politician. One of the most influential industrial entrepreneurs of his age, he became an administrator of the Banque de France and a representative in parliament of the Seine department. He invented the first European cashmere tissues, and created the 'shawls of Ternaux', woven from Tibetan and Nubian wool. His large Château d'Auteuil is presently housing the Lycée Jean-Baptiste Say.

4 Ternaux ainé (1818), Paris, 52 pp. On pp. 33–50, a letter from Say to Ternaux, dated 5 September 1818, is reproduced. Ternaux writes in his introduction:

> I have tried to let myself be deeply influenced by everything that the most distinguished authors on the subject, such as Adam Smith, Turgot, Galiani, Necker, and Say have written on this matter; but I must confess that, doubtful about my own insights, I would have found it difficult to decide to present and publish my project of a Compagnie de prévoyance, if I would not have been encouraged by one of them whom I have even consulted. Of the answer I have received, containing a number of more developed remarks and considerations, useful to my project, I gratefully use the permission he has given me to include it in this memorandum.

5 Say to anon., 4 June (1818?); Hashimoto photocopies collection.

6 Say to Thénard, 1818; *Mélanges et Correspondance*, pp. 520–525. Louis Jacques Thénard (1777–1857) was a very successful chemist, and the author of a widely used and translated textbook. From 1808 he was a professor of chemistry at the University of Paris. He and Say had known each other at least since 1816, when he wrote a letter of thanks after receiving a copy of Say's *Traité*:

> This is no equal exchange. You give me a first class work, the extreme merit of which is recognised in all civilised countries, a work that will not change and that will still be read in the coming centuries, while I have offered you one that will pass by like all other elementary works.

7 Archives Nationales, Paris: *Séances du Conseil de Perfectionnement du Conservatoire des Arts et Métiers*. Charles Dupin (1784–1873) was a naval engineer and mathematician. In 1818 he was elected to the Académie des Sciences. He encouraged the establishment of schools and libraries, the founding of savings banks, the construction of roads and canals and the use of steam power.

8 As from January 1820, Say kept a very summary *Comptes Courants*, as a sequel to his *Journal des Affaires personnelles*. Under the management of Horace, his private capital went up again: in September 1826, it stood at just over 38,000 F. After 1828, only a few expenses for Charles and Andrienne Comte have been recorded.

9 Liesse (1901). Liesse was Say's distant successor at the chair of 'Economie Industrielle et Statistique'. In his article, he acknowledges having consulted the Say papers with regard to Say's lecture notes and the students' letters he received.

10 Say papers; tables of content, *Cours du Conservatoire*.

11 Ibid. April 1824: *As from April 14, the precautions I have to take and the rule of life I have to follow as a consequence of my attack of 4 April, do not allow me to resume my lectures of this year.*

12 Liesse (1901) p. 35.

13 Ibid. p. 40.

14 Mill [1873] p. 51. He continued:

> He lived a quiet and studious life, made happy by warm affections, public and private. He was acquainted with many chiefs of the Liberal party, and I saw various noteworthy persons while staying at his house; among whom I have pleasure in the recollection of having once seen Saint-Simon, not yet the founder of either a philosophy or a religion, and considered only as a clever *original.*

15 Say papers, dossier G 385 *Principe d'Utilité.*

16 Quoted in Liesse (1901) p. 50.

17 Ibid. p. 54.

18 A letter of 7 March 1822 from John Cowell, secretary of the Political Economy Club, informed Say that he had been elected as 'honorary member' (a possibility created for foreigners not permanently domiciled in England); Say papers, A 79–33. Ricardo, Malthus, James Mill and Robert Torrens had founded this society in 1821. Ricardo had proposed Say's honorary membership: Political Economy Club, *Minutes etc.* (Centenary Volume 1921) pp. XVI, 11–13, 18.

19 Adler (on behalf of the Danish prince) to Say, 17 June 1823; Say papers, A-1. The letter accompanied a copy of the Danish translation of Say's *Traité.*

20 In the Say papers, these letters have been kept together in a separate third file of letters received, together with a number of Say's answers to specific students' questions.

21 Say (1820), Paris and London (Bossange).

22 Say to Sismondi, 16 August 1820; Hashimoto photocopies collection.

23 James (1979) p. 366.

24 *The Morning Chronicle* was founded in 1769. It was bought by James Perry in 1789, bringing the journal firmly down on the Whig side. The content often came from journalists labelled as radicals, a dangerous connotation in the aftermath of the French Revolution. Several charges of libel and seditious libel were levelled against the newspaper and its contributors at one time or another, Perry being sentenced to three months in gaol in 1798.

25 John Crawfurd (1783–1868) was a Scottish physician, colonial administrator and diplomat, and author. He is best known for his work on Asian languages, his *History of the Indian Archipelago* and his role in founding Singapore.

26 Perry to Say, 22 September 1820; Say papers, A 105–75.

27 See Blaug (1997) for the close relationship between the two theories.

28 Schumpeter (1954) pp. 615–625.

29 Sowell (1972).

30 Baumol (1977) (the article only discusses seven versions).

31 Sismondi to Say, 18 May 1823; Say papers, A 115–96 mondi. J.C.L. Simonde de Sismondi (1773–1842) was born in Geneva. He was a bank clerk, farmer and professional author of economics and history. He wrote: 1. *Tableau de l'agriculture toscane* (1801); 2. *De la richesse commerciale*, 2 vols (1803); 3. *Historie des républiques italiennes du moyen age*, 16 vols; 4. *Nouveaux principes d'économie politique*, 2 vols (1819); 5. *Histoire des français*, 31 vols. As a philosopher on liberty, he influenced Benjamin Constant. As an economist, Schumpeter labelled him as 'thoroughly prolabour'; by others he is ranked among the early socialists.

32 Schumpeter (1954) p. 620. He continues: 'The professional world has laughed at him ever since.'

33 In the second edition of the *Traité* (II p. 152n) he comments on Napoleon's statement on the large number of casualties in the battle of Eylau (1807): 'One Parisian night will compensate it all.' Say's angry human capital approach counters with the comment: 'It takes one night, and after that twenty years of care and expenses, to shape a man whom the cannon slaughters in an instant.'

34 Sismondi to Say from Geneva, 3 September 1820; Say papers, A 115–94. Say's first note reads in French: 'C'est une seule et même chose.' Emphasis by Sismondi.

35 Sismondi and Say (1824) in *Revue Encyclopédique*; translation by Forget (1999) p. 174.

36 *Traité* [5th edn. 1826] var. I p. 261.

37 *Traité* [4th edn. 1819] var. I p. 137.

38 J.-B. Say (1836), *Mélanges et Correspondence*, p. 219: '...ma théorie demeure entière'. Sowell (1972) wrongly translated this as: 'My theory of markets *becomes* complete'. See Chapter 10 below.

39 Sismondi (1827); J.-B. Say's copy (now in the library of A. Heertje) with some of his annotations cut off by the binder – my guesses inserted (emphasis added).

40 Baumol (1977) p. 160.

41 Forget (1999) p. 175.

42 *Traité* (1803) I p. 389. Of course he was standing on the shoulders of the *French predecessors of Malthus* (the title of J.J. Spengler's book, 1942).

43 Say to Prévost, 19 March 1810; published by Kitami (1999).

44 *Traité* (1814) II p. 148 n1.

45 The anarchist philosopher William Godwin (1756–1836) was the husband of the feminist Mary Wollstonecraft. In 1793 he published *An Inquiry concerning Political justice*, and in 1820 *Of Population*, an essay against Malthus. One letter by him is kept in the Say papers, dated 1822 (A 30–38); it is a brief introduction of Henry Rosser (1799–1822), the author of a pamphlet supporting Godwin against Malthus. (Rosser drowned on this visit to Paris.)

46 Schumpeter (1954) p. 580 n7.

47 *Mélanges et Correspondance*, pp. 238–239.

48 Everett to Say, 18 February 1824; Say papers, A 84–42. French translation in *Mélanges et Correspondance*.

49 Everett (1826). Say's manuscript note in Say Papers, carton H 392 *Population*.

50 Everett to Say, 1829; Say papers, A 84–43. Apart from the specific subject under consideration, Everett's letter offers another example of the widely accepted division between the 'modern British [Ricardian] school' in economics, and the followers of Say.

51 Guillaumont (1969) p. 65.

52 De Brême to Say, 20 April 1819 and 30 October 1820; Say papers, A 73–24 and A 73–25.

53 Say to De Gérando, 30 March 1819; Hashimoto photocopies collection.

54 'Z.' (1824).

55 Klotz (2010).

56 Ibid. pp. 412–413.

57 Ibid. p. 434.

58 Say to Bentham, 1823; British Museum add. mss.

59 Julie Deloche Say, English Diary 1825; in Raoul-Duval family papers.

60 The Combination Act 1799, titled *An Act to prevent Unlawful Combinations of Workmen* prohibited trade unions and collective bargaining by British workers. An additional act was passed in 1800. Sympathy for the plight of the workers brought repeal of the acts in 1824. Lobbying by Francis Place played a role in this. However, in response to the series of strikes that followed, the *Combination Act of 1825* was passed, which allowed labour unions but severely restricted their activity.

61 Wallas (1918) pp. 237–238. Joseph Hume (1777–1855) was a Scottish doctor and radical MP. In March 1823 he had sent a pamphlet on health and economy to Say; Say papers, A 34–42.

62 Mill to Say, 25 May 1825; published by A. Heertje in *History of Political Economy*, vol. III no. 2 (1971) pp. 417–418.

63 In the first edition ch. XXVIII, *Du produit des colonies*; in editions 2–6 ch. XIX, *Des Colonies et de leurs produits.*

64 *Traité* (var.) p. 404.

65 Ibid. p. 405.
66 Ibid. p. 407; from the fourth edition (1819) a footnote was added:

> It must be remarked that the free worker, whose day wage is paid more dearly than the slave's, executes a job which, if less troublesome, is almost always more costly because of the intelligence and talent it requires. Generally watchmakers and tailors are free labourers.

67 Ibid. pp. 412–413.
68 *Lettre de Mr. Jean Baptiste Say, auteur du Traité d'Economie Politique, à Mr. Polidore Martelly, négociant, à Londres*; 4 pp. printed by J. McCreery, Tooks Court, Chancery Lane, London. Say's letter was dated 9 April 1822. Polidore Martelly shows up in trading partnerships in London and Haiti in the early 1820s. It is evident that he had a personal interest in setting up his business in Port-au-Prince as a foreigner, and therefore he may have made Say's letter public.
69 Alexandre Pétion (1770–1818) was the son of a French colonist and a freeborn woman of colour. In 1806 he was elected president of the South Haitian Republic. He actively supported Simon Bolivar (with money, soldiers and ammunition) in return for a promise to abolish slavery in South America. Say writes about him in the Letter to Polidore Martelly:

> *Ah! Petion! You honest and sweet soul, whose hand I shook more than once in our philanthropical reunions, when we flattered ourselves with the prospect of seeing slavery destroyed and all colonies growing in independence, in wealth, and in happiness, could you have thought that proposals destructive for economic liberty ... what? destructive for the natural rights of man, could be pronounced by one of your fellow citizens, and that he would not be ashamed at pleading for institutions which our old tyrants in Europe would not even dare to re-establish!*

70 Adam Hodgson, *A letter to M. Jean-Baptiste Say, on the comparative expense of free and slave labour*; Liverpool 1823, 55 pp. with a 17 pp. appendix. An American edition was published in the same year, as well as a second English one, including Say's reply.
71 The pamphlet's reviewer in the *Revue Encyclopédique* (1823) even remarked: 'It seems that in Europe no work on political economy can inspire confidence, if it has not, so to speak, obtained the sanction of our famous fellow-countryman.'
72 *Cours à l'Athénée* [1819] ed. Steiner (1996a) p. 213.

9 The final years

1 Its full title was: *Revue encyclopédique ou analyse raisonnée des productions les plus remarquables dans la littérature, les sciences et les arts*. It was a successor to: *Annales encyclopédiques* (1817–1818), which had followed up the *Magasin encyclopédique* (1795–1816). Its founder Marc Antoine Jullien (1775–1848) had been a young Jacobin during the French Revolution, close to Robespierre and Condorcet. Like Say, he transformed from a supporter to a critic of Bonaparte. During the *Restauration*, he was a journalist and educational reformer.
2 Forget (1999) includes most – but not all – of his articles in her bibliography.
3 Nardin (1965).
4 Say to Jullien, 22 July 1824; Amsterdam University Library mss. 65 Ee. Jullien commented in the margin upon the society: *Sorte de mouvement historique qui appartient à nos annales de la civilisation.*
5 Say (1824a).
6 Quoted in Nardin (1965) p. 108.
7 Ibid. p. 111.
8 Moody to Say, 25 March 1828; Say papers, A 103–70.

9 J.-B.S. 'On the progress of useful arts', in *Revue Encyclopédique*, February 1824, pp. 481–482.

10 J.-B.S. (1826) in *Revue Encyclopédique* pp. 116–119 (original emphasis).

11 Say to anon. [doubtlessly Jullien] 1827, in Hashimoto (2004) p. 228.

12 Say to Jullien, 30 September 1825, in Hashimoto (1971).

13 Say to Schnitzler, 20 September 1832, in Hashimoto (2004) p. 235.

14 Schumpeter (1954) p. 492.

15 Thomas Tooke (1774–1853) was an economist and statistician, and one of the founders of the Political Economy Club. The six-volume *History of Prices* is his best-known work. George Grote (1794–1871) was a banker, political radical and MP, and classical historian. He was the author of *A History of Greece*. His wife Harriet was the biographer of the Dutch painter Ary Scheffer, and of her husband. John Austin (1790–1857) was a legal philosopher and professor of jurisprudence at the University of London. His wife Sarah was an editor and translator of German.

16 Say to Place, 11 and 27 November 1825, 18 January 1826; British Museum add. mss. 35152–229–235.

17 Sarah Austin to Say, 6 December 1831; Say papers, A 66–4.

18 Harriet Grote to Say, 23 July 1828; Say papers, A 88–47: *Business goes on smoothly – money is very abundant. interest 3 p.cent and sometimes even less.*

19 Say papers: Bentham to Say, 4 June 1818 on *Petit Volume*; 4 August 1823 on Count Toreno who in spite of a personal introduction had been allowed no further than the doorstep, *even if he would have been King Toreno.* Say to Bentham, 9 September 1828 on General O'Connor: *he was in a way to salvation as numbering himself among my disciples; though it does not appear that he has left all to follow me.*

20 Say to Place, 12 September 1824; B M add. mss. 35153–227.

21 Bentham to Say, undated (after 1825); Say papers, A 67–15.

22 R. Doane and Bentham to Say, 11 March 1820; Say papers, A 67–10.

23 Bentham to Say, 11 September 1818; Say papers, A 67–8. Peregrine Bingham (1788–1864) was an English legal writer and police magistrate; he was a friend of John and Sarah Austin.

24 Quoted in Schoorl (1982) p. 13. Unlike the Say papers, the ring has not survived in the Raoul-Duval family (the descendants of Octavie Say and Charles Raoul-Duval).

25 Sinclair to Say, 1 January 1821 and 28 April 1834; Say papers, A 114–92 and 93. Sir John Sinclair (1754–1835) was a Scottish politician, writer on finance and agriculture and the first person to use the word *statistics* in the English language, in his pioneering work, *Statistical Account of Scotland* (21 volumes).

26 Henry James to Say, 31 July 1822; Say papers, A 93–55. O'Brien (1994).

27 Say to Tooke, 14 May 1825, in *Mélanges et Correspondence*, pp. 525–526.

28 Cazenove to Say, 20 March 1828; Say papers, A 76–29 (original emphasis). John Cazenove (1788–1879), a businessman of Huguenot descent, was a supporter and friend of Malthus, who proposed him for membership of the Political Economy Club. In *A Reply to Mr. Say's Letters to Mr. Malthus* (1821) and in other publications he criticised Say's Law.

29 Say to Cuvier, 3 October 1826, in Hashimoto (1971) p. 225.

30 Daru to Say, 2 November 1826; Say papers, A 19–27.

31 Andrieux to Say, 10 December 1826; Say papers, A 3–4.

32 Say to anon. (Andrieux?), 3 August 1828, in Hashimoto photocopies collection: *I have paid tribute to the Académie Française with the first volume of my Cours Complet d'Economie politique: hereby accept the second which I beg you to present to it. By placing it under your aegis, I am sure of having an excellent protector.*

33 Handwritten copy by Say of his letter to Raynouard, 9 November 1829; glued into vol. 1 of the *Cours Complet* in A. Heertje's library.

34 The lawyer and novelist Jean Ch.P. Lacretelle (1766–1855) was an Academy member from 1811. He wrote to Say in January 1830: *Thanks to your persevering cares and to*

the sagacity of your excellent mind, the torch lit by the Quesnays, the Gournays and the Turgots, does no longer throw a flickering light.

35 Letter of Andrieux, 12 July 1830: *I cannot or must not announce to you anything positive; for the Academy has not, and I believe will not, pronounce itself definitely before the first of August; I will only tell you (but keep this for yourself; as it must be kept a secret) that the Commission is of the best disposition with regard to your work; that not only it sees it as a very good book, written to advance and propagate the Science of political economy; but that it also believes that a book intending to inspire the love of work and of economy is useful to everybody. Your presence, at the session of St. Louis, is not indispensable, but perhaps you would be glad to assist.*

36 Say to Deterville, [July?] 1828 in *Copies de Lettres*.

37 *Acta*, 3 December 1829 and 10 January 1830.

38 *Acta*, 27–29 July 1830: *Revolution, Charle [sic] X is dethroned. We learn about it while staying with my brother Louis in Nantes.*

39 *Acta*, 29 September and 2 October 1930.

40 Archives Nationales, dossier F 17–13556, file 24: *Chaire d'Economie Politique*. In all countries mentioned, a translation of Say's *Traité* had been published.

41 Archives Nationales, dossier F 17–13551: *Procès verbaux* of the professorial nominations.

42 Ibid. dossier F 17–13556, dossier 24; Silvestre de Sacy, the ministerial administrator, advised to adopt the advice of the professorial committee 'without mentioning Mr. Blanqui, or anybody else. Approved by the minister.' Antoine Isaac, Baron Silvestre de Sacy (1758–1838), was a French orientalist, professor of Arabic languages and rector of the University of Paris. As a member of the Committee of Public Instruction he was involved in Say's nomination. In 1816 he had written to Say, thanking him for a copy of the *Traité*: Silvestre de Sacy to Say, 25 June 1816; Say papers, A 57–67.

43 Ibid. Dossier F 17–3856: *Etats des Traitemens*. *Acta*, 4 June 1831.

44 Division of Say's estate, document of 14 December 1832; Raoul-Duval family papers.

45 *Archives Nationales*, dossier Conservatoire and dossier F17–13556, file 24.

46 Say [1821] in Steiner (1996a) p. 309.

47 Dossiers numbered *K* in Say papers. The forthcoming edition of Say's *Politique pratique* as a volume of his *Oeuvres Complètes* will enable further study on his political thought, and may lead to publications comparable to Donald Winch's *Adam Smith's Politics* (1978).

48 The full manuscript text of these sessions was used by Say in his utility essay, and is therefore absent in the edition of Steiner (1996a). The subject matter was labelled by Say in his remaining notes as 'Summary analysis' for the fourth, and 'Analytical table' for the fifth lecture of 1819. Steiner has annotated the points which were indeed used by Say in his utility essay; these are discussed in the next chapter. See Steiner (1996a) pp. 167–168.

49 Say (1827).

50 Ibid. p. 3.

51 Ibid. p. 20.

52 Say (1828).

53 Say (1827) p. 21.

54 Ibid. p. 27.

55 Say (1826b) p. 302.

56 Ibid. p. 266.

57 Ibid. p. 267.

58 Ibid. p. 269.

59 Ibid. p. 270: 'Bonaparte detested political economy; not because he understood any of it, but by instinct, and because arbitrariness does not want to be tied by any principle.'

60 Ibid. p. 271.

61 Ibid. p. 273.
62 Say (1828).
63 Ibid. p. 30.
64 Say (1836) p. 460.

10 Among masters, peers and students

1 Groenewegen (2002).
2 Steiner (1998a).
3 Say wrote summarising as well as critical notes in the margin of his own copy of *The Wealth of Nations*. Both have been edited by Hitoshi Hashimoto (1980, 1982).
4 *Wealth of Nations* (5th edn. 1789), Say's copy I, 119.
5 Say papers, F 375–2; Say crossed out his original first sentence: *An English journal, while giving much praise to my work, accuses me of...*
6 Say to Cowell, 22 April 1822; *Mélanges et Correspondance*, p. 439.
7 J.-B. to Louis Say, 21 April 1822; ibid. p. 543. Letter of 1827 in *Mélanges et Correspondance* (1848) p. 545.
8 Undated note in Say papers; also quoted by Tiran (1995) p. 44.
9 Etienne Dumont (1759–1829) was a Genevan pastor and legal scholar, best known as the editor of several of Bentham's works, starting in 1802. In 1789 he went to France and worked with Mirabeau on the *Courrier de Provence*; this must have been the occasion of his first meeting with Say. He moved to England where he worked closely with Bentham, and returned to Geneva in 1814.
10 This is plausibly argued by Whatmore (2000) p. 2007. Forget (1999) strangely neglects the influence of Bentham, and Palmer (1997) is doubtful if Say already knew his work in 1803.
11 Kitami (2003) p. 687.
12 Ibid. p. 688.
13 Bentham to Say, 11 March 1820; Say papers, A 67–10. Franz-Xaver Swediaur (1748–1824) was an Austrian-born doctor, author of a treatise on syphilis. Ricardo had dinner with him in Paris in 1817, and Say introduced him to Francis Place in 1818.
14 Bentham to Say, 19 October 1823; Say papers, A 67–12. Does Bentham refer here to Ricardo's *Principles*, or to one of his own works?
15 Say papers, Dossier G 385, Principe d'Utilité; taken from his lecture notes for 1819 at the Athénée (original emphasis):

> *But digging deeper into this subject we wished to know wherein consisted not the estimated, but the real utility of things. ... We have seen that this principle which we called the* principle of utility, *far from being opposed to the strictest moral principles, was entirely in conformity with these, and that – when applied to the relations between governments and the people, or the people mutually – it was worthy of human beings who had arrived at their highest level of maturity; worthy of the perfect man.*

16 Say papers, Dossier G 385.
17 Say (1836), 'Essai sur le Principe de l'Utilité', in *Mélanges et Correspondance d'Economie Politique*, pp. 665–676.
18 Say to Dumont, 5 March 1829; quoted by Kitami (2003) p. 690.
19 Say to Dumont, 10 May 1829; quoted by Kitami (2003) pp. 690–691.
20 Say to Malthus, July 1827, in *Mélanges et Correspondance* (1836) p. 645.
21 Say [1820] in Steiner (1996a) p. 242.
22 Say (1836) p. 346.
23 Schumpeter (1954) p. 491.
24 Say to Malthus, 24 February 1827, *Mélanges et Correspondance* p. 639.

25 Ibid. p. 640; Say's adaptation of his law consisted of admitting the possibility of unemployment by the introduction of new machinery, and of considering the necessity of compensating government spending.
26 Malthus to Say, n.d. [1827], ibid. pp. 640–644.
27 Say to Malthus, July 1827, ibid. p. 644.
28 Roggi (1972) p. 963.
29 Say (1826a) (original emphasis).
30 Ibid. pp. 112–114.
31 Say to Sismondi, 29 August 1828; quoted by Steiner (2003) p. 355.
32 See Kitami (2003).
33 Claude Adrien Helvétius (1715–1771) was a French materialist philosopher. His most famous work is *De l'Esprit* (1758). He influenced Beccaria with regard to penal law, and Bentham with regard to utilitarianism. François Jean de Beauvoir, Marquis de Chastellux (1734–1788) was a French general, author and member of the Académie Française. He served with the French troops in the American War of Independence. In 1772 he published *De la Félicité Publique* (a copy of which was owned by Say). In 1774 he wrote the *Éloge de M. Helvétius*. In one of the population chapters of the *Cours Complet* (1836, p. 381 n1) Say called Chastellux' work 'one of the most recommendable books of the last century', and its author 'an equally bright thinker and fine author'.
34 Say papers, third dossier *Correspondance*; nine answered letters A 121, 1–9; 12 unanswered A 129bis-140; seven unnumbered letters classified as *difficultés*, numbered A-G, with answers attached.
35 Say papers, A 129bis-30 (anon. and undated).
36 Say papers, A 129bis-28 (Balthasard); unnumbered (Balland), annotated as 'answered'.
37 Johnson to Say, 5 March 1829; Say papers, A 129bis-26.
38 Velez to Say, 30 December 1823; Say papers, A 129bis-34.
39 Say's unnumbered answer to student letter of 19 February 1830, A 129bis-19; Say papers.
40 Bidaux to Say, 1823; Say papers, A 129bis-35 to 38.
41 Letter of 8 February 1821; Say papers, third dossier *Correspondance*, A-9.
42 Say papers, F 380–47; dossier *Etudes, Récommendations à moi-même*.

11 Alive after 200 years

1 Sowell (1972).
2 Say to Malthus (1826), *Mélanges et Correspondance*, pp. 204–208.
3 Sowell (1974) pp. 47–48.
4 Anikin (1975) pp. 303–304.
5 Ibid. p. 305.
6 Palmer (1997).
7 Ibid. p. 5.
8 Whatmore (2000).
9 Ibid. p. 219.
10 Hollander (2005).
11 Ibid. p. 227.
12 Ibid. p. 94.
13 Say, *Traité* (1817), as quoted by Hollander (2005) p. 118 (my translation).
14 Ibid. pp. 187–188.
15 Ibid. p. 276.
16 Kurz and Gehrke (2003). Their chapter is a translation of their conference paper in English, which to some extent explains their use of the Prinsep translation as the only source for the *Traité*. I comment upon their ideas at some length as these are an

illustration of the continuing struggle between objectivist (Ricardian? Sraffian??) and subjectivist (Saysian) economists.

17 Ibid. p. 217.
18 Ibid. p. 216.
19 In the preceding chapter I argued along the same lines with respect to Malthus, Sismondi and Say: their methodological differences were small, but they held fundamentally different views of society. But Say and Ricardo embraced different paradigms and also differed in their ideas of society. It may seem remarkable that they agreed on the validity of Say's Law, but this can be explained in either system.
20 For example they write that Say believed that the improvement of machinery would never cause unemployment (p. 224). In the fourth to sixth editions of the *Traité*, however, Say mitigated this conclusion by introducing two important hypotheses: 1. that the introduction of machinery would be a slow process, allowing for adjustment of employment; 2. that governments would undertake precautionary measures like public works or colonisation (Say, *Traité* (var. I) p. 137).
21 Kurz and Gehrke (2003) p. 231.
22 Ibid. p. 235.
23 Ibid. p. 256.
24 Steiner (2003).
25 Ibid. pp. 350–355.
26 Ibid. p. 347.
27 Steiner (1998b, 1996a, 1996b).
28 Forget (1999).
29 Ibid. pp. 123–124.
30 Ibid. p. 173.
31 Tiran (1994).
32 Tiran (1995) p. 36: Galiani, Verri, Locke, Quesnay, Turgot, Thornton, Hume, Montesquieu and Smith are all quoted by Say.
33 Béraud (1992).
34 Tiran (1995) pp. 37–38.
35 Ibid. p. 39 n 1, n 2.
36 Rothbard (1995).
37 Ibid. p. 43.
38 Kates (2000).
39 Ibid. p. 10.
40 Ibid. p. 75.
41 Kates (2003).
42 Skousen, in Kates (2003) p. 106.
43 Keen, in Kates (2003) p. 208.
44 Horwitz, in Kates (2003) p. 96.

Archival sources

Quotations from manuscript sources of more than one sentence are printed in italics. Unless otherwise stated, all translations from the French are the author's.

Say papers, Bibliothèque Nationale, Paris
Amaury Duval papers, Musée Rolin, Autun
Jeremy Bentham papers, University College London
Francis Place papers, British Museum, London
Dossiers of professorial nominations, Archives Nationales, Paris
J.-B. Say letters, University Library Amsterdam
Raoul-Duval family papers, Château du Vaudreuil, Eure
Hashimoto photocopies collection, Institut Triangle, Université Lyon 2 *Lumière*

References

Anikin, A. (1975), *A Science in its Youth (Pre-Marxian Political Economy)*. Progress Publishers, Moscow

Baumol, W.J. (1977), 'Say's (at least) eight Laws, or what Say and James Mill may really have meant', *Economica* 44, pp. 145–161

Béraud, A. (1992), 'Ricardo, Malthus, Say', in A. Béraud and G. Faccarello (eds) *Nouvelle histoire de la pensée Economique* vol. I pp. 365–508. La Découverte, Paris

Bergeron, L. (1972), 'Douglas, Ternaux, Cockerill: aux origines de la mécanisation de l'industrie lainière en France', *Revue Historique*, pp. 67–80

Blanc, E. (2003), 'Tableau Chronologique', in J.-P. Potier and A. Tiran (eds), *Jean-Baptiste Say: nouveaux regards sur son oeuvre*. Economica, Paris, p. 741

Blaug, M.J. (5th edn 1997), *Economic Theory in Retrospect*. Heinemann, London

Comte, Ch. (1834), 'Notice historique', in J.-B. Say, *Mélanges et correspondence*

Dorigny, M. and B. Gainot (1998), *La Société des Amis des Noirs 1788–1799: Contribution à l'histoire de l'abolition de l'esclavage*. UNESCO, Paris

Everett, A.H. (1826), *Nouvelles Idées sur la Population, avec des remarques sur les Theories de Malthus et de Godwin*; avec une nouvelle préface de l'auteur. Renouard & Sautelet, Paris

Flandrin, J.-L. (1976), *Familles, parenté, maison, sexualité dans l'ancienne société*. Hachette, Paris

Forget, E.L. (1999), *The Social Economics of Jean-Baptiste Say: Markets and Virtue*. Routledge, London – New York

Groenewegen, P. (2002), 'The French connection', in P. Groenewegen, *Eighteenth Century Economics: Turgot, Beccaria and Smith and Their Contemporaries*, pp. 125–143. Routledge, London – New York

Guillaumont, P. (1969) [PhD thesis 1964], *La Pensée démo-économique de Jean-Baptiste Say et de Sismondi*. Editions Cujas, Paris

Hashimoto, H. (1971), 'Les lettres inédites de Jean-Baptiste Say', *Treatises of Shikoku Christian College* no. 20

Hashimoto, H. (1980), 'Notes inédites de J.-B. Say qui couvrent les marges de la Richesse des Nations et qui la critiquent', Kyoto Sangyo University, *Economic and Business Review* 7, pp. 53–81

Hashimoto, H. (1982), 'Notes inédites de J.-B. Say qui couvrent les marges de la Richesse des Nations et qui la résument', Kyoto Sangyo University, *Economic and Business Review* 9, pp. 31–133

Hashimoto, H. (2004), *15 lettres inédites de J.-B. Say et 5 lettres inédites d'Horace Say*. Kyoto Sangyo University

Hodgson, A. (1823), *A letter to M. Jean-Baptiste Say, on the comparative expense of free and slave labour.* Hatchard & Son, London

Hollander, S. (2005), *Jean-Baptiste Say and the Classical Canon in Economics.* Routledge, London – New York

Holtman, R. (1967), *The Napoleonic Revolution.* Lippincott, Philadelphia

Horwitz, S. (2003), 'Say's Law of Markets: An Austrian Appreciation', in S. Kates (ed.), *Two Hundred Years of Say's Law*. Edward Elgar, Cheltenham, pp. 82–98

Israel, J. (2011), *Democratic Enlightenment.* Oxford University Press, Oxford

James, P. (1979), *Population Malthus: His Life and Times.* Routledge & Kegan Paul, London

Kadish, A. and K. Tribe (eds, 1993), *The Market for Political Economy: The Advent of Economics in British University Culture, 1850–1905.* Routledge, London – New York

Kates, S. (2000), *Say's Law and the Keynesian Revolution: How Macroeconomic Theory Lost its Way.* Edward Elgar, Cheltenham

Kates, S. (ed. 2003), *Two Hundred Years of Say's Law: Essays on Economic Theory's Most Controversial Principle.* Edward Elgar, Cheltenham

Keen, S. (2003), 'Nudge nudge, wink wink, say no more', in S. Kates (ed.), *Two Hundred Years of Say's Law*. Edward Elgar, Cheltenham, pp. 199–209

Kitami, H. (1999), 'Trois lettres inédites de Jean-Baptiste Say à Pierre Prévost', *Bulletin de la Société Franco-Japonaise des Sciences Economiques* no. 21, pp. 52–58

Kitami, H. (2003), 'Jean-Baptiste Say et Etienne Dumont', in J.-P. Potier and A. Tiran (eds), *Jean-Baptiste Say: nouveaux regards sur son oeuvre.* Economica, Paris, pp. 683–697

Kitchin, J. (1966) [dissertation Paris 1956], *Un Journal 'philosophique': La Décade (1794–1807).* Minard, Paris

Klotz, G. (2010), 'Jean-Baptiste Say et les ingénieurs des Ponts et Chaussées (1803–1850)', in A. Tiran (ed.), *Jean-Baptiste Say: influences, critiques et postérité.* Editions Classiques Garnier, Paris, pp. 409–442

Koolman, G. (1971), 'Say's conception of the role of the entrepreneur', *Economica* XXXVIII(151), pp. 269–286

Kurz, H. and Chr. Gehrke (2003), 'Say et Ricardo', in J.-P. Potier and A. Tiran (eds), *Jean-Baptiste Say: nouveaux regards sur son oeuvre.* Economica, Paris, pp. 215–263

Landes, D.S. (1966), 'Technological change and development in Western Europe', in *The Cambridge Economic History of Europe* vol. VI, pp. 504–521. Cambridge University Press, Cambridge

Lécuyer, B. and A.R. Oberschall (1968), 'The Idéologues and the Institut', in *International Encyclopedia of the Social Sciences* vol. XV. Macmillan, New York

Levan-Lemesle, L. and J. Hecht (eds, 1986), *Les problèmes de l'institutionnalisation de l'économie politique en France au XIXe siècle.* Presses Universitaires, Grenoble

Liesse, A. (1901), 'Un professeur d'Economie politique sous la Restauration: J.-B. Say au Conservatoire des Arts et Métiers', *Journal des Economistes*, pp. 161–174

Mill, J.S. (1952) [1873], *Autobiography* (ed. The World's Classics). Oxford University Press, London – New York – Toronto

Nardin, J.-C. (1965), 'Le Libéria et l'opinion publique en France, 1821–1847', in *Cahiers d'études africaines* vol. V–XVII, pp. 99–100

O'Brien, D.P. (ed. 1994), *Foundations of Monetary Economics* vol. VI: The Non-Conformists. Edward Elgar, Cheltenham

Palmer, R.R. (1997), *J.-B. Say: An Economist in Troubled Times.* Writings selected and translated by R.R. Palmer. Princeton University Press, Princeton

Picavet, F. (n.d.), 'Idéologie, Idéologiste, Idéologue', *La Grande Encyclopédie*, part 20-II. La Grande Encyclopédie S.A., Paris

Potier, J.-P. (2006), 'Les traductions du *Traité*', in J.-B. Say [var. 2006], *Traité d'Economie Politique* vol. I* pp. LIII–LXXXI

Potier, J.-P. (2010), 'Les traducteurs du *Traité d'Economie Politique*', in A. Tiran (ed.), *Jean-Baptiste Say: influences, critiques et postérité*. Editions Classiques Garnier, Paris, pp. 131–176

Potier, J.-P. and A. Tiran (eds, 2003), *Jean-Baptiste Say: nouveaux regards sur son oeuvre*. Economica, Paris

Presser, J. (3rd edn 1960), *Napoleon: historie en legende*. Elsevier, Amsterdam

Regaldo, M. (1976), *Un Milieu Intellectuel: La Décade Philosophique (1794–1807)* (PhD thesis Lille)

Ricardo, D. (1819), *Principes d'Economie Politique et de l'Impôt*, trad. F.S. Constancio, notes de J.-B. Say. Paris

Ricardo, D. (ed. P. Sraffa 1951–1973), *Works and Correspondence*. Cambridge University Press, Cambridge

Roggi, P. (1972), 'Sette lettere inedite di J.-B. Say a J.C.L. Sismondi', in *Rivista di politica economica*, pp. 963–979

Rothbard, M. (1995), 'J.B. Say: the French tradition in Smithian clothing', in M. Rothbard, *Classical Economics: An Austrian Perspective on the History of Economic Thought* vol. II pp. 3–45. Edward Elgar, Cheltenham

Say, Jean-Baptiste (1789), *De la liberté de la presse*. Paris

Say, Jean-Baptiste (1794), *La Science du Bonhomme Richard, par Benjamin Franklin, précédée par un Abrégé de la Vie de Franklin, par J.B. Say*. La Décade, Paris

Say, Jean-Baptiste (1800), *Olbie*. Déterville, Paris

Say, Jean-Baptiste (1803), *Traité d'Economie Politique*. Crapelet, Paris

Say, Jean-Baptiste, *Traité* (second to fourth edition 1814, 1817, 1819). Déterville, Paris

Say, Jean-Baptiste (1826), *Traité* (fifth edition). Rapilly, Paris

Say, Jean-Baptiste (1815), *De l'Angleterre et des Anglais*. Arthus Bertrand, Paris

Say, Jean-Baptiste (1817a), *Petit Volume, contenant quelques aperçus des hommes et de la société*. Déterville, Paris

Say, Jean-Baptiste (1817b), Anon. [J. Bentham – J.B. Say], *De l'influence ministérielle sur les élections en Angleterre*; 'De l'imprimerie de Bossange', Paris

Say, Jean-Baptiste (1818a), *De l'Importance du Port de la Villette*. Paris

Say, Jean-Baptiste (1818b), *Des Canaux de Navigation dans l'état actuel de la France*. Paris

Say, Jean-Baptiste (1818c), *Copie de la lettre adressée par* M.J.-B. SAY *à Messieurs les Membres du Conseil d'Administration de la Compagnie d'Assurances générales* (privately printed)

Say, Jean-Baptiste (1820), *Lettres à M. Malthus sur différens sujets d'Economie Politique, notamment sur les causes de la stagnation générale du commerce*. Bossange, Paris

Say, Jean-Baptiste (transl. K.H. Rau 1821), *Malthus und Say über die Ursachen der jetztigen Handelsstockung*. Perthes und Besser, Hamburg

Say, Jean-Baptiste [1822], *Lettre de Mr. Jean Baptiste Say, auteur du Traité d'Economie Politique, à Mr. Polidore Martelly, négociant, à Londres*; 4 pp. printed by J. McCreery, Tooks Court, Chancery Lane, London

Say, Jean-Baptiste (1824a), 'De la Première colonie formée par les Américains en Afrique', in *La Revue Encyclopédique* vol. 24, pp. 5–18

Say, Jean-Baptiste (1824b), 'J.-B.S.' review in *Revue Encyclopédique*, February, pp. 481–482

Say, Jean-Baptiste (1826a), 'De la crise commerciale d'Angleterre', in *Revue Encyclopédique*, September, pp. 40–45

Say, Jean-Baptiste (1826b), 'Economie Politique', in *Encyclopédie Progressive*, pp. 217–304

Say, Jean-Baptiste (1826c), 'J.-B.S.' review in *Revue Encyclopédique*, January, pp. 116–119

Say, Jean-Baptiste (1827), *De l'objet et de l'utilité des statistiques* (Extrait de la *Revue Encyclopédique*, September)

Say, Jean-Baptiste (1828), 'De l'Influence des futurs progrès de l'Economie politique sur le sort des nations', in *Revue Encyclopédique*, January, pp. 14–34

Say, Jean-Baptiste (1828–1829), *Cours Complet d'Economie Politique Pratique*, vol. I–VI. Rapilly, Paris

Say, Jean-Baptiste (1836), *Cours Complet d'Economie Politique Pratique, suivi des Mélanges, Correspondance et Catéchisme d'economie Politique*. H. Dumont, Brussels

Say, Jean-Baptiste (1848, ed. Ch. Comte, E. Daire and H. Say), *Oeuvres Diverses de J.-B. Say*. Guillaumin, Paris

Say, Jean-Baptiste (2006 var.), *Oeuvres Complètes I, II*; Variorum edition of editions 1–5 and posthumous 6 (1841) of the *Traité*, ed. C. Mouchot, A. Tiran a.o.

Schoorl, E. (1980), *Jean-Baptiste Say: Hoofdstukken uit zijn leven en economisch denken* (PhD thesis University of Amsterdam). PET, Amsterdam

Schoorl, E. (1982), 'Bentham, Say and Continental Utilitarianism', *The Bentham Newsletter* no. 6, pp. 8–18

Schoorl, E. (2001), 'Loi des Débouches (Say's Law)', *Dictionnaire des Sciences Economiques*, pp. 257–259. Presses Universitaires de France, Paris

Schoorl, E. (2003), 'Towards a new biography of J.-B. Say', in J.-P. Potier and A. Tiran (eds), *Jean-Baptiste Say: nouveaux regards sur son oeuvre*. Economica, Paris, pp. 699–714

Schoorl, E. (2010), 'Please print my article first in this issue', in A. Tiran (ed.), *Jean-Baptiste Say: influences, critiques et postérité*. Editions Classiques Garnier, Paris, pp. 219–249

Schmidt, C. (1911), 'Jean-Baptiste Say et le blocus continental', in *Revue d'histoire des doctrines économiques et sociales*, vol. IV, pp. 148–154.

Schumpeter, J.A. (1954), *History of Economic Analysis*. George Allen & Unwin, London

Shovlin, J. (2006), *The Political Economy of Virtue: Luxury, Patriotism and the Origins of the French Revolution*. Cornell University Press, Ithaca – London

Sismondi, J.C.L. de (2nd edn 1827), *Nouveaux Principes d'Economie Politique*. Delaunay, Paris

Skousen, M. (2003), 'Say's Law, Growth Theory and Supply-Side Economics', in S. Kates (ed.), *Two Hundred Years of Say's Law*. Edward Elgar, Cheltenham, pp. 99–106

Smith, A. (5th edn 1789) *An Inquiry into the Nature and Causes of the Wealth of Nations*; J.-B. Say's annotated copy, Bibliothèque de l'Institut, Paris

Sowell, T. (1972), *Say's Law: An Historical Analysis*. Princeton University Press, Princeton

Sowell, T. (1974), *Classical Economics Reconsidered*. Princeton University Press, Princeton

Sowell, T. (2006), *On Classical Economics*. Yale University Press, New Haven

Stedman Jones, G. (2008), *An End to Poverty? A Historical Debate*. Columbia University Press, New York

Steiner, Ph. (ed. 1996a), *Jean-Baptiste Say, Cours d'économie politique* [1819] *et autres essays*. Flammarion, Paris

Steiner, Ph. (1996b), 'J.-B. Say et les colonies', in F. Demier and D. Diatkine (eds), *Le Libéralisme à l'Epreuve: Smith et l'Economie Coloniale*. Maison des Sciences de l'Homme, Paris

Steiner, Ph. (1997), 'La theorie de l'entrepreneur chez Jean-Baptiste Say et la tradition Cantillon-Knight', *l'Actualité Economique, Revue d'analyse économique* 73(4), pp. 611–627

Steiner, Ph. (1998a), *La 'science nouvelle' de l'économie politique*. Presses Universitaires de France, Paris

Steiner, Ph. (1998b), 'Jean-Baptiste Say: the entrepreneur, the free trade doctrine and the theory of income distribution', in G. Faccarello (ed.), *Studies in the History of French Political Economy: From Bodin to Walras*, pp. 196–228. Routledge, London – New York

Steiner, Ph. (2003), 'La théorie de la production de J.-B. Say', in J.-P. Potier and A. Tiran (eds), *Jean-Baptiste Say: nouveaux regards sur son oeuvre*. Economica, Paris, pp. 325–360

Steiner, Ph. (2010), 'J.-B. Say et les alterations de sa correspondance avec David Ricardo', in A. Tiran (ed.), *Jean-Baptiste Say: influences, critiques et postérité*. Editions Classiques Garnier, Paris, pp. 557–577

Teilhac, E. (1927), *L'Oeuvre économique de Jean-Baptiste Say*. Alcan, Paris

Ternaux ainé (1818), *Mémoire sur les moyens d'assurer les subsistances de la ville de Paris, par l'établissement d'une compagnie de prévoyance*. Paris

Tiran, A. (1994), *J.-B. SAY: Les écrits sur la monnaie, la banquet et la finance* (PhD thesis Université Lyon 2 *Lumière*, Lyon)

Tiran, A. (ed. 1995), *Jean-Baptiste Say, Manuscrits sur la monnaie, la banque et la finance*. Cahiers Monnaie et Financement, Université Lyon 2 *Lumière*, Lyon

Tiran, A. (ed. 2010), *Jean-Baptiste Say: influences, critiques et postérité*. Editions Classiques Garnier, Paris

Valynseele, J. (n.d.) [1971], *Les Say et leurs alliances*. Privately printed, Paris

Wallas, G. (1918), *The Life of Francis Place, 1771–1854*. Knopf, New York

Whatmore, R. (2000), *Republicanism and the French Revolution: An Intellectual History of Jean-Baptiste Say's Political Economy*. Oxford University Press, Oxford

Winch, D. (1978), *Adam Smith's Politics: An Essay in Historiographic Revision*. Cambridge University Press, Cambridge

'Z.' (1824), 'De l'Enseignement de l'Economie politique', in *Revue Encyclopédique*, January, p. 238

Index of names

Thénard, baron Louis Jacques 107
Théremin, Charles 24
Thomasson, factory owner 75, 76
Tiran, André 9, 14, 17, 166, 173–5
Toscan, Georges 11
Tooke, Eyton 120, 135
Tooke, Thomas 125, 135, 138, 149
Treuttel & Wurtz, booksellers 98, 99
Trower, Hutches 93
Turgot, Anne Robert Jacques 6, 32, 43, 65, 126, 152

Ustery, bookseller Paul 62

Velez, Cuban economist 164
Vernes, François 15, 16, 23, 27

Verri, Pietro 65, 121, 154
Volney, Constantin François 14
Voltaire 31, 38

Wadström, Carl Bernhard 19
Wadström, Mrs. 19
Warden, Mr. 46
Washington, George 92, 128
Watt, James 76
Whatmore, Richard 6, 9, 12, 24, 30, 166, 167, 178
Whitney, Eli 164
Widmer, Samuel 90
Wilberforce, William 129
Williams, Helen Maria 10, 18, 19
Wyburn sisters 74

Taylor & Francis

eBooks

ORDER YOUR FREE 30 DAY INSTITUTIONAL TRIAL TODAY!

FOR LIBRARIES

Over 23,000 eBook titles in the Humanities,
Social Sciences, STM and Law from some of the
world's leading imprints.

Choose from a range of subject packages or create your own!

▶ Free MARC records

▶ COUNTER-compliant usage statistics

▶ Flexible purchase and pricing options

▶ Off-site, anytime access via Athens or referring URL

▶ Print or copy pages or chapters

▶ Full content search

▶ Bookmark, highlight and annotate text

▶ Access to thousands of pages of quality research
at the click of a button

For more information, pricing enquiries or to order
a free trial, contact your local online sales team.

UK and Rest of World: **online.sales@tandf.co.uk**

US, Canada and Latin America:
e-reference@taylorandfrancis.com

www.ebooksubscriptions.com

ALPSP Award for
BEST eBOOK
PUBLISHER
2009 Finalist

Taylor & Francis eBooks
Taylor & Francis Group

A flexible and dynamic resource for teaching, learning and research.